Cornelia Schleime

Herausgegeben von/Edited by Eckhard Hollmann & Jürgen Krieger

Texte von/Texts by Wolfgang Büscher, Christiane Bühling & Cornelia Schleime

Zungenschlaf

Cornelia Schleime

Arbeiten auf Papier Works on Paper

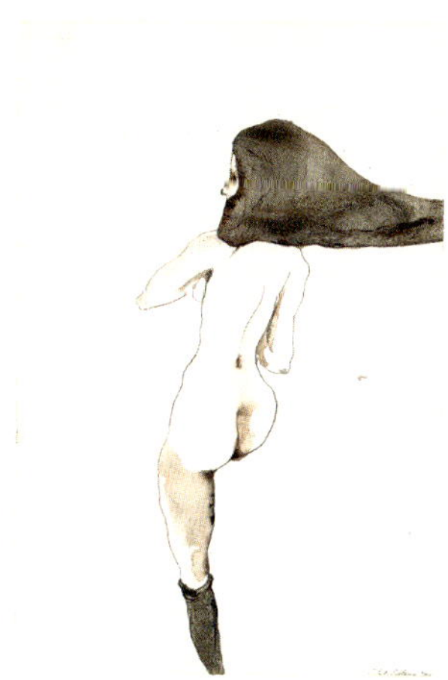

Inhalt

Content

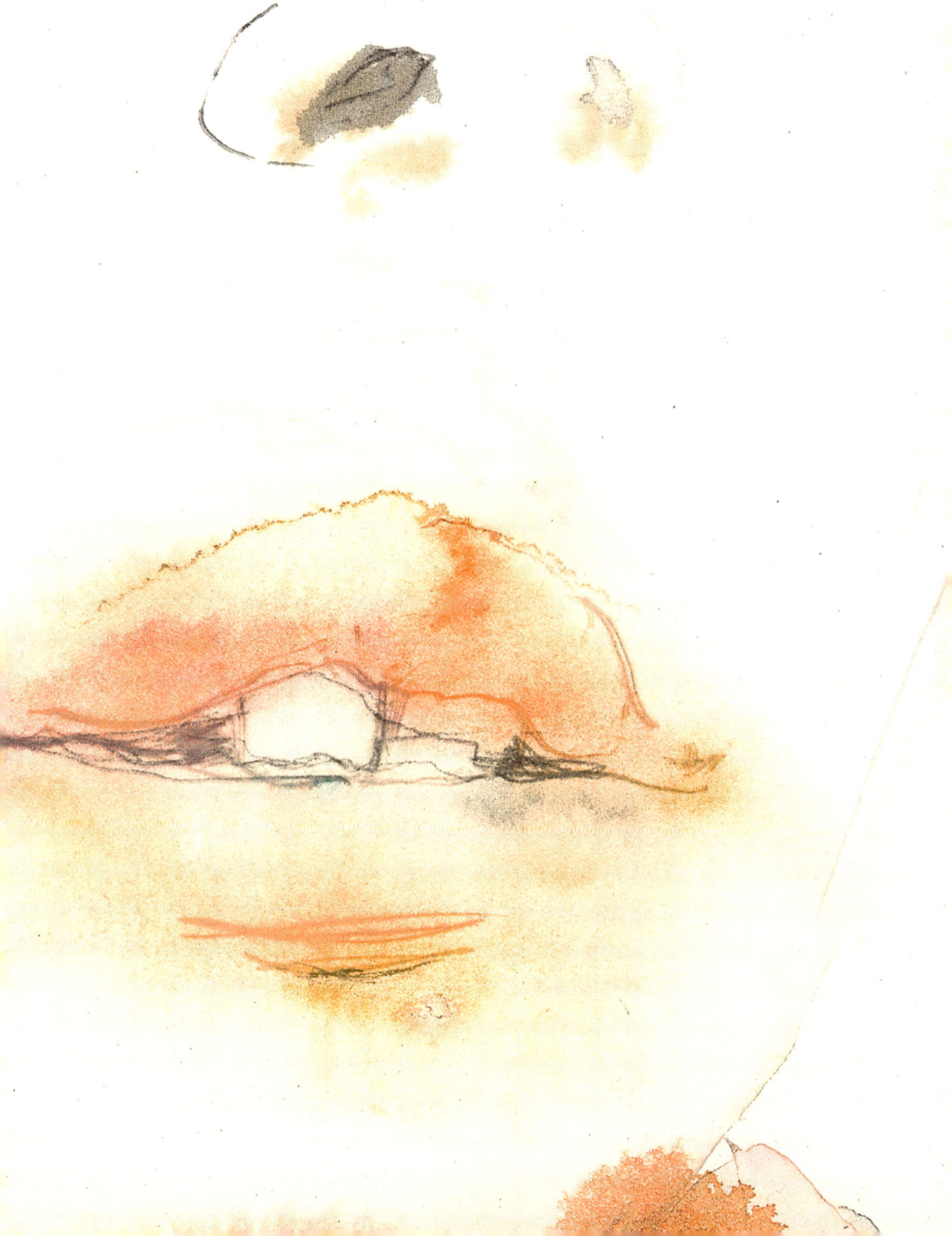

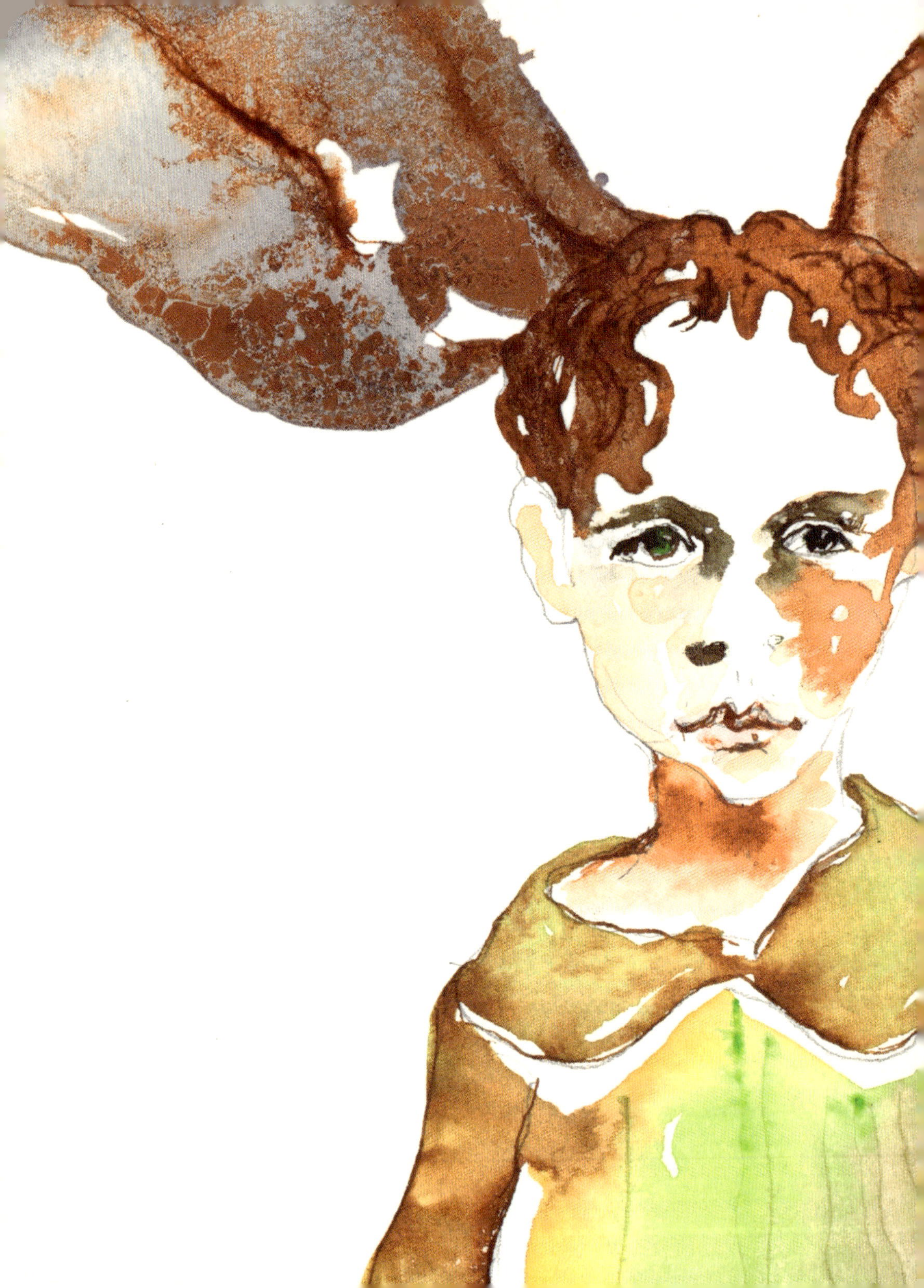

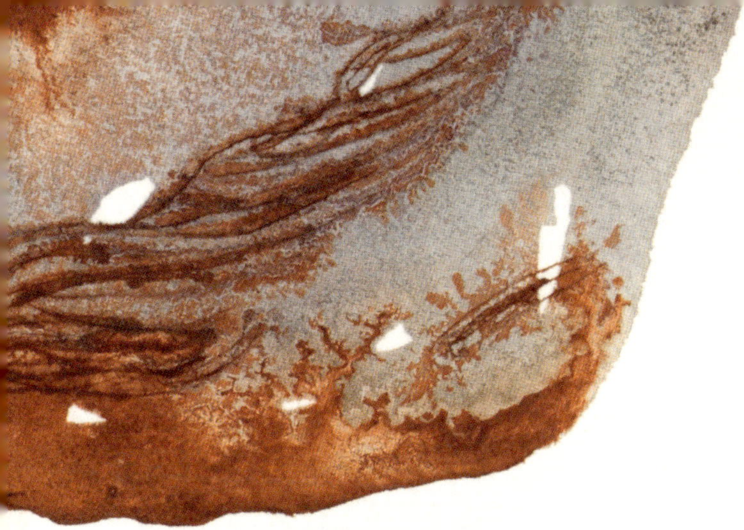

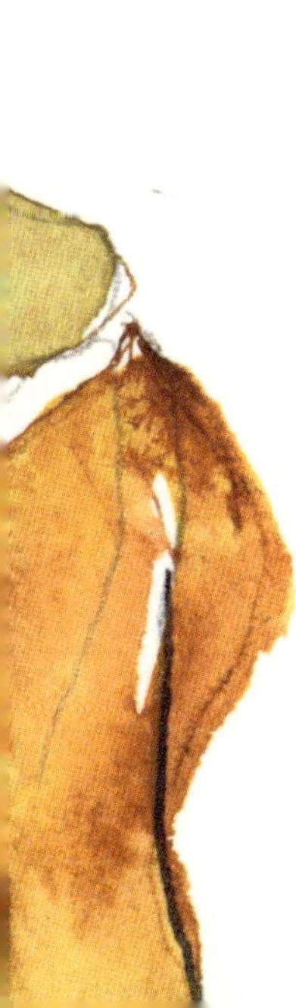

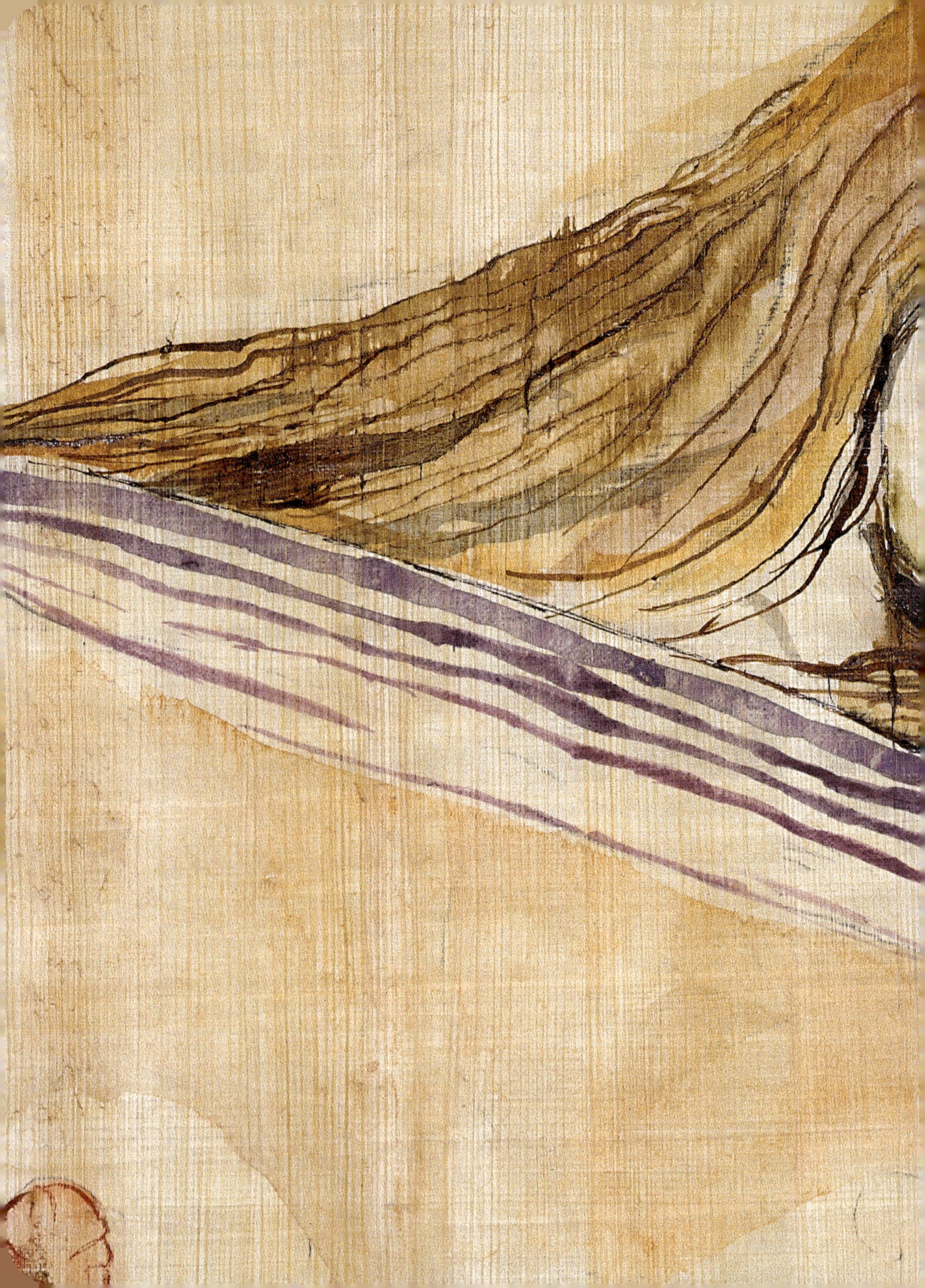

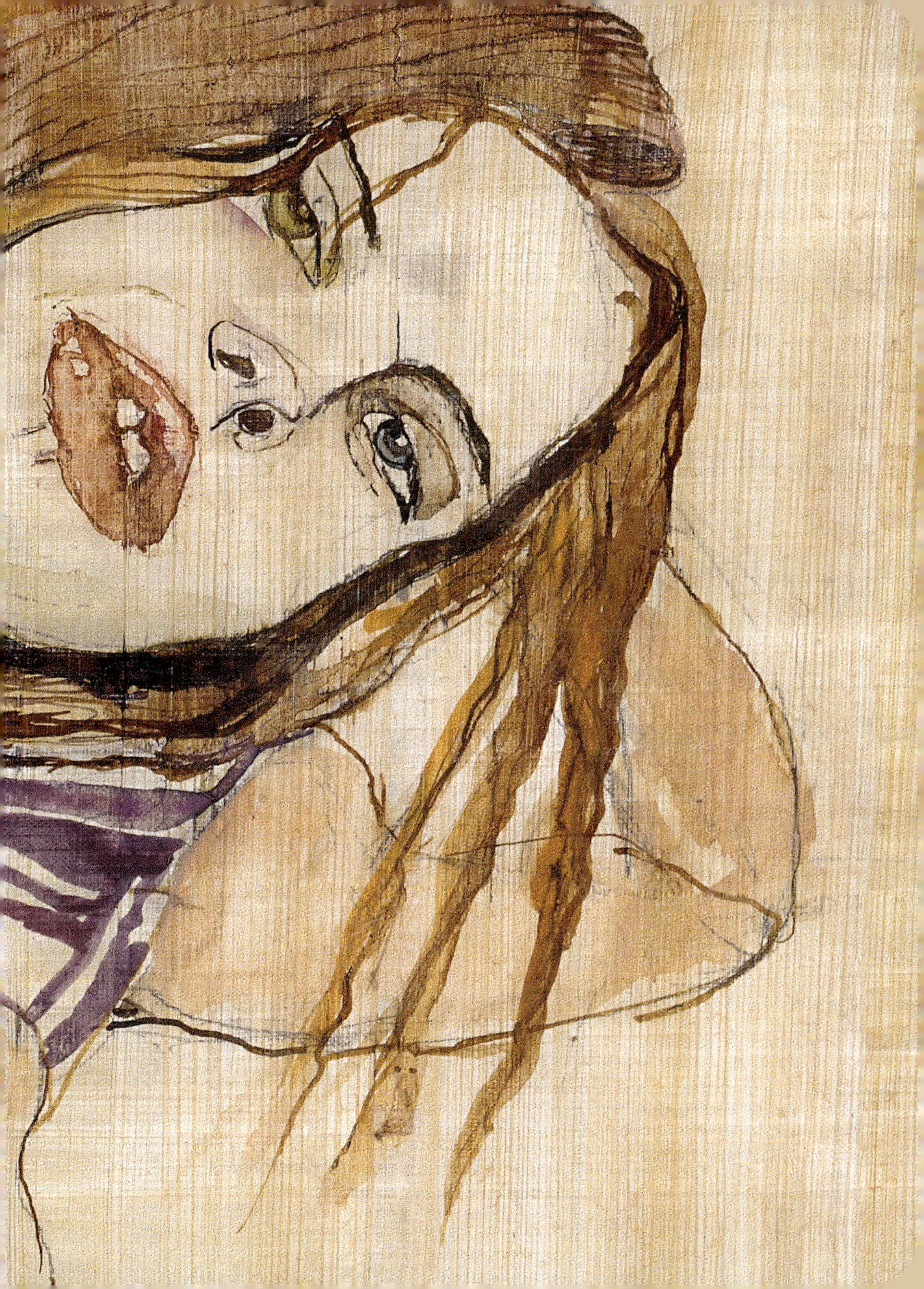

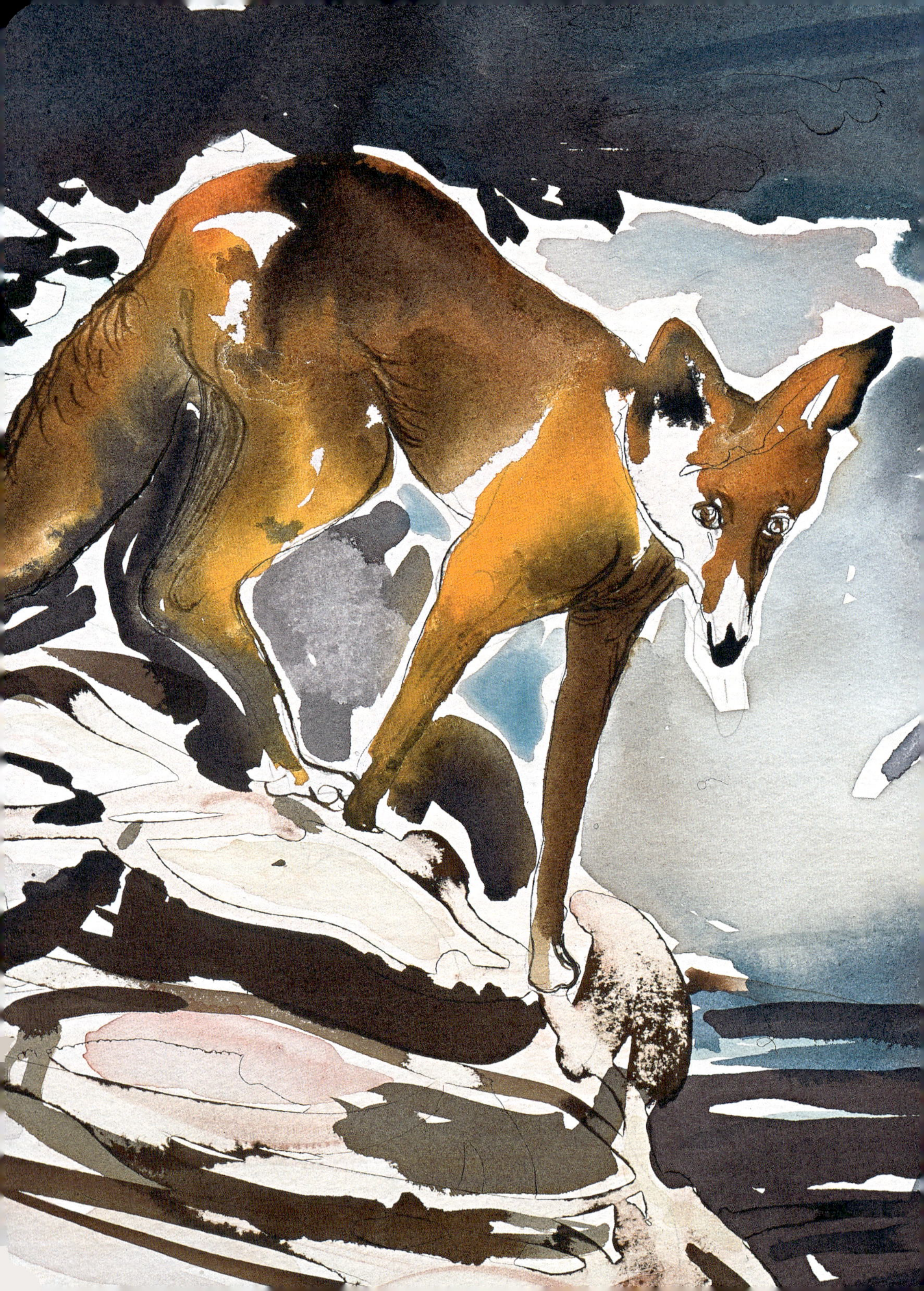

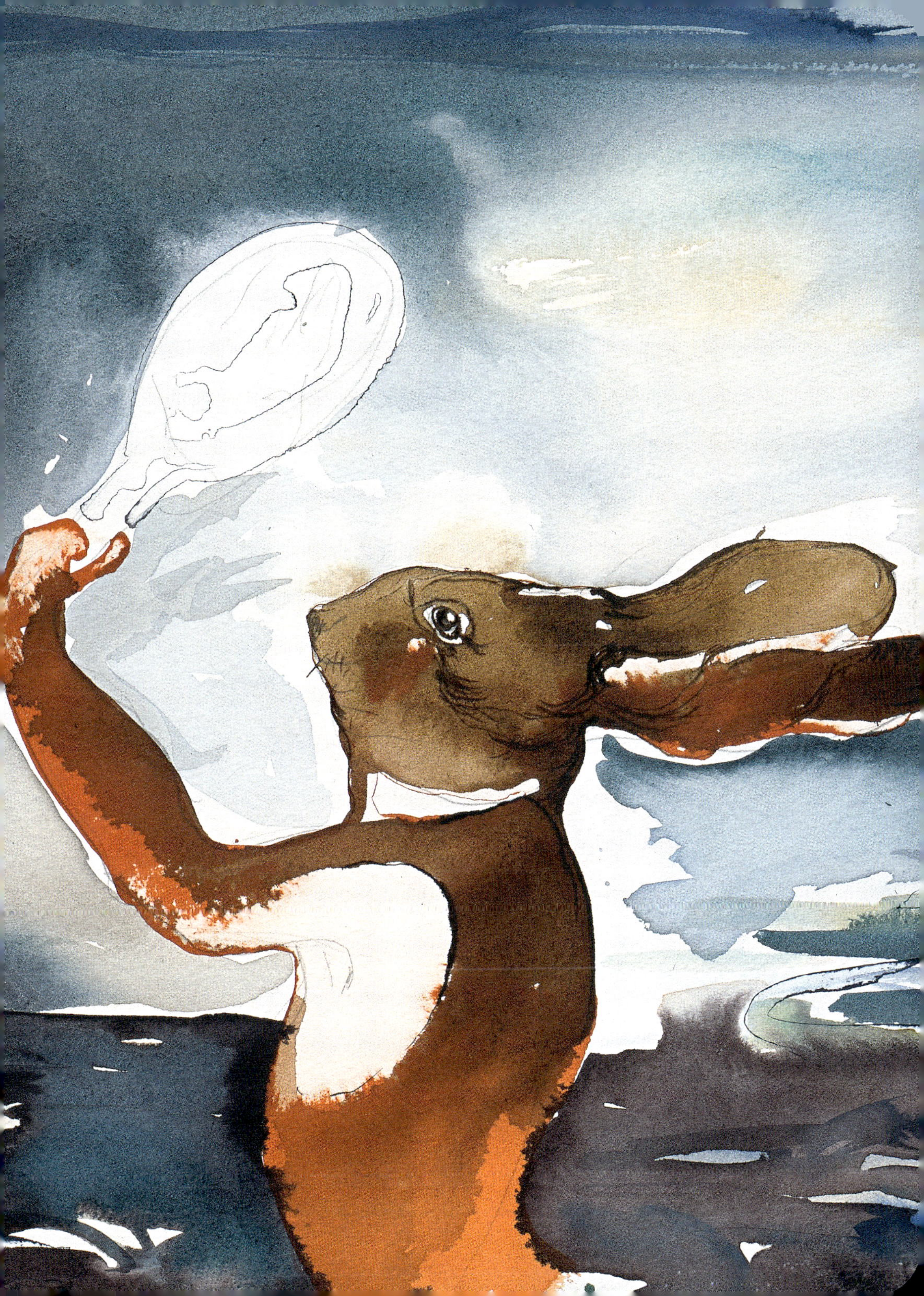

Interview

Wolfgang Büscher im Gespräch mit
Cornelia Schleime, Berlin 10. November 2011

Wolfgang Büscher Vor uns auf dem Tisch liegt ein schwarzbraunes, körniges Bild: „Der Hodenbruch". Ein Mann ist zu sehen, dem etwas groß und schwer zwischen den Beinen hängt. Was ist da los?

Cornelia Schleime Das war in Dresden, wir Studenten gingen damals oft in die Pferdegaststätte, da gab es Pferdefleisch, das war billig. Die anderen sagten: Guck mal, da drüben ist wieder der mit dem Hodenbruch. Ich guckte immer hin, wenn der durchs Lokal ging, aber ich sah nichts. Ich wusste nicht, was die anderen meinten. Dann, eines Tages im Zug nach Berlin, kommt ein Mann auf mich zu mit einem Riesenbeutel zwischen den Beinen. Es war der Mann aus der Pferdegaststätte.

W.B. Was hat es mit dem körnigen Farbauftrag auf sich?

C.S. Ich habe das Bild schon im Westen gemacht, 1984. Damals nach der Ausreise aus der DDR hatte ich sehr wenig Geld. Von einem türkischen Wirt habe ich mir Kaffeesatz geholt, den gab es ja umsonst, und ihn in die Farben gemischt. Ich war immer auf der Suche nach rauhen, nicht glatten Oberflächen, als Ostler interessiert einen glattes Papier nicht.

W.B. Wie ist das Bild entstanden, vom Hoden her?

C.S. Vom Kopf her. Es ist ein automatisches Arbeiten, erst war der Kopf da, dann ein Arm, der Körper, dann kam irgendwann die Erinnerung an den Hodenmann.

W.B. Das glatte Gegenteil von Konzeptkunst?

Interview

Wolfgang Büscher in Conversation with Cornelia Schleime, Berlin 10 November 2011

Wolfgang Büscher Lying on the table in front of us is a blackish-brown, grainy picture: "Der Hodenbruch" (Scrotal Hernia). It shows a man with something large and heavy hanging between his legs. What is it about?

Cornelia Schleime It was in Dresden. At that time we students often went to the restaurant serving horse meat. It served horse meat, which was cheap. The others always said: Look, there's that man with the scrotal hernia again. I always watched him walking across the restaurant but I couldn't see anything. I didn't know what the others meant And then, one day when I was on the train to Berlin, a man walked towards me with a huge bulge between his legs. It was the man from the restaurant serving horse meat.

W.B. What is the reason for the grainy paint application?

C.S. I painted the picture in the West in 1984. I had very little money in those days after leaving the GDR. I used to collect the coffee grounds from a Turkish restaurant owner; they were free, and I used to mix them into the paint. I was always searching for rough surfaces which weren't smooth: artists from the East are not interested in smooth paper.

W.B. How did you produce the picture? Starting with the scrotum?

C.S. I started with the head. I worked automatically; first there was the head, then an arm and the body, and then at some point I remembered the man with the scrotal hernia.

C.S. Ja. Ich mag Konzeptkunst auch nicht so sehr. Die schneidet die Kunst vom Erlebten ab, von Träumen, vom Unterbewussten. Als ich in den Westen kam, kam hier gerade die Konzeptkunst auf, da waren wir aus dem Osten so eine kleine Gemeinschaft – die aus dem Osten im Westen. Es kam zu unserer Gruppenausstellung „Malstrom" im Haus am Waldsee in West-Berlin. Das hatte fast eine politische Dimension: Die neuen Wilden des Westens erlebten gerade einen Einbruch, nun kamen wir, die neuen Wilden des Ostens. Das Feuilleton des Westens nannte uns den „Untergrund vom Prenzlauer Berg". Das waren wir nicht. Wir waren eine Gruppe von Individualisten. Anfangs war der Westen für uns die totale Fremde, dann kam diese Gruppenausstellung, und ich fühlte mich schon wieder eingezwängt unter eine Überschrift. Ich wurde so viele Jahre lang vorgestellt als die aus dem Ost-Untergrund. Meine Malerei schaute sich keiner an. Die Zeitungen schrieben immer nur über meine Geschichte. Nicht über meine Bilder.

W.B. Und dann Amerika.

C.S. Anderthalb Jahre war ich dort, 1988/89 – da habe ich alles abgeschüttelt. Ich dachte, das ist ein tolles Leben in Amerika: mit dem Auto herumfahren und ein Reisetagebuch machen. Bis ich keine Lust mehr hatte, herumzufahren und wieder nach New York ging, dort habe ich mich wohlgefühlt. Und dann ging die Mauer auf, neue Themen setzten sich durch, nun endlich verschwand die einengende Betrachtung auch meiner Arbeit.

W.B. The very opposite of conceptual art?

C.S. Yes. I am against conceptual art anyway. It separates art from experience, from dreams, from the subconscious. When I came to the West conceptual art was just starting to appear. We artists from the East were such a small community – the artists from the East in the West. We presented our group exhibition "Malstrom" in the Haus am Waldsee in West Berlin. It assumed almost political dimensions: The new Wild Ones of the West were just in decline and then along we came, the new Wild Ones from the East. The Feuilleton des Westens called us the "underground from Prenzlauer Berg". That's not what we were. We were a group of individualists. At the beginning the West was completely foreign to us, and then came this group exhibition and yet again I felt I had been forced in under a single heading. My works were shown for many years as the artist from the underground in the East. Nobody looked at my paintings. The newspapers always only wrote about my story. Not about my pictures.

W.B. And then America.

C.S. I was there for a year and a half in 1988/89 – and I shook off everything. I thought what a fantastic life it was in America: driving around in a camper van and just sending my travel diaries to the gallery owner in Berlin. Until I didn't want to do that any more and went back to New York again, where I felt at home. And then the Wall opened up and new topics came to the fore; and then the narrow-minded approach to my work also disappeared at last.

W.B. Manche Maler zeichnen wie nebenbei. Andere zeichnen, um große Bilder vorzubereiten. Wie ist es bei Ihnen?

C.S. Zeichnen ist bei mir nie Vorbereitung. Ich kann nur in Extremen leben. Klein oder groß. Nie Mittelformate, erst jetzt sind einige entstanden. Wenn ich große Bilder male, bin ich körperlich ausgelaugt. Nach großen Bildern entlasse ich mich ins Zeichnen. Ich finde, die Zeichnung ist für mich das autonomste Ausdrucksmittel – das, das mir am meisten liegt. Zeichnungen sind wie Gedichte. Fragte man mich, was würdest du am liebsten machen, wäre die Antwort: unterwegs sein. Reisetagebücher zeichnen und schreiben. Alles variiert, auch die Schrift darin. Mal ist eine Seite eng beschrieben, mal ist nur ein Vögelchen auf einer Seite – das Spielerische, Experimentierfreudige steckt da mehr drin als im Malen großer Formate, das Verträumte.

W.B. Sie haben etliche Serien gezeichnet.

C.S. Eigentlich interessiert mich die Serie nicht so sehr. Es geht meist um die eine Zeichnung darin. Zeichnen ist für mich eigentlich wichtiger als große Bilder zu malen. Bei den Bildern gehe ich auf volles Risiko. An einem Abend schaue ich das Bild an, das ich gerade male, und denke, na gut, das war nix, kippe Schellack drüber und gehe schlafen. Am anderen Morgen hat sich die Suppe ihren Weg gesucht über das Bild und ich sehe es mit anderen Augen.

W.B. Das Bild muss leiden?

C.S. Das Bild muss nass werden. Ich kann sehr gut mit Pfützen arbeiten beim Zeichnen, ich hau sie aufs Blatt,

W.B. Some artists draw as a sideline, as it were. And others draw when they are preparing large pictures. What about you?
C.S. Drawing, for me, is never preparation. I can only live in extremes. Small or large. Never medium-sized formats; only now have I produced a few of those. When I paint big pictures I am physically drained. After big pictures I allow myself the relief of drawing. I think that for me drawing is the most autonomous form of expression – the one that comes most naturally to me. Drawings are like poems. If you were to ask me what I would most like to do, the answer would be: to travel. To draw and write in a travel diary. Everything varies, even the writing. Sometimes a page is closely written and sometimes there is only a bird on a page – there is more of the playful, experimental element than in painting large formats, like in a trance.
W.B. You have drawn a large number of series.
C.S. I'm not really so interested in series. Mostly it is just about a single drawing. For me, drawing is really more important than painting large pictures. With pictures I risk all odds. One evening I may look at the picture I am just painting and think okay, it's no good, so I pour shellac over it and go to bed. The next morning the viscous brew has spread out across the picture and I see it in a different light.
W.B. So the picture has to suffer?
C.S. The picture has to get wet. When I am drawing I can work very well with puddles; I slosh them onto the paper and then apply the pen: "oh, just look, yes, that's the start of a leg".

geh dann mit der Feder rein – oh, da ist ja, da entsteht ja ein Bein.

W.B. Die Zeichnungen entstehen fast organisch?

C.S. Als Kind musste ich einmal lange im Krankenhaus liegen, da habe ich immer die Wände vor mir gehabt, auf denen der Putz abblätterte und die Farbe fleckig geworden war, ich sah immerzu Figuren darin. Vielleicht hat mein Zeichnen etwas damit zu tun. Es zieht sich jedenfalls durch von der DDR bis heute. Ich habe immer gezeichnet.

W.B. Sie sagten, Sie mögen kein glattes Papier. Warum nicht?

C.S. Die Dresdner Tradition war mir zu piefig – Zeichnen als Vorstudie zum Bild. Weil ich das Zeichnen als selbständiges Element gesehen habe. Dann wollten sie mich dort auf Grafik trimmen. Ich sollte meine Zeichnungen in Grafik umsetzen. Ich liebe Bücher, solche mit original gezeichneten Bildern darin. Aber diese Grafik-Editionen liebe ich nicht. Es muss immer das Original sein, wie bei den Naturwissenschaftlern früher, die ihre Berichte selbst schrieben und illustrierten. Damals in der DDR bin ich zusammen mit einem Malerfreund in ein verlassenes Schulgebäude eingestiegen, dort fanden wir eine Menge alter Landkarten, die habe ich dann bemalt. Ich komme von der Zeichnung her, vom Papier. Ich liebe Materialien wie Pergament, Japan-Papier, auch Hotelpapier, wo oben ein Hotelname draufsteht und unten eine Faxnummer – fragile Papiere eben.

W.B. Wohin in aller Welt sind Sie seit 1984 gereist?

C.S. Die erste Reise im Westen ging im August 1985 nach

W.B. So the drawings are created almost organically?

C.S. As a child I once had to spend a long time in hospital; all the time the walls were there in front of me and the plaster was flaking off and the paint was marked, and so I kept on seeing figures on them. Maybe my drawing has something to do with that. At any rate it runs through from the GDR to the present day. Drawing is something I have always done.

W.B. You said you don't like smooth paper. Why not?

C.S. I found the tradition in Dresden too stuffy – drawing as a preliminary study for a picture. Because I saw drawing as an independent element. And then they wanted to make me into a graphics specialist. I was supposed to transfer my drawings onto prints. I love books, the kind with original pictures drawn in them. But I don't like these editions of prints. It must always be the original, like the scientists in the old days, who wrote and illustrated their reports themselves. In those days in the GDR I climbed into an abandoned school building with a painter friend. We found a lot of old maps there which I then painted. I start out from the drawing, from paper. I love materials like parchment, Japan paper and also hotel paper, where the hotel's name is at the top and underneath you have a fax number – delicate papers, in fact.

W.B. Whereabouts have you travelled since 1984?

C.S. My first journey in the West was to Crete in August 1985. During that trip I produced a travel diary with texts and drawings, including some from photos. I stitched

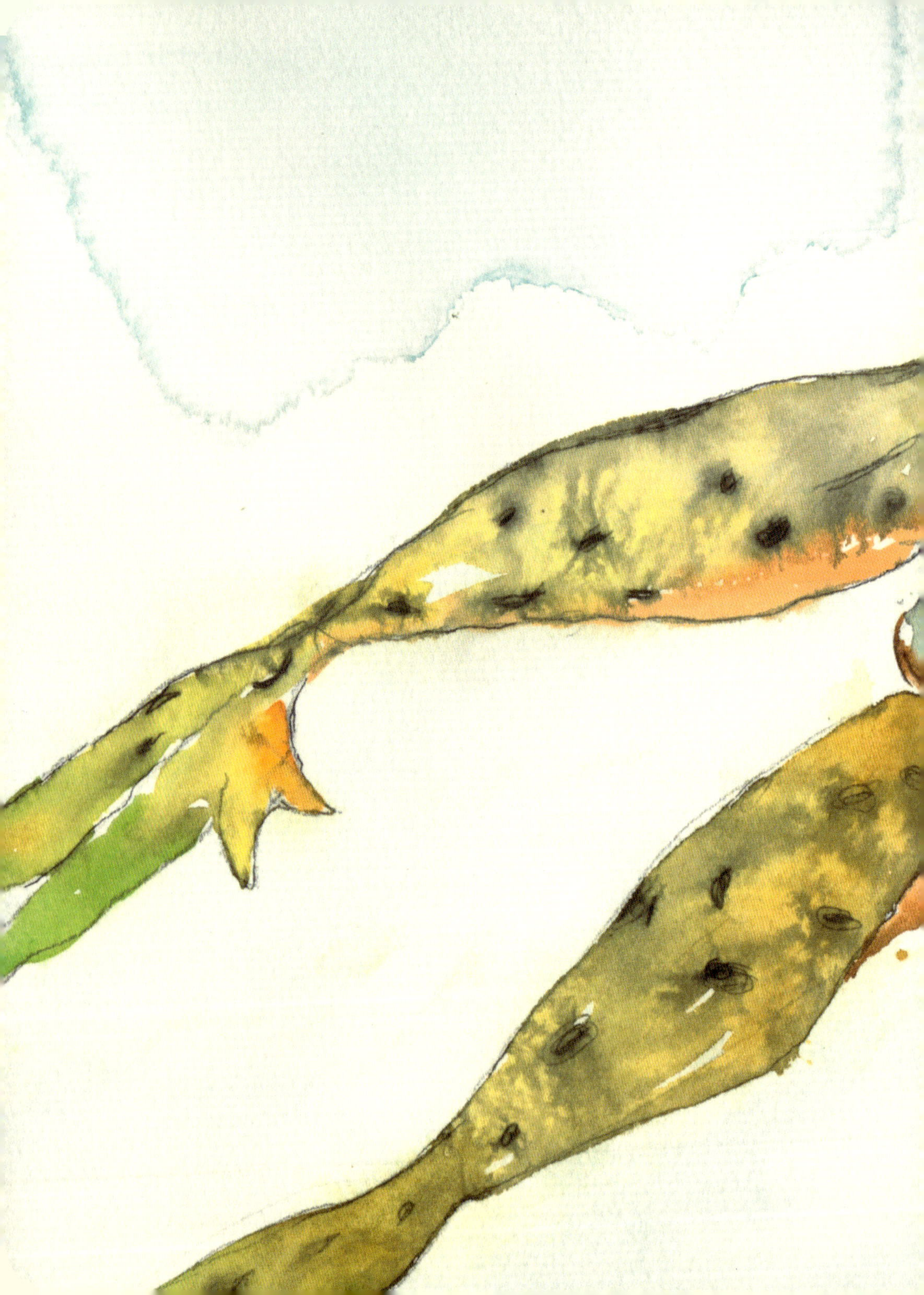

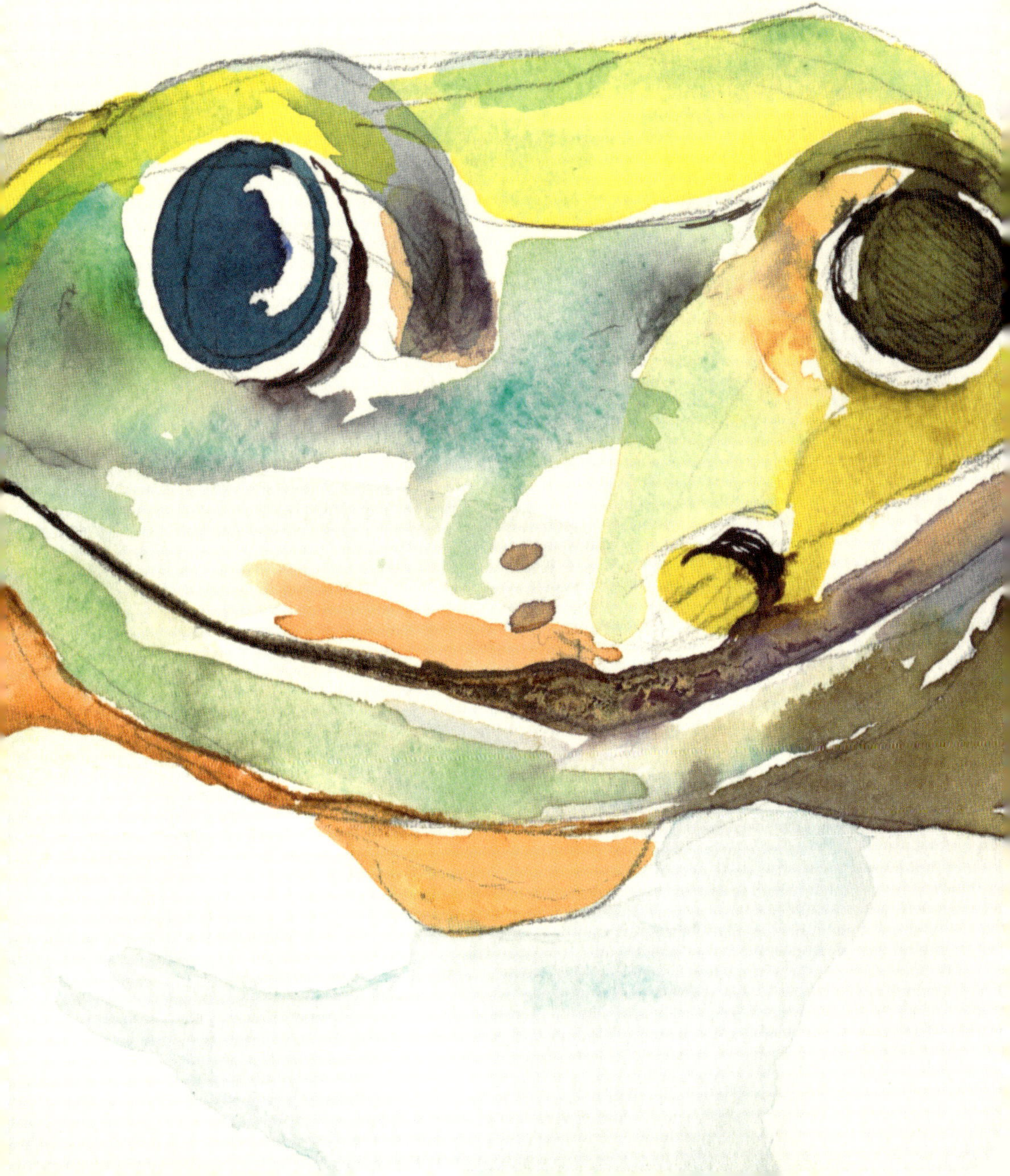

Kreta. Dabei entstand ein Reisetagebuch mit Texten und Zeichnungen, auch solchen aus Fotos heraus. Das Buch habe ich selbst genäht. Es folgten Reisen nach Afrika, Kuba, Gomera, Los Angeles, Hawaii, Italien, in die Türkei, Irland, Schottland, Bali, Sansibar und ins Canyonland in den USA. Wenn ich weg bin, schalte ich komplett ab. Umso größer war der Schock, als ich gegen Ende der Griechenlandreise merkte: Mein Buch ist weg! Ich bin mit dem Bus die ganze Strecke zurückgefahren, die ich gerade gekommen war. Ich war geradezu hysterisch, bin auf die Straße gerannt, habe Busse angehalten und sie durchsucht nach meinem Buch, bin in die Polizeistation gelaufen – nichts. Am Ende saß ich auf einer Bank und heulte. Da sehe ich was, es lehnt am Pfosten eines Busschildes, der Wind blättert darin – ein Buch. Mein Buch. Es grenzte an ein Wunder, es war eines der größten Glücksgefühle, die ich je erlebt habe.

W.B. All diese Reisetagebücher sind nie ausgestellt worden oder als Reprint erschienen?

C.S. Ein einziges Reprint gibt es, das Tagebuch der Hawaii-Reise. Sonst wurden die Reisetagebücher nie gezeigt. Ich selbst sehe sie auch lange Jahre nicht. Sie liegen hier. Ich lagere vieles von meinem Werk. Ich behalte auch Bilder, gebe sie nicht auf den Kunstmarkt. Eines der Bücher ist im Rücken mit einer Wurstpelle beklebt. Am Anfang hat's noch ein bisschen gestunken, jetzt riecht's nicht mehr. Manchmal freue ich mich über meine Buchnähkunst, ich nehme dazu weißen dicken Zwirn und nähe sie alle selbst, und ich nehme echten Buch-

the book myself. That was followed by trips to Zanzibar, Gomera, Los Angeles, Hawaii, Italy, Turkey and Canyonland in the USA. When I am away I switch off completely. So the shock was all the greater when I noticed toward the end of the trip to Greece that my book had disappeared! I retraced by bus the entire route I had just travelled. I was quite hysterical and ran out into the road, stopped the buses and searched them for my book and then I went to the police station – nothing. I finally sat down on a bench and burst into tears. And then I saw something propped up against the post with the bus sign. The wind was leafing through it – a book. My book. It seemed like a miracle; it was one of the most intense feelings of happiness I have ever experienced.

W.B. And all these travel diaries have never been exhibited or published as reprints?

C.S. There is just one reprint: the diary of my trip to Hawaii. Otherwise my travel diaries have never been exhibited. I don't look at them myself for years afterwards either. They lie here. I store lots of my works. And I keep pictures and don't release them for sale on the art market. One of the books has a sausage skin stuck onto the spine. It stank at bit at the beginning, but now it doesn't smell any more. Sometimes I like the books I have stitched myself; I use thick thread and stitch them all myself and I use proper bookbinder's glue. It's important that it doesn't tear; the book must be really strong.

W.B. What made you decide to produce picture books like this; was it just because of your travelling?

binderleim. Wichtig ist, dass es nicht reißt, das Buch muss richtig fest sein.

W.B. Wie kamen Sie darauf, solche Bilderbücher herzustellen, einfach durch das Reisen?

C.S. Ich hatte mal eine Wohnung, noch in Ost-Berlin, die war so klein, dass ich darin nicht malen konnte, da habe ich mit den Büchern angefangen. Ich könnte auch im Knast überleben, ich muss nur was zu fummeln haben. Und ich bin ja nicht nur Malerin, ich bin Künstlerin. Ich habe einen Roman geschrieben, und jetzt mache ich eben dieses Buch mit den Zeichnungen.

W.B. Jetzt haben Sie viel Platz, zumal draußen in Brandenburg, wo Sie seit einigen Jahren auch leben. Hat das Landleben Sie und Ihre Arbeit verändert?

C.S. Es hat schon etwas verändert. Ich bin selbstbewusster geworden. Es ist eine andere Intensität der Arbeit da draußen. Ich versinke in der Arbeit – keine Künstler, die vorbeikommen; kein Rumtingeln auf Vernissagen; keine komischen Empfänge, zu denen man geht; keine Ablenkung. Ich werde zum Bauern. Essen zum Beispiel ist auf dem Land viel elementarer als in der Stadt. Ich esse dreimal warm. Man wird sperriger, auch radikaler. Für Arbeiten auf Papier ist die Stadt besser: eine Höhle, und zeichnen will ich in der Höhle. Malen geht draußen auf dem Land besser, gerade wenn die Jahreszeit trübe wird. Im Sommer ist die Ablenkung durch die Natur stärker. Die meisten Bilder male ich von Oktober bis März. Das ist meine Schweigescholle da draußen.

C.S. I once had a flat; that was still in East Berlin, and it was so small that I couldn't paint in it. That was when I started making books. I could even survive in prison; all I need is something to fiddle with. And I'm not just a painter; I am an artist. I have written a novel, and now I'm making this book with the drawings.

W.B. Now you have plenty of room, especially out in Brandenburg, where you have lived for some years. Has country life changed you and your work?

C.S. Yes, it has changed some things. I have become more sure of myself. Work assumes a different intensity out there. I become immersed in my work – there are no artists who come by, and there's no doing the rounds of exhibition openings, no funny receptions that one goes to; no distractions. I become a farmer. Food, for example, is far more elemental in the country than in town, I eat three hot meals a day. You become more awkward, more radical. For work on paper the city is better: a cave, and I like drawing in a cave. Painting is better in the country, especially when it's the gloomier season of the year. In summer nature is more of a distraction. I paint most pictures in January, February and March. Out there is where I retire to my hermit's cell.

W.B. Have you become less of an urban animal?

C.S. When I'm in my flat in Berlin, a colleague will call me and say: Hey, there's a new bar opening up near your place, come on over. So I go there and think, my God, what are they talking about? He's got a Bentley – and now he's got a Bentley too. And so it goes on the whole time. Nobody ever

W.B. Sind Sie unstädtischer geworden?

C.S. Wenn ich in meiner Wohnung in Berlin bin, ruft ein Kollege an: Du, da eröffnet gerade eine neue Bar bei dir in der Gegend, komm doch hin. Dann geh ich hin und denke, Gott, was reden die denn? Der da hat'n Bentley – und der hier hat jetzt auch'n Bentley. So geht das die ganze Zeit. Über Kunst wird nicht mehr gesprochen. Nur darüber, wo wann welche Ausstellung ist. Der Typus des Künstlers hat sich verändert. Auf einmal laufen sie alle mit solchen Retro-Brillen herum. Auf dem Land geht es ziemlich karg zu und spröde, das sehe ich schon. Die Frau aus dem Vorderhaus sagt mir: Die Blumen, die muss sie aber jetzt reinstellen, es gibt Frost – die redet mich in der dritten Person an. Die Gespräche in der Stadt sind oft langweilig. Auf dem Land geht's schärfer zu: Letzte Nacht hab ich ein Wildschwein falsch geschossen, ein inneres Organ getroffen, das Fleisch ist versaut. Oder: Die Sau war zu schwer, um sie abzutransportieren.

W.B. Über die Enge und die Bedrückungen in der DDR müssen wir nicht diskutieren – dennoch: Hatte die Stille der DDR für einen jungen Künstler nicht den Vorteil, sich ungestörter entwickeln zu können? Ohne dass ein heiß laufender Kunstmarkt ihm sein halbgares Zeug aus dem Atelier reißt und ihn zwingt, zu tanzen, bevor er tanzen kann?

C.S. So still war es nun auch nicht. Wir waren ja in gewisser Weise im Widerstand, da gibt es immer was zu tun. Aber das, was wir taten, war auch ein wenig hoffnungslos, da

talks about art. Only about where and when which exhibition is taking place. Artists as such are a different type these days. Suddenly they are all running around wearing these retro glasses. Out in the country everything is pretty austere and rough, I agree that's how it is. The woman from the front house tells me: "She must bring the flowers in, there's going to be a frost – she addresses me in the third person". The conversations in the city are often boring. Out in the country it's harsher: Yesterday evening I shot a wild boar but hit it in the wrong place; I hit one of the inner organs and the meat is ruined. Or: The old sow was too heavy to carry back home.

W.B. There is no need to discuss the narrowness and oppression in the GDR – but all the same: didn't the quiet of the GDR have an advantage for young artists in that they could develop without being disturbed? Without an overheated art market snatching their half-finished works from their studios and forcing them to dance before they were able to?

C.S. It wasn't as quiet as all that. We were part of the resistance, to some extent, and there was always something to do. But what we did was also a bit helpless, because the repression against us simply became more acute. We were banned from working et cetera. Those who were free had to cope with the art market and we had to cope with the politics of dictatorship. But what I am trying to achieve in art has nothing to do either with politics or with the art market. Both here and there, the art market and politics are only side effects.

sich die Repression gegen uns noch verschärfte. Berufsverbot et cetera. Hatten die einen in der Freiheit mit dem Kunstmarkt zu tun, hatten wir mit der diktatorischen Politik zu tun. Aber was ich in der Kunst anstrebe, hat weder mit der Politik noch mit dem Kunstmarkt zu tun. Ob hier oder da sind Kunstmarkt und Politik nur Begleiterscheinungen.

W.B. Was empfanden Sie nach dem Mauerfall, gerade aus den USA zurückgekehrt? Trafen Sie alte Kollegen aus der DDR?

C.S. Wenn Kollegen aus dem Osten zu mir kamen, wollten die ihre alte Conny haben. Die Enttäuschung stand ihnen im Gesicht, wenn sie die nicht fanden: Ach, du malst jetzt Porree? Es gibt auch eine falsche Suche nach Seele im Osten. Es war ein ganz anderes Leben dort, immer ging es um Sinnfragen. Keine Ironie, immer nur dagegen sein, immer nur Melancholie und tiefer Ernst. Natürlich gibt es auch die guten Ost-Künstler, die zeichnen sich dadurch aus, dass sie in der alten und in der neuen Zeit Bescheid wissen – die zum Beispiel wissen, es gibt heute ganz neue, feinere, ironische Arten von Provokation. Aber es ist auch etwas verloren gegangen. Der Ostler meiner Generation, wenn er Künstler kannte, hat immer das Chronologische gesehen, die Entwicklung einer Kunst: Aha, da fängt er abstrakt an, und jetzt wird's figurativ, jetzt wird's dies und das. Der Westen sieht nicht die Linie, er sieht nur den Punkt: Aha, so und so ist der. In der Ausstellung, im Katalog muss alles zueinander passen – die Show steht. Man guckt nicht zurück, nur nach vorn.

W.B. What did you feel after the fall of the Wall, when you returned from the States? Did you meet your old colleagues from the GDR?

C.S. When colleagues from the East came to see me they wanted to find their old Conny again. The disappointment was writ plain on their faces when they didn't find her: Oh, so now you're painting leeks? In the East there is also a lot of false soul-searching. It was a completely different country there and it was always a matter of questions of meaning, No irony, always being against things, never anything but melancholy and deep seriousness. Of course there are also good artists from the East; they distinguish themselves by being at home in both the old and the new era. For example, they know that today there are completely new, subtler ways of provoking. But something has been lost as well. The "Easterners" of my generation, if they knew artists, always saw the chronological development in art: Aha, now he's starting to paint abstract pictures, and now it's becoming figurative, and now it's becoming this and that. The "Westerner" doesn't see the line, he only sees the point: Aha, so that's what it's like. In the exhibition, in the catalogue, everything has to be just so – the show is complete. People don't look back, they only look forwards.

W.B. Was your "Pope" series intended to be ironic?

C.S. Not at all! In the last picture in the series Wojtyla is eating a red girl – that was when I stopped because that went over the top and became ironic. Carrying the Cross: If someone says to me: "That's rubbish," then I say to them, "You

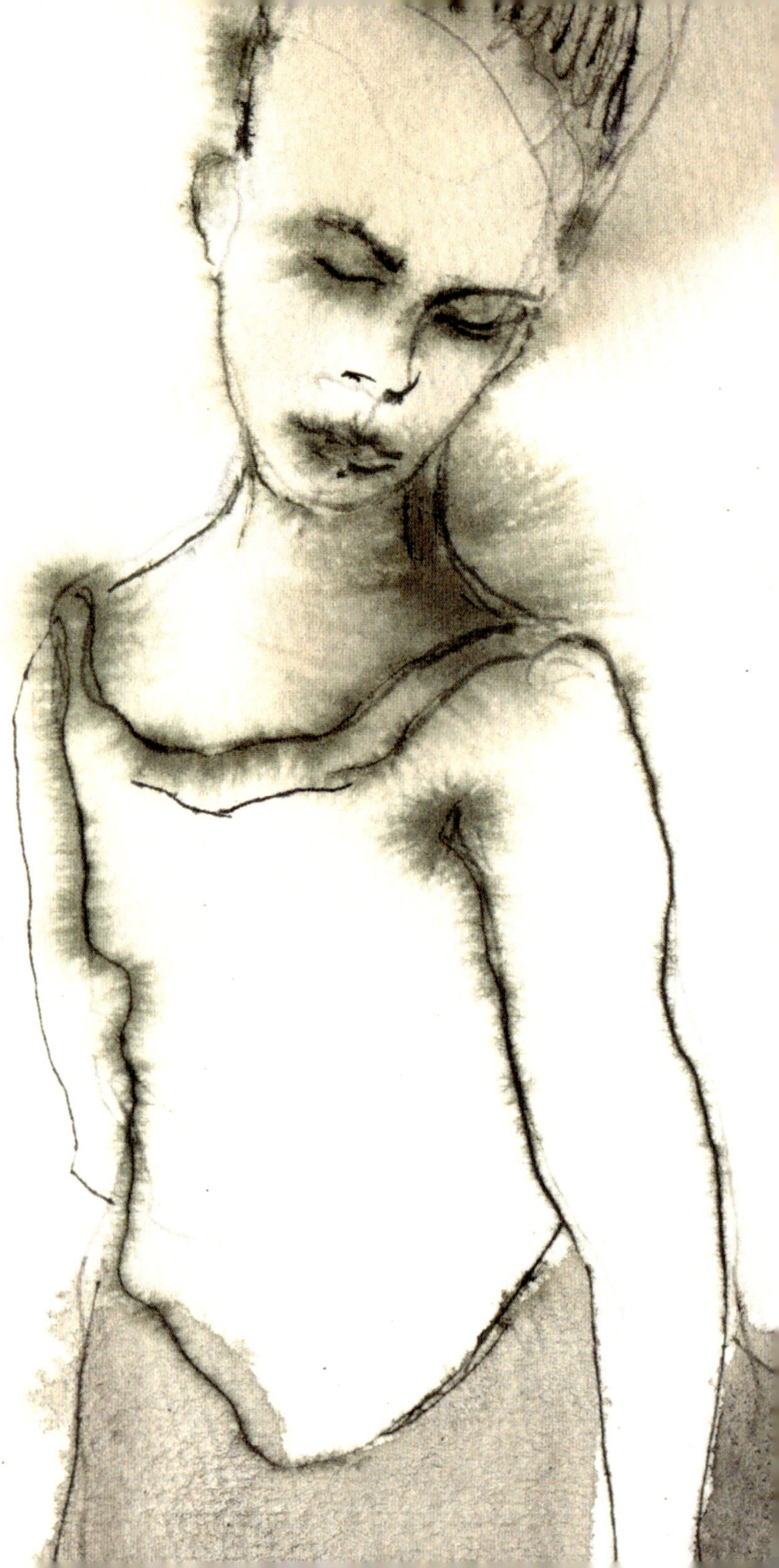

W.B. Ihre Papst-Serie, war das auch Ironie?
C.S. Gar nicht! Das letzte Bild der Serie, da küsst Woytila so ein rotes Mädchen – da habe ich aufgehört, da kippte es, da kam die Ironie. Das Kreuz tragen: Wenn mir jemand sagt, das ist doch Quatsch, dann sage ich, du verstehst nichts. Alle sagten, als der Papst so krank war, jetzt solle er zurücktreten. Ein Unding! Er hat das Kreuz zu tragen. Es ist so wie ein Künstler, der hat ja auch ein Ideal. Eine ganz große Geste ist, dass Woytila seinem Attentäter verziehen hat. Und er war ja auch ein schräger Vogel, er kommt von der Kunst, vom Theater her. Ich kann diese kritische Diskussion nicht ertragen. Ironie! Ich würde doch nie ein Bild aus Ironie anfangen. Ironie ist gut, wenn sie sich einschleicht. Aber doch nicht als fester Vorsatz: Jetzt male ich mal ironisch. Die Auseinandersetzung mit dem Papst hat meine Haltung gehärtet. Er kann doch nicht sagen: Treibt ab. Ich hab's selbst gemacht, aber ich habe auch die Zeichnung gemacht, wo die Embryonen um den Papst herumschwirren. Wenn das Frauenbild Maria ist, kann der Papst die Frauen nicht zur Abtreibung ermuntern. Eine Abtreibung ist doch nicht wie einen Pickel ausdrücken. Fürchten die, die das ganz normal finden, denn gar nicht, dass sie das verfolgt?
W.B. Sie sind katholisch aufgewachsen?
C.S. Meine erste bewusste Zeichnung hieß „Das Paradies", das war im Religionsunterricht. In dieser Zeichnung habe ich geschafft, was ich in der Kirche mit acht, neun, elf

haven't understood anything." When the Pope was so ill everyone said he should abdicate. What nonsense! He has to bear the Cross. It's like an artist; he, too, has an ideal. The fact that Wojtyla forgave his attacker was a great gesture. And he was an eccentric character too; he came from the arts scene, from the theatre. I can't stand these critical discussions. Africa, the AIDS victims, and the Pope is to blame – I can't stand these do-gooders and their posturing. So that is it who goes to Africa and sacrifices themselves? The Catholic nuns. Irony! I would never start painting a picture with an ironic aim in mind. Irony is fine when it creeps in. But not as a set resolution: So now let's be ironic. The dispute with the Pope has made me harden my resolve. He can't say, "Have an abortion!" I have had one myself but I also produced the drawing where the embryos are hovering around the Pope. If the Virgin Mary is the role model for women, the Pope cannot encourage women to have an abortion. An abortion is not like squeezing out a spot. And those who find it completely normal, are they not afraid that it will haunt them?

W.B. Did you grow up as a Catholic?

C.S. The first drawing I can remember was called "Paradise", and I drew it during Religious Education. In this drawing I succeeded in achieving what I couldn't necessarily achieve at church at the age of eight, nine, eleven – for the very first time I was completely oblivious. I didn't like going to Church, but afterwards when I left with the congregation I experienced feelings of happiness. Wojtyla was the first

Jahren nicht unbedingt geschafft habe – ich bin komplett versunken, zum ersten Mal. Ich bin ja ungern in die Kirche gegangen, aber hinterher ist man mit der Gemeinde rausgegangen, da habe ich ein Glücksgefühl gehabt. Mit Woytila habe ich zum ersten Mal einen alten Menschen gemalt, sonst waren es immer Kinder oder schöne Frauen gewesen. Hier war es ein Gesicht als Landschaft: die ganze Welt, Berge, diese Stirn, da ist alles drin. „Totus tuus" aus dieser Serie ist mein wichtigstes Bild – wo der Papst den Tod umarmt.

W.B. Oder den sterblichen Menschen.

C.S. Er ist aber schwarz.

W.B. Ja.

C.S. Vielleicht weil der Schwarze sich noch umarmen lässt, anders als hier, hier ist alles verkopft.

W.B. Sind Bilder mächtiger als Zeichnungen?

C.S. Bei Bildern ist meine Aggression stärker – hundert Prozent. Zeichnungen vertragen das nicht, fast gar nicht. Bilder fange ich verträumt an, und dann muss ich sie kaputtmachen. Dann geht es weiter. Jetzt zeichne ich gerade Köpfe. Die kleinen Zeichnungen gelingen fast immer, aber bei den Köpfen ist viel Ausschuss.

W.B. Wie kommen die Gesichter zu Ihnen?

C.S. Anfangen. Einfach anfangen. Einmal hatte ich eine von der Vogue auf dem Blatt. Aber das ist dann nur so ein flüchtiger Blick auf ein Titelfoto, mehr nicht. Das Zeichnen löst sich gleich wieder davon und geht seinen eigenen Weg.

W.B. Setzen Sie dem Papier auch physisch zu, so wie der Leinwand?

time I painted an old person; before that it was always children or beautiful women. And here you have a face like a landscape: the whole world, mountains, this brow, it contains everything. “Totus tuus” in this series is my most important picture – where the Pope embraces Death.

W.B. Or Man in his mortality.

C.S. But he’s black.

W.B. Yes.

C.S. Perhaps because the black man allows himself to be embraced, unlike here where everything is so full of meaning.

W.B. Are pictures more powerful than drawings?

C.S. In pictures my aggression is stronger – definitely. Drawings can’t take it, hardly at all. I start pictures in a dreamy state, and then I have to destroy them. And then it continues. At the moment I am drawing heads.

The small drawings are almost always successful, but when it comes to the heads there are always a lot of failures.

W.B. How do the faces come to you?

C.S. By starting. Just starting. Once I ended up with one from Vogue on my sheet of paper. But then it’s only a fleeting glimpse on a cover photo, no more than that. The drawing detaches itself immediately and goes its own way.

W.B. Do you treat the paper physically in any way, as you do the canvas?

C.S. What interested me with these heads was drawing onto the wet paper. I’m not telling a story and it’s not a matter of anatomical correctness. In my mind’s eye I can always see the portraits of the deceased person on the coffins of

C.S. Bei diesen Köpfen hat es mich interessiert, in das nasse Papier hinein zu zeichnen. Man erzählt keine Geschichte, es geht nicht um anatomische Korrektheit. In meinem Kopf sind dabei immer die Totenporträts auf altägyptischen Särgen. Ich kann mit Köpfen nichts anfangen, bei denen man erkennt, dass sie aus unserer Zeit sind. Es muss so sein, dass die Zeit gerinnt. Ich suche nach dem Ausdruck beim Zeichnen. Ich will nicht Realität, ich will Gegenrealität. Ich will auf Bildern nicht sehen, was ich auf der Straße sehen muss. Viele mögen ja meine dominanten Frauen, aber ich liebe die Entrückten, die Verträumten.

W.B. Sie verwenden eigensinnige Papiere – muss es immer Papier sein?

C.S. Am liebsten würde ich auf Wände malen, eine Kirche ausmalen. Möglichst keine Begrenzungen haben, nicht mal die einer Leinwand. Wenn ich im Fernsehen etwas über Galaxien sehe, könnte ich mich reinsteigern: dass der Raum sich weitet.

W.B. Wie muss man sich Ihren Umgang mit den Farben vorstellen?

C.S. Ich würde die Farbfläschchen nie so benutzen, wie sie sind. Ich mische alle Farben ab. Wenn man eine tolle rote Lippe malen will, muss alles andere grau, braun, morastig sein. Dann müssen Unfarben aufs Blatt. Schöne Farben ergeben ein Bild: So machen es die Dilettanten, wenn sie Aquarelle malen. Wenn ich nur drei Farbtöne habe, provoziert es mich sehr, daraus was zu machen. Ich habe auch nur drei Pinsel, einen dünnen, einen dicken, einen flachen.

ancient Egypt. I have no use for heads where you recognise immediately that they are of our time.
It's inevitable that time passes. I try to express that in my drawings. I'm not attempting to create reality, I'm aiming for counter-reality. On pictures I don't want to see what I have to look at in the streets. Lots of people like my dominant women, but I like the other-worldly ones, the dreamers.

W.B. You use unusual papers - does it always have to be paper?

C.S. I'd prefer above all to paint on walls, to decorate a church. If possible to have no limits at all, not even those of the canvas. When I see something on television about galaxies I could really get obsessed with the way that space expands.

W.B. How should we see your use of colours?

C.S. I would never use the bottle of paint just as it is. I always mix all the colours. If you want to paint nice red lips then everything else has to be grey, brown, mud-coloured. Then you need non-colours on the sheet. Pretty colours create a picture: that's how amateurs paint when they produce watercolours. If I only have three colours it spurs me on to make something of it. And I only have three brushes: a thin one, a thick one and a flat one. Having a lot doesn't make things better, it makes them worse. I have never seen another studio with so little in the way of materials and so few brushes. And the pens are just the same; one is crooked and one blots.

W.B. You are in your element when it's wet and damp, dripping and daubing?

Das Viele macht nichts besser, eher schlechter. Ich habe noch kein anderes Atelier gesehen, das so wenig Material, so wenige Pinsel hat. Bei den Federn ist es genauso, eine ist schon schief, eine kleckst.

W.B. Das Nasse und Feuchte, das Triefen und Klecksen ist Ihr Element?

C.S. Wenn der Prozess richtig zustande kommt, dann kleckst und trieft alles. Ich habe mir bei alten Meistern oft angeschaut, wie die das machen: einen goldenen Ring zum Beispiel. Sie machen es mit Dreck – nur dieser eine, kleine goldene Punkt leuchtet aus dem Dreck heraus.

C.S. If the process develops the right way, then everything is daubed and dripped. I have often studied the old masters to see how they do it: paint a golden ring, for example. They use dirt – and just the one little golden dot shines out of the dirt.

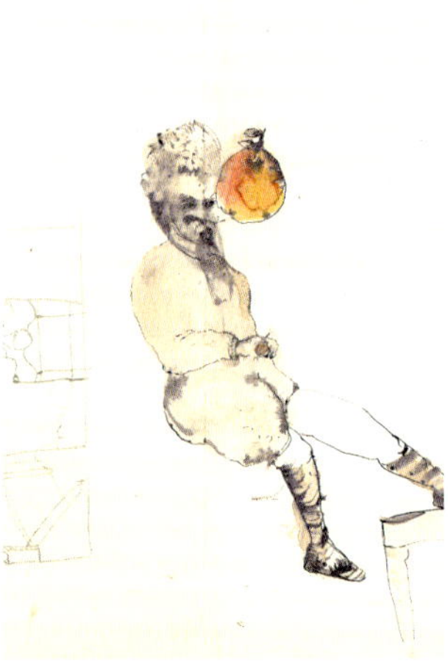

1984–1987

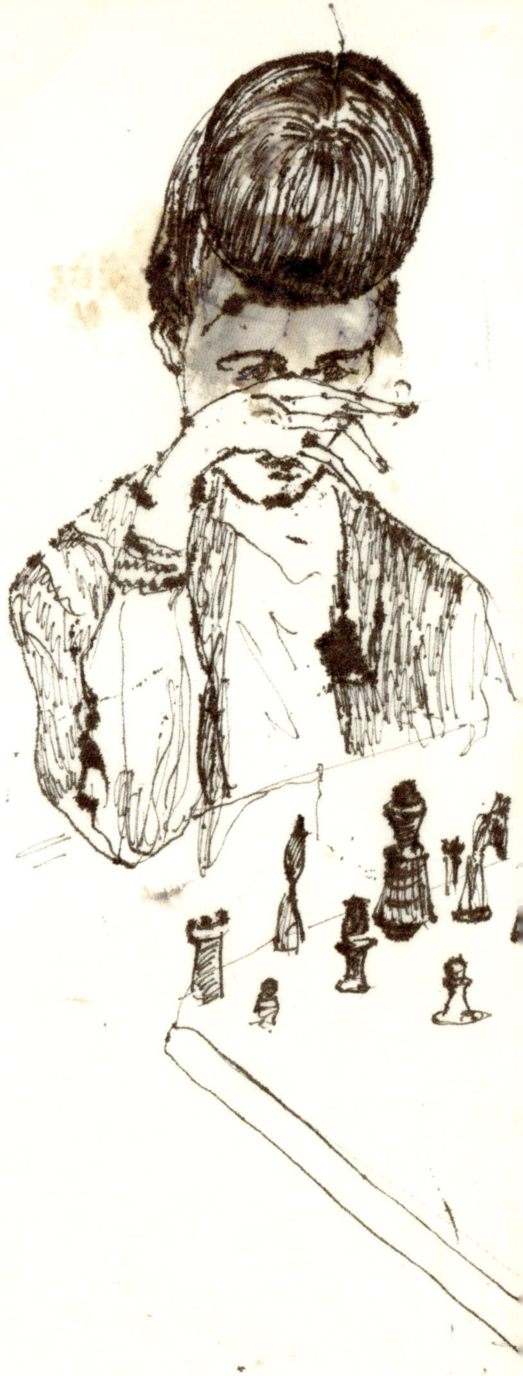

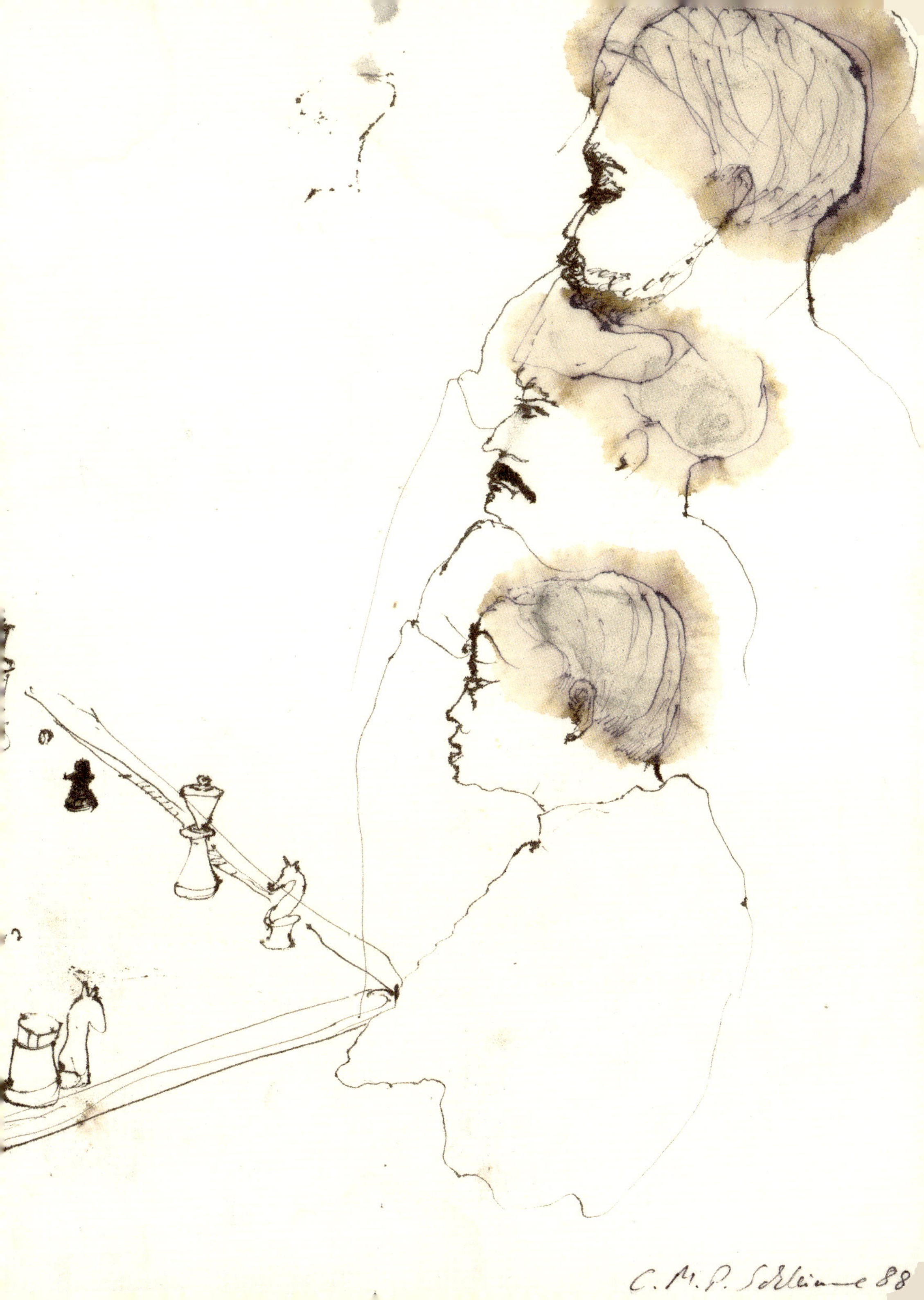
C. M. P. Schleime 88

vorhergehende Seite previous page **Moritz, Schachspiel** 1988
Tusche auf Japanpapier Indian ink on Japan paper 53 x 74 cm

Konfuser Nachmittag 1984
Japanpapier auf Vlies kaschiert Japan paper laminated on fleece
82 x 55 cm

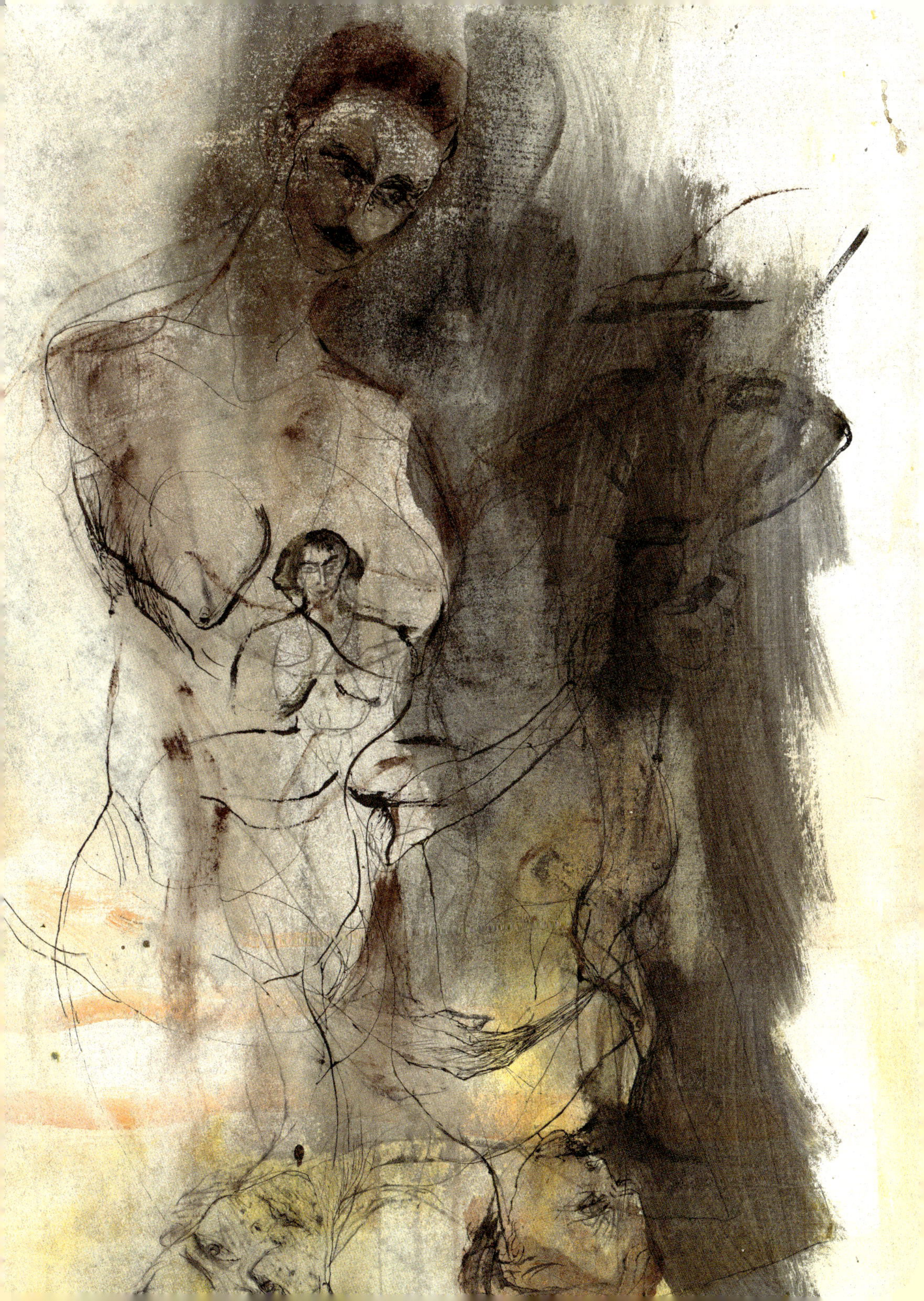

Willi Willmann 1986

Tusche & Grafit auf Zeitungspapier Indian ink & graphite on newspaper 55 x 82 cm

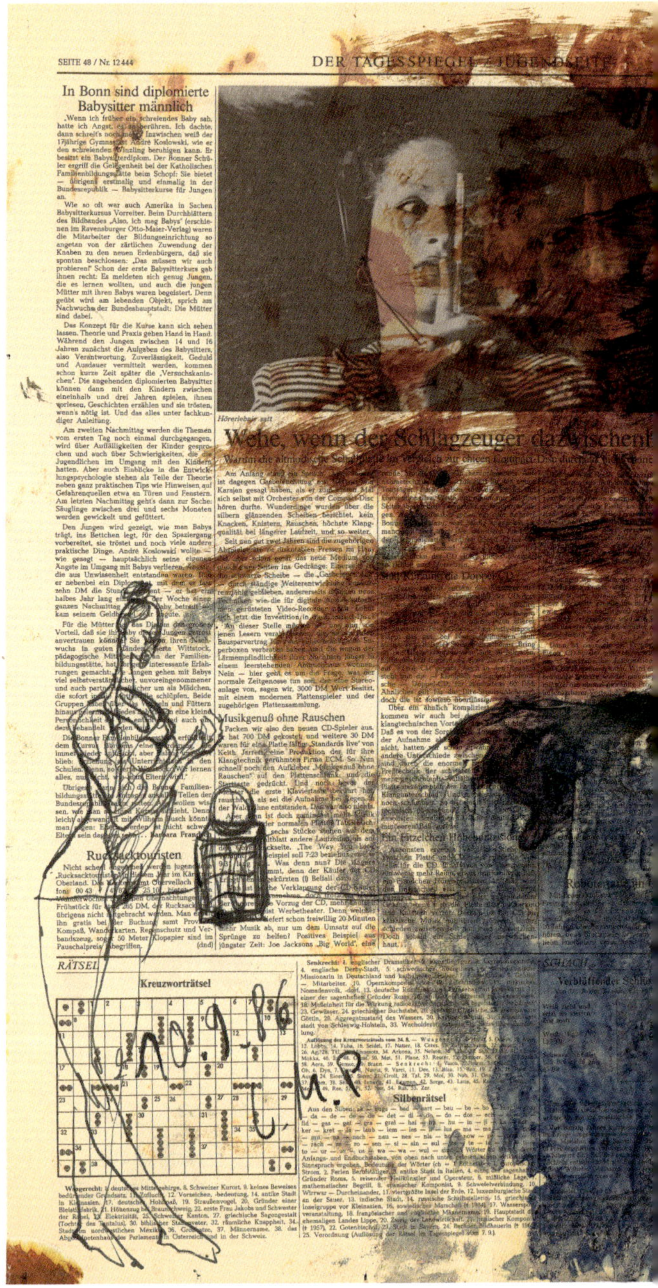

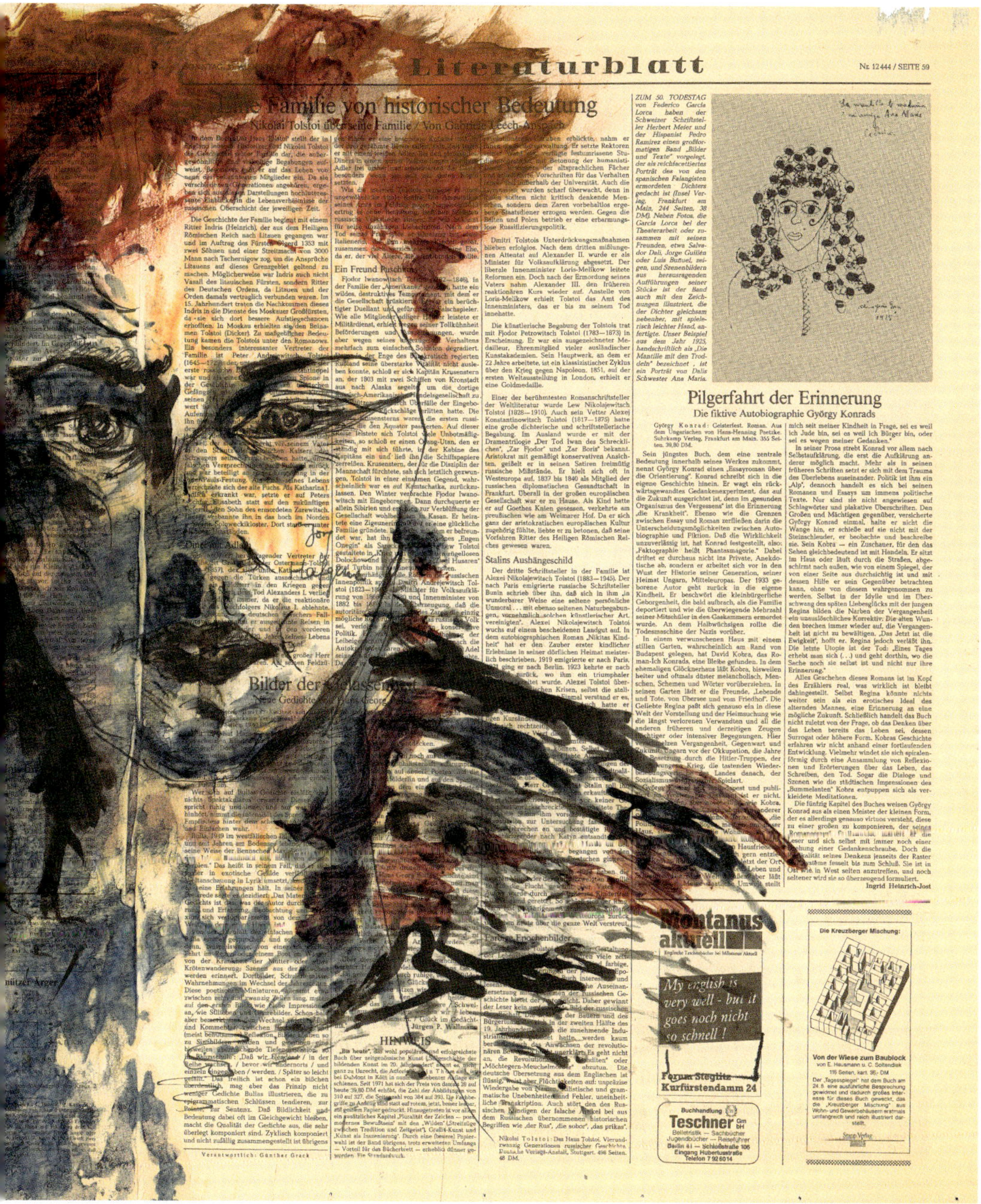
Literaturblatt
Nr. 12444 / SEITE 59
Familie von historischer Bedeutung
Ein Freund Puschkins
Stalins Aushängeschild
Bilder der Gelassenheit
HINWEIS
Pilgerfahrt der Erinnerung
Die fiktive Autobiographie György Konrads
Ingrid Heinrich-Jost
Montanus aktuell
My english is very well - but it goes noch nicht so schnell!
Forum Steglitz
Kurfürstendamm 24
Teschner
Die Kreuzberger Mischung:
Von der Wiese zum Baublock

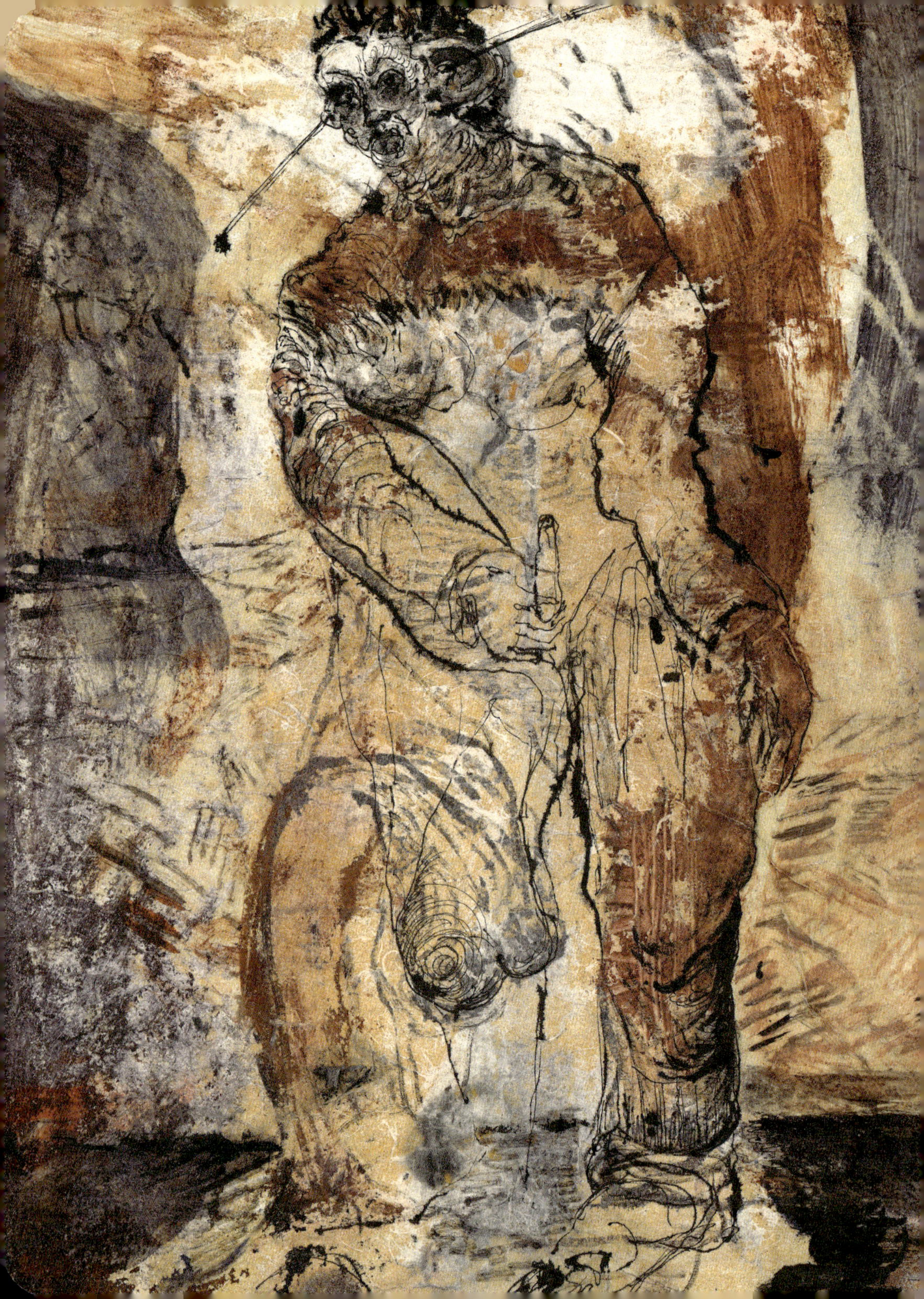

Der Hodenbruch 1984
Japanpapier auf Vlies kaschiert & Tusche
Japan paper laminated on fleece & Indian ink
82 x 55 cm

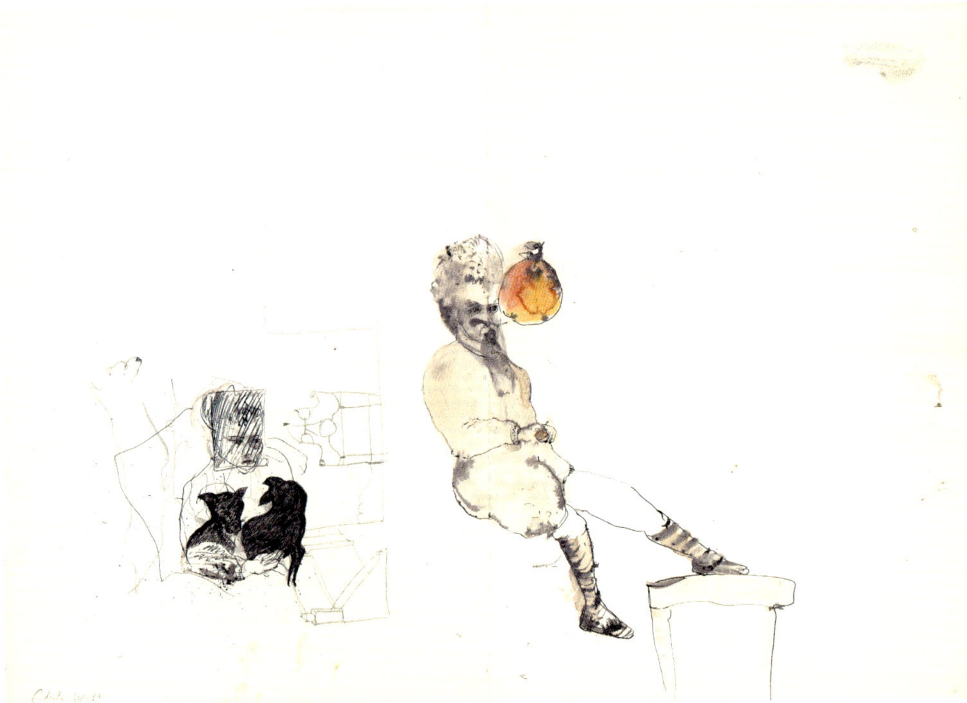

Moritz mit Sonnenbrand 1987
Tusche & Aquarell & Grafit auf Papier
Indian ink & watercolour & graphit on paper
63 x 88 cm

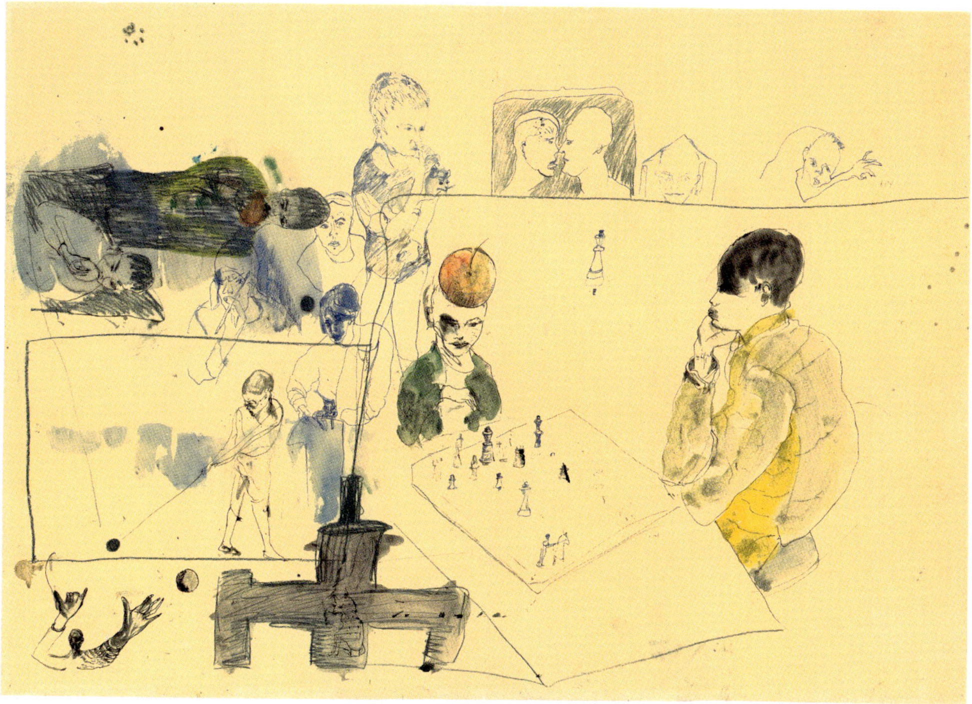

Moritz mit Früchten 1987
Tusche & Aquarell & Grafit auf Papier
Indian ink & watercolour & graphit on paper
71 x 98 cm

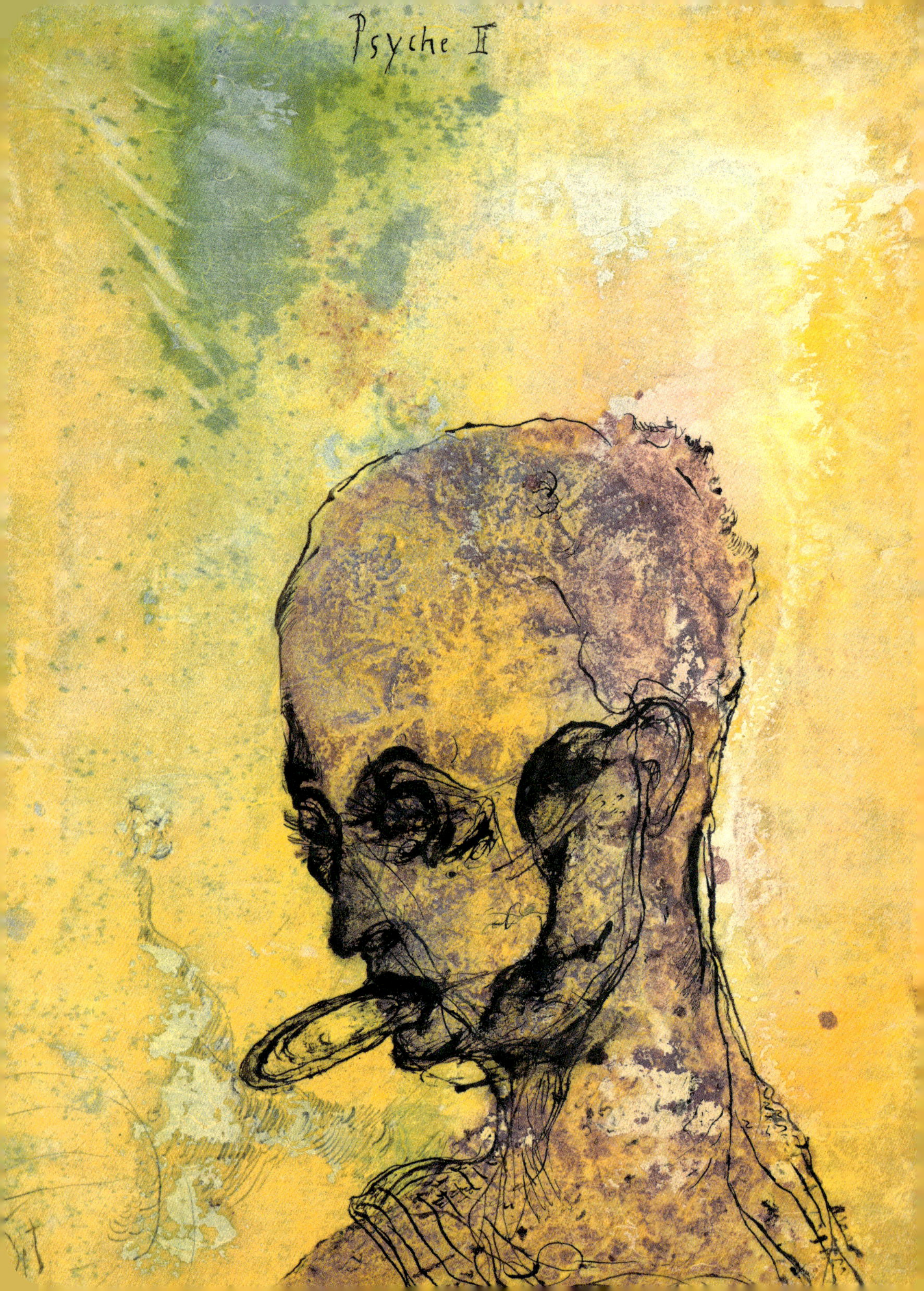
Psyche II

linke Seite left page **Psyche II** 1986
Japanpapier auf Vlies kaschiert & Tusche
Japan paper laminated on fleece & Indian ink 76 x 56 cm

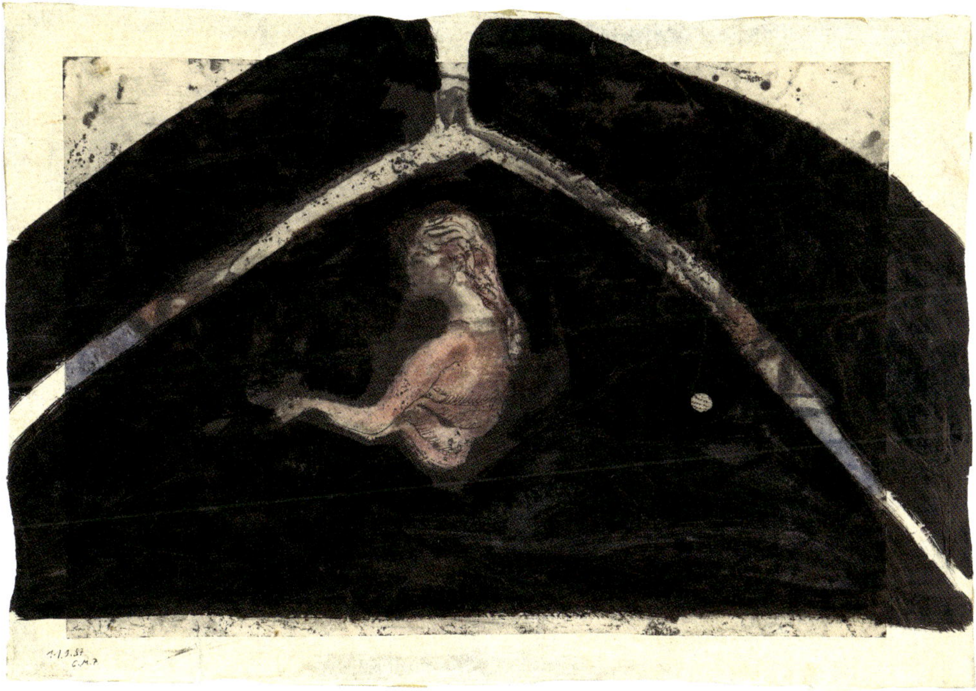

Wille zur Abstraktion 1987
Collage & Tusche auf Papier Collage & Indian ink on paper
59 x 86 cm

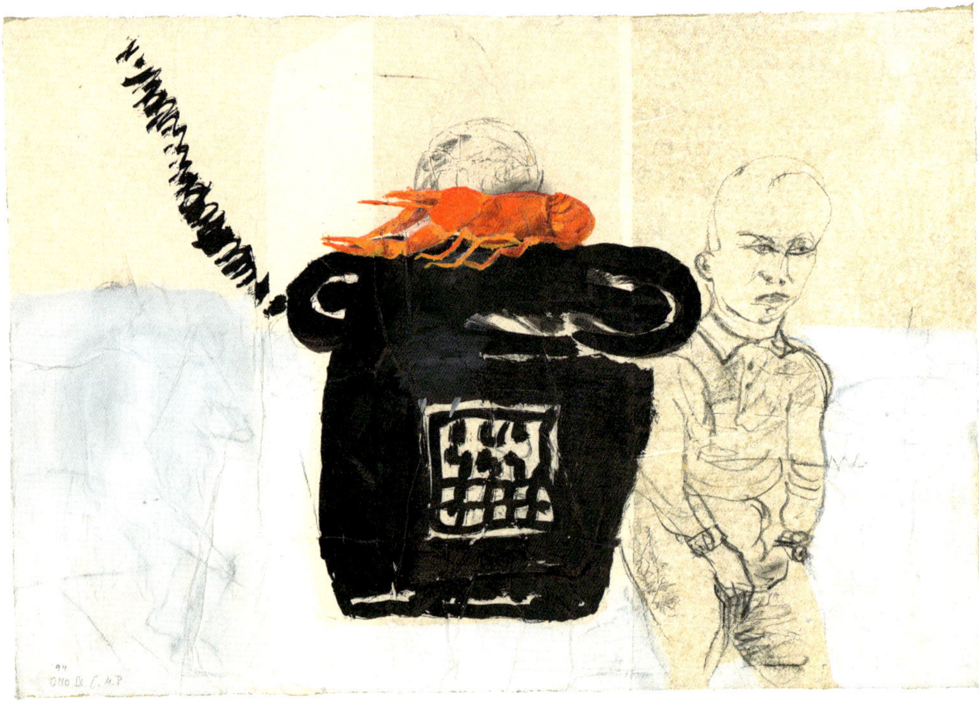

Krebsgang am Telefon 1987
Japanpapier auf Vlies kaschiert & Gouache, Grafit
Japan paper laminated on fleece & gouache, graphite
56 x 76 cm

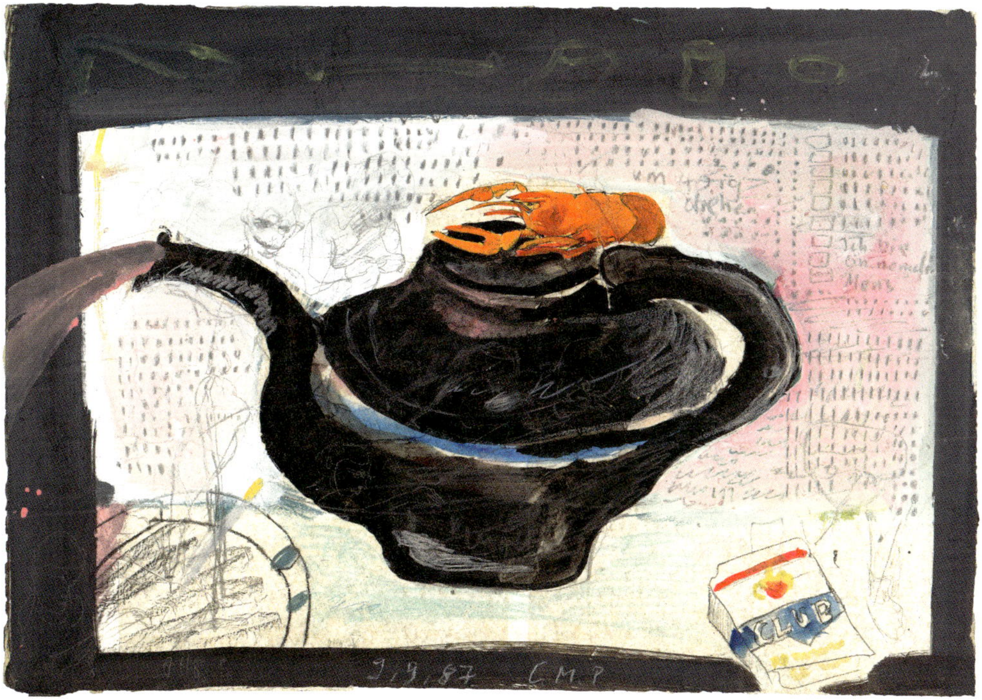

Willkommen im Krebsclub 1987
Japanpapier auf Vlies kaschiert & Gouache, Grafit
Japan paper laminated on fleece & gouache, graphite
56 x 76 cm

Gondeln
In Reih & Glied
gekettet

Lydia
Arizona
Libell

der sie besitzt
darf mit ihnen kreisen
darf sie berühren
bis er sich spiegeln
kann

kein Fremder
darf sie je fortbewegen

hier spricht nur Daumenver-
ständigung
von Mann zu Mann

es ist die Geliebte
die dem Owner nicht
widerspricht
da die Geliebte
niemals spricht

es ist diejenige, die
er nicht verlässt
auch wenn sie trunken
im Hafen schunkelt

der Wind nur
der Wind nur
darf sie ihm nehmen

Cornelia Schleime

Gondolas
tethered
one behind the other

Lydia
Arizona
Libell

he who owns them
may circle with them
may touch them
until he can mirror
himself

no stranger
may ever move them to another place

thumb communication is all
that's spoken here
from man to man

it is the mistress
who does not
contradict the owner
as the mistress
never speaks

it is the one whom
he will not leave
even if she sways drunkenly
in the harbour

the wind alone
the wind alone
may take her from him

Cornelia Schleime

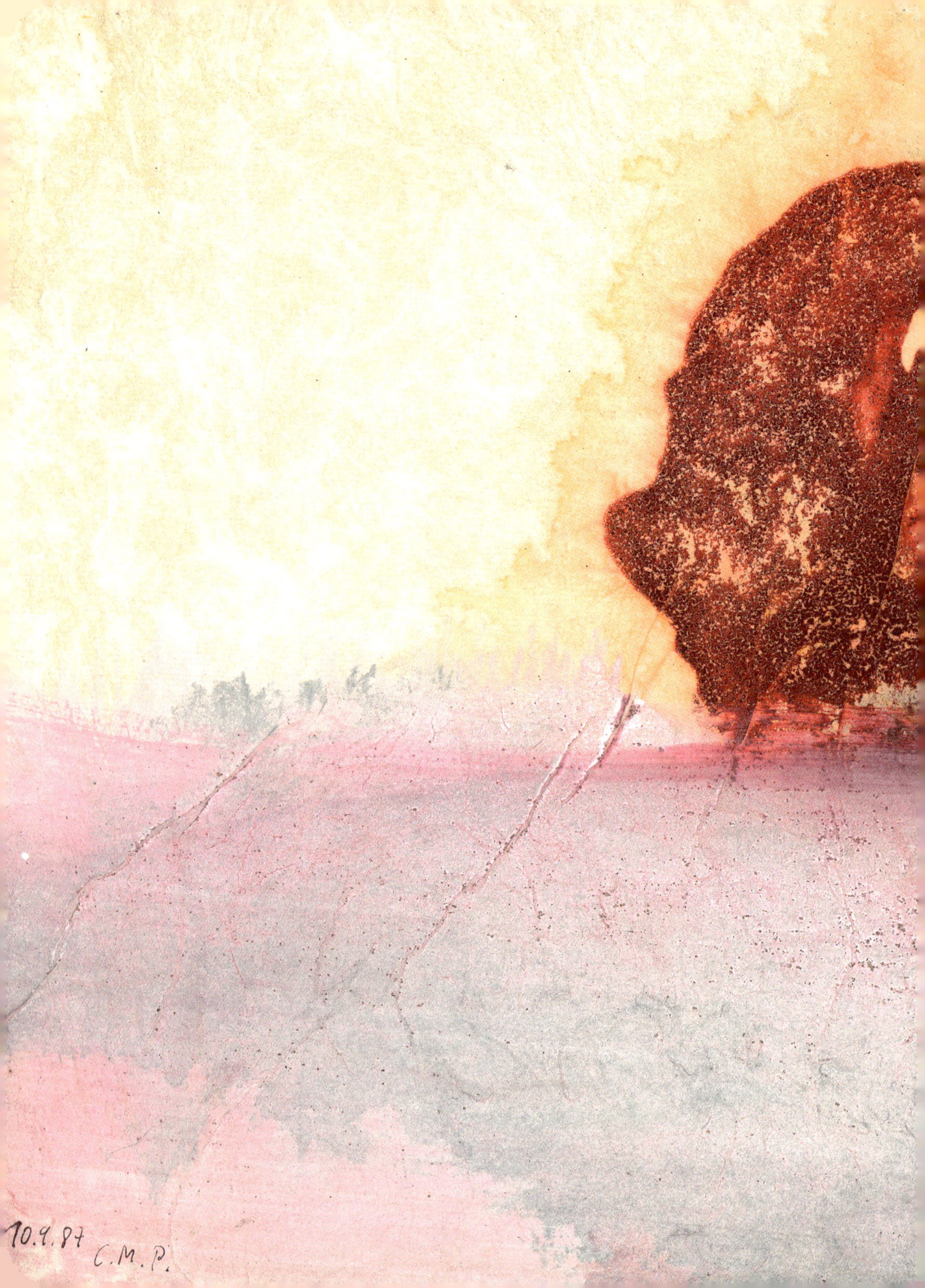
10.9.87
C.M.P.

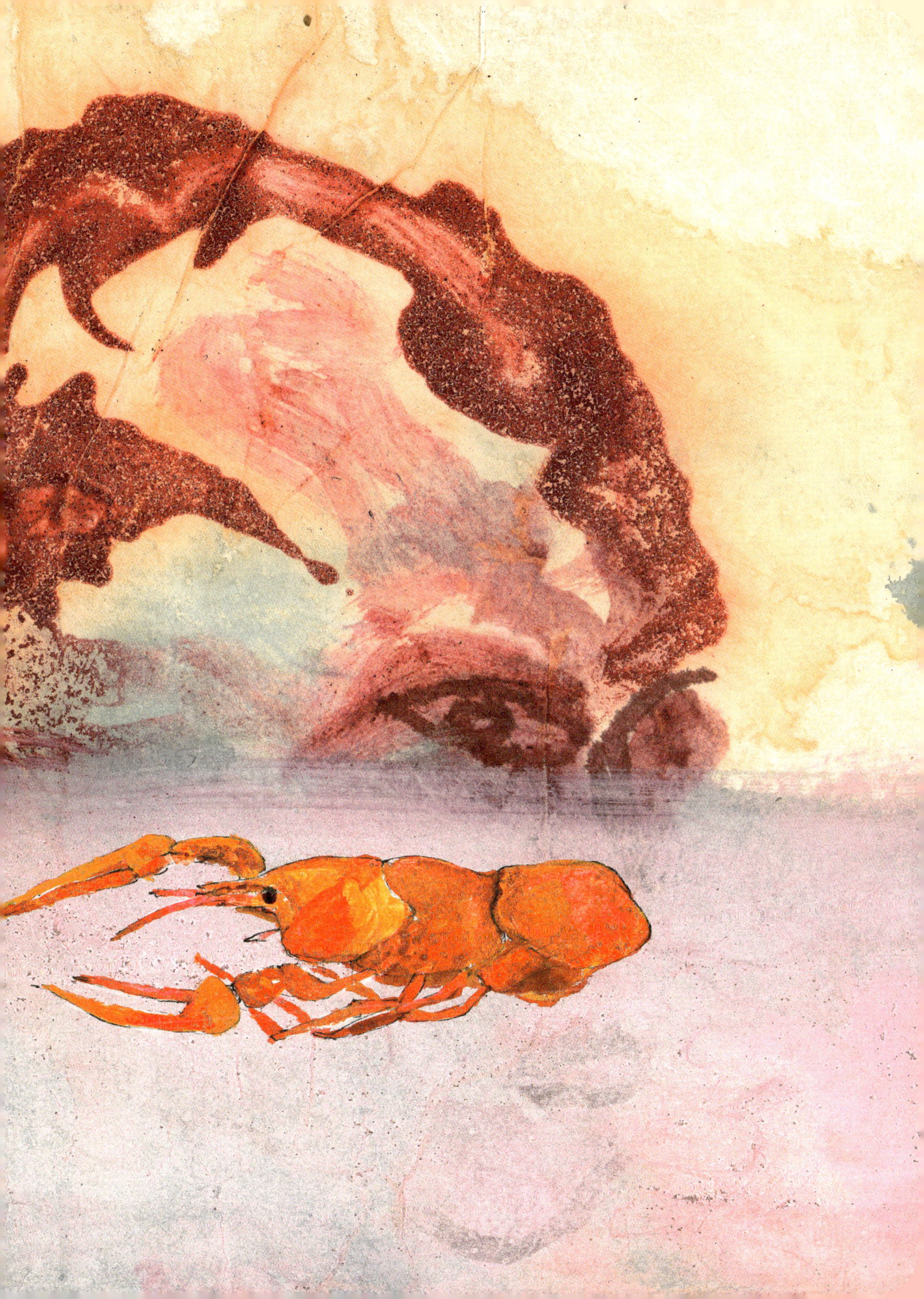

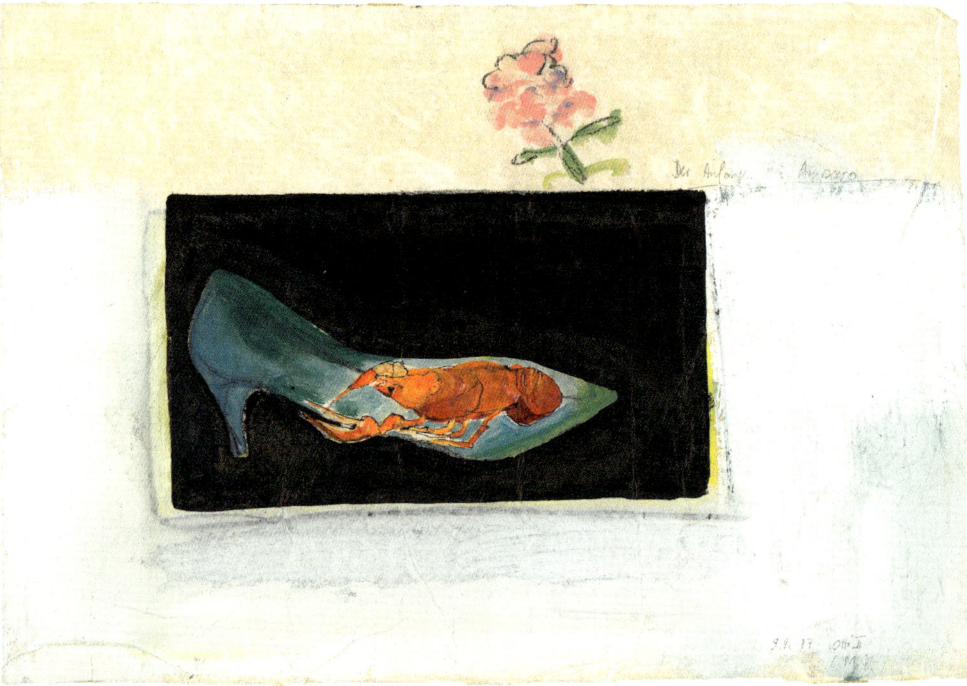

Cinderella 1987
Japanpapier auf Vlies kaschiert & Gouache, Grafit
Japan paper laminated on fleece & gouache, graphite
55 x 76 cm

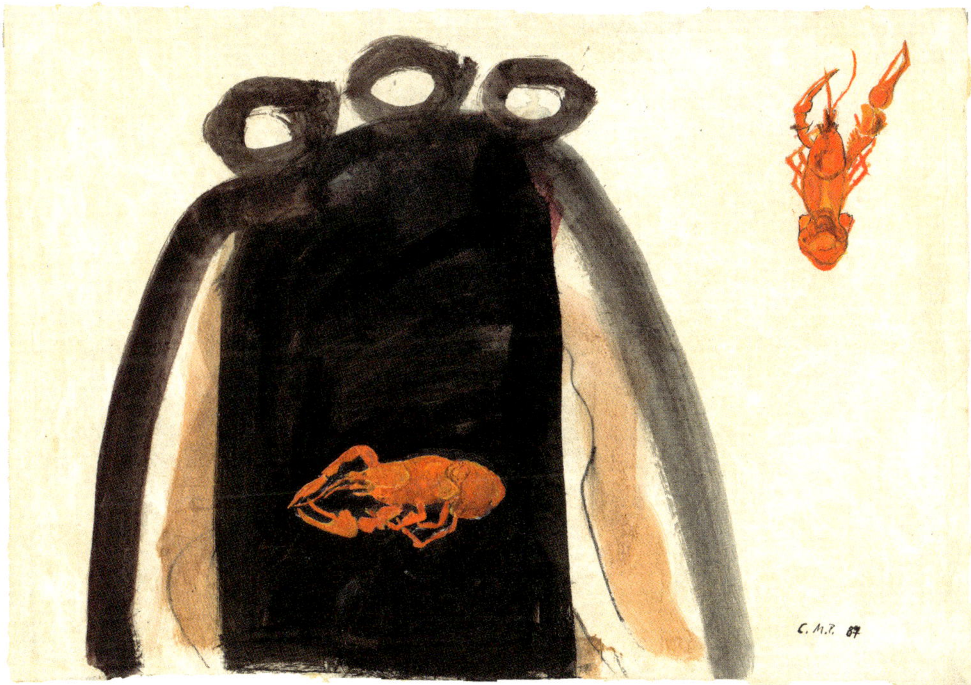

Upside down 1987

Japanpapier auf Vlies kaschiert & Gouache, Grafit

Japan paper laminated on fleece & gouache, graphite

55 x 76 cm

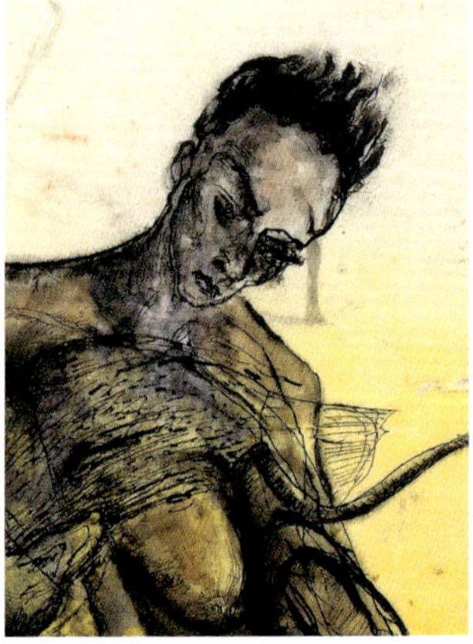

1988–1998

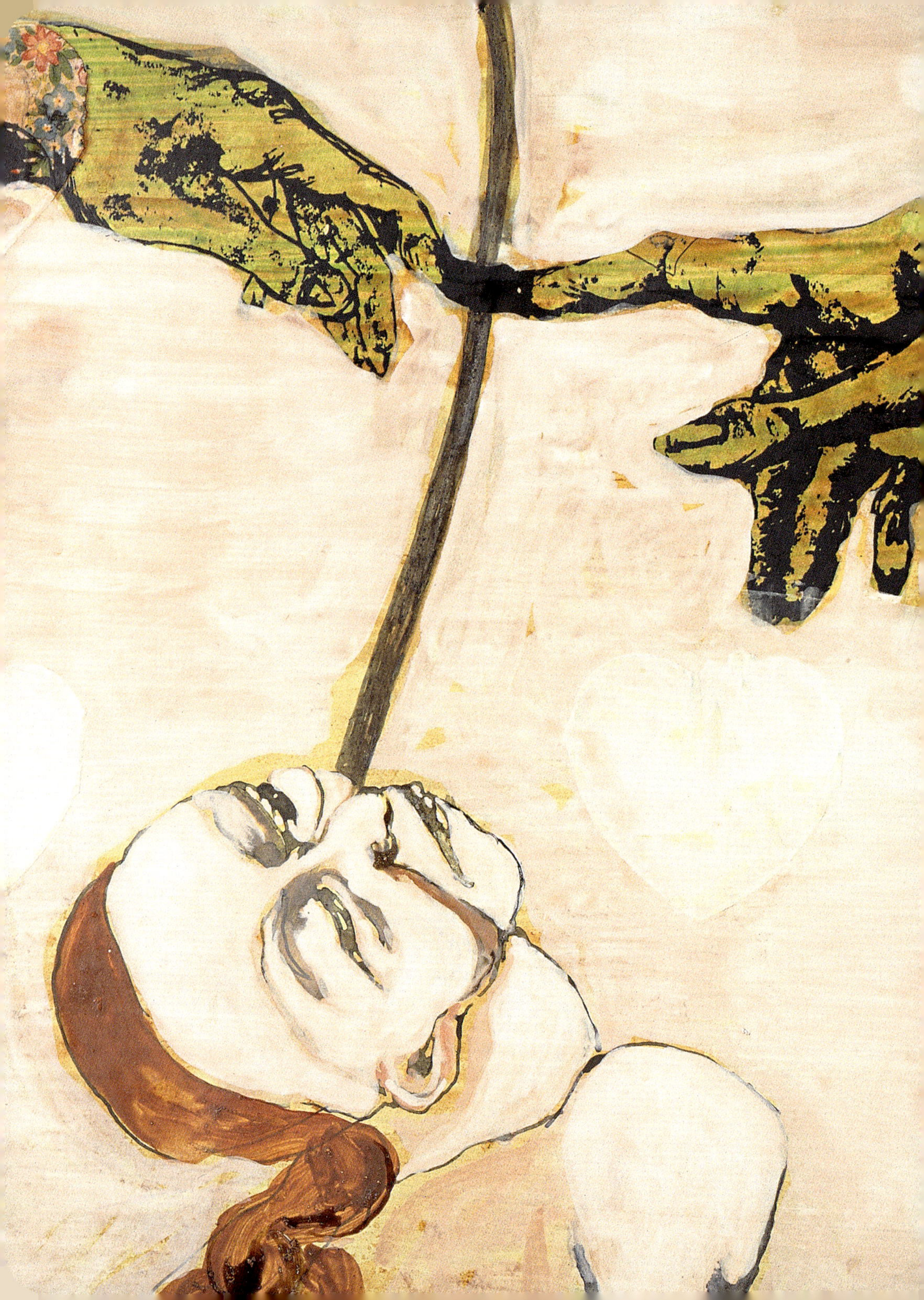

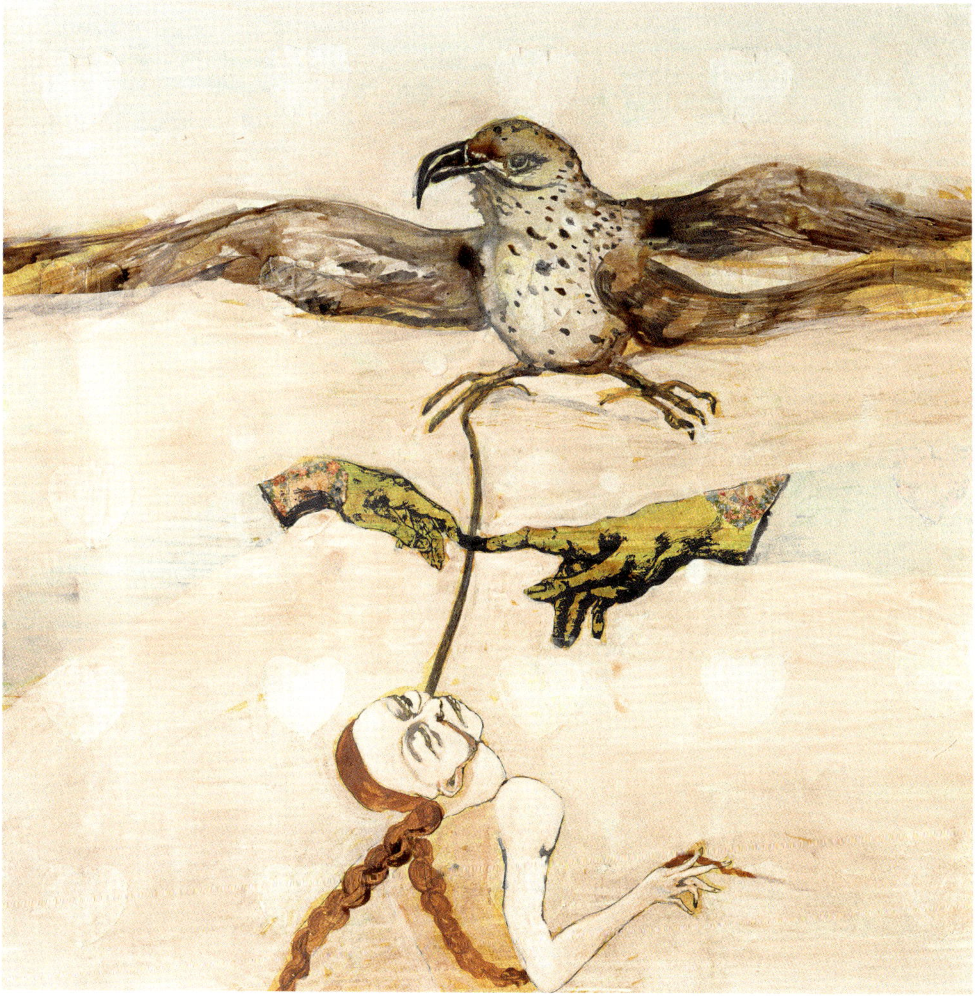

aus der Reihe „Finger Gottes“ 1988
Mischtechnik auf Siebdruck Mixed media on screen print
60 x 60 cm

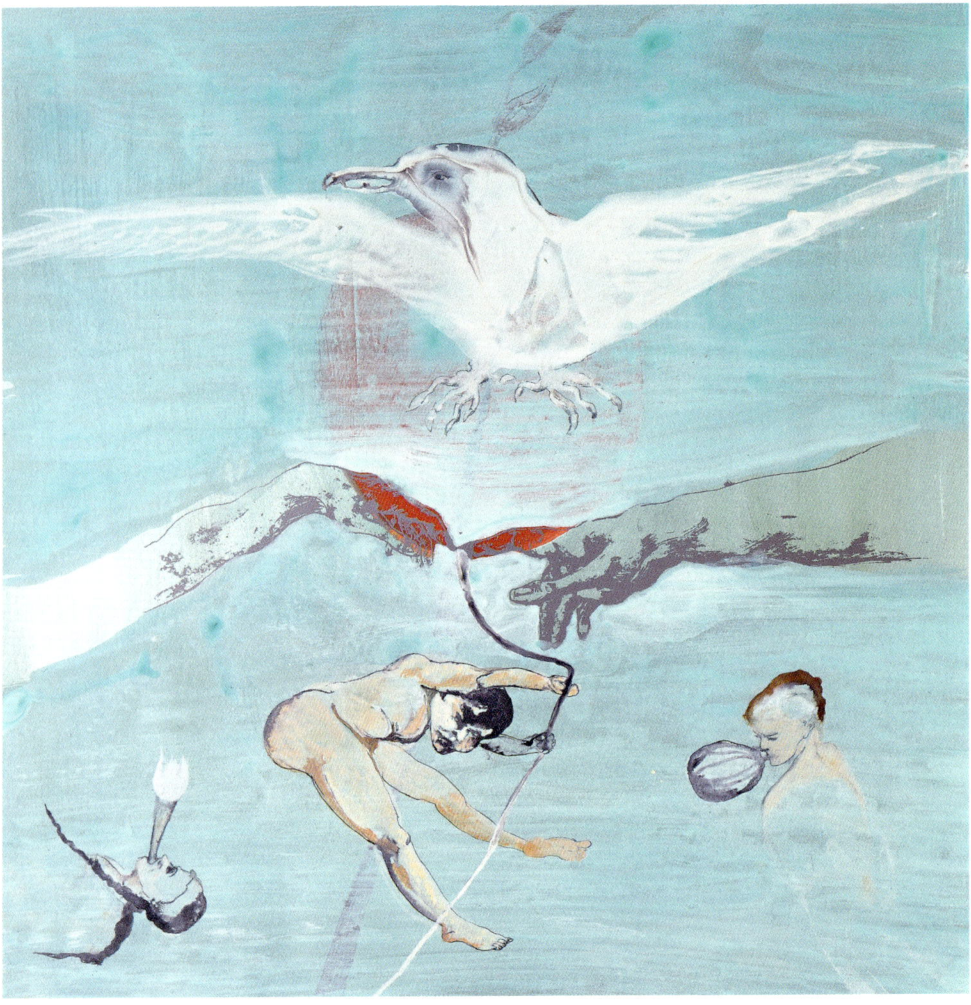

aus der Reihe „Finger Gottes" 1988
Mischtechnik auf Siebdruck Mixed media on screen print
60 x 60 cm

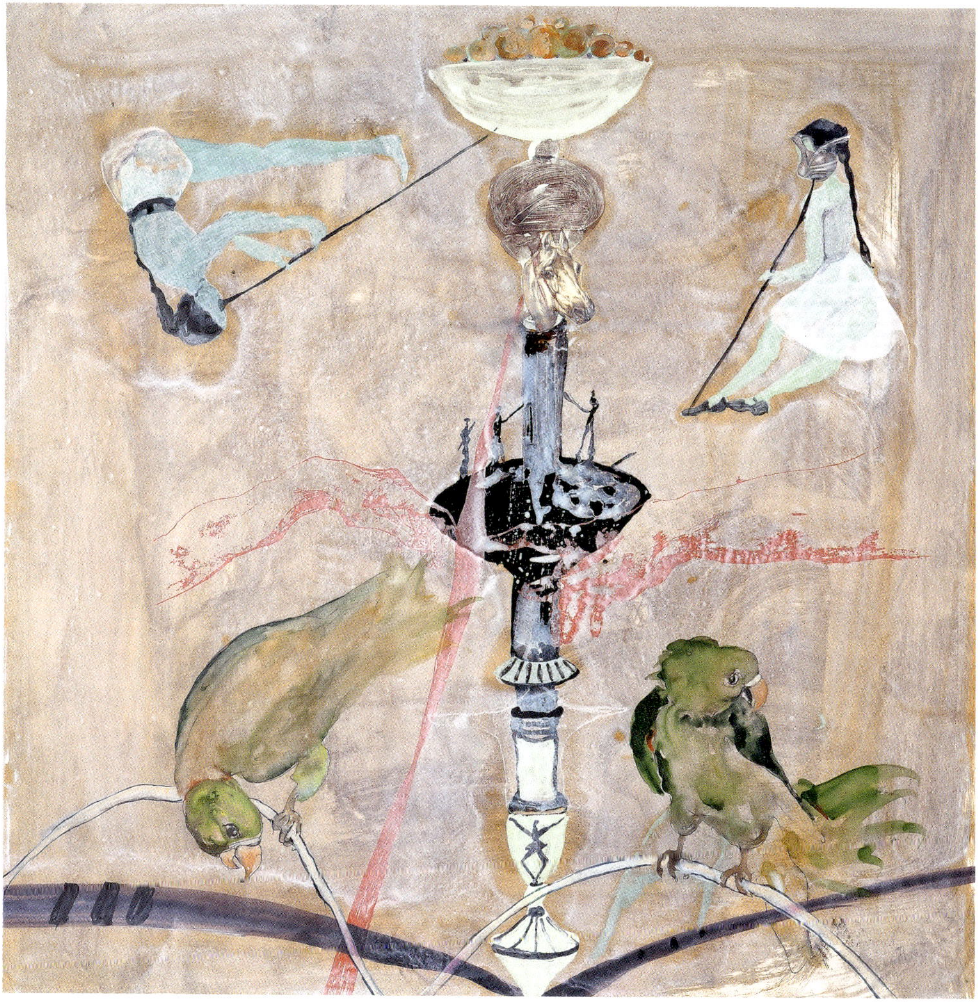

aus der Reihe „Finger Gottes“ 1988
Mischtechnik auf Siebdruck Mixed media on screen print
60 x 60 cm

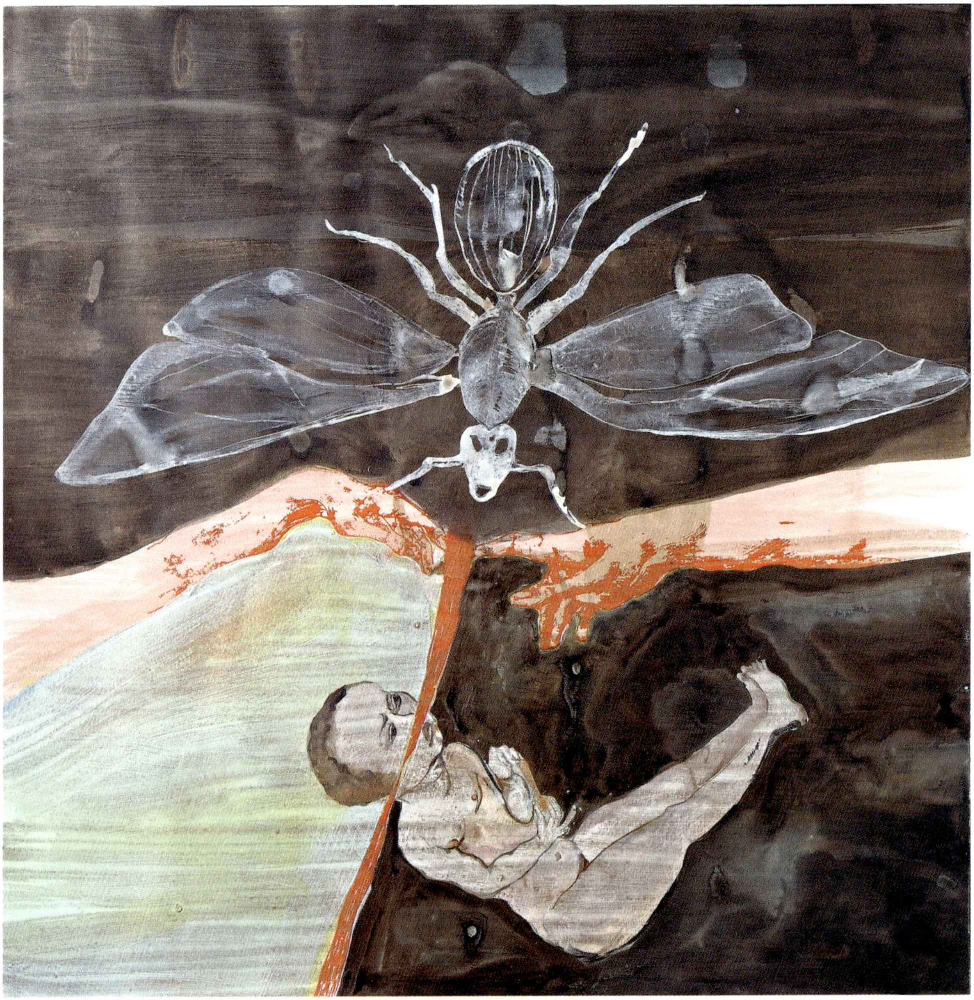

aus der Reihe „Finger Gottes" 1988
Mischtechnik auf Siebdruck Mixed media on screen print
60 x 60 cm

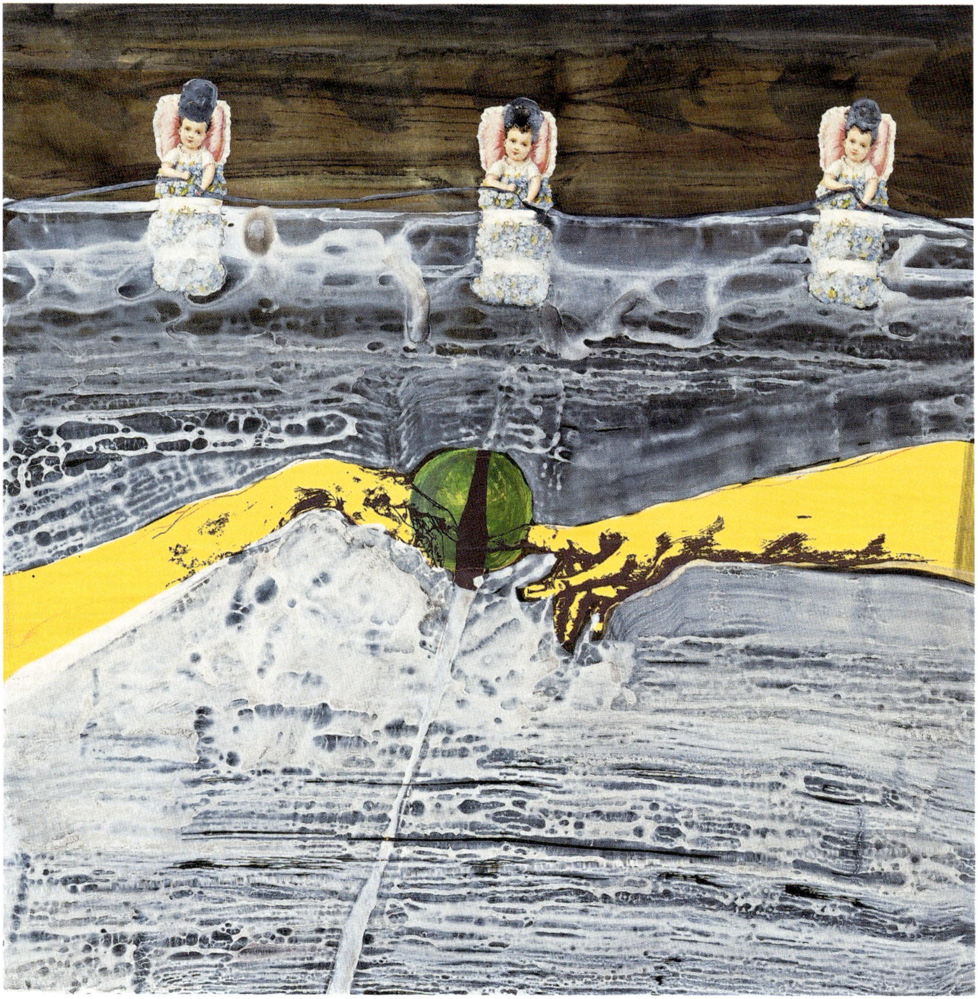

aus der Reihe „Finger Gottes" 1988
Mischtechnik auf Siebdruck Mixed media on screen print
60 x 60 cm

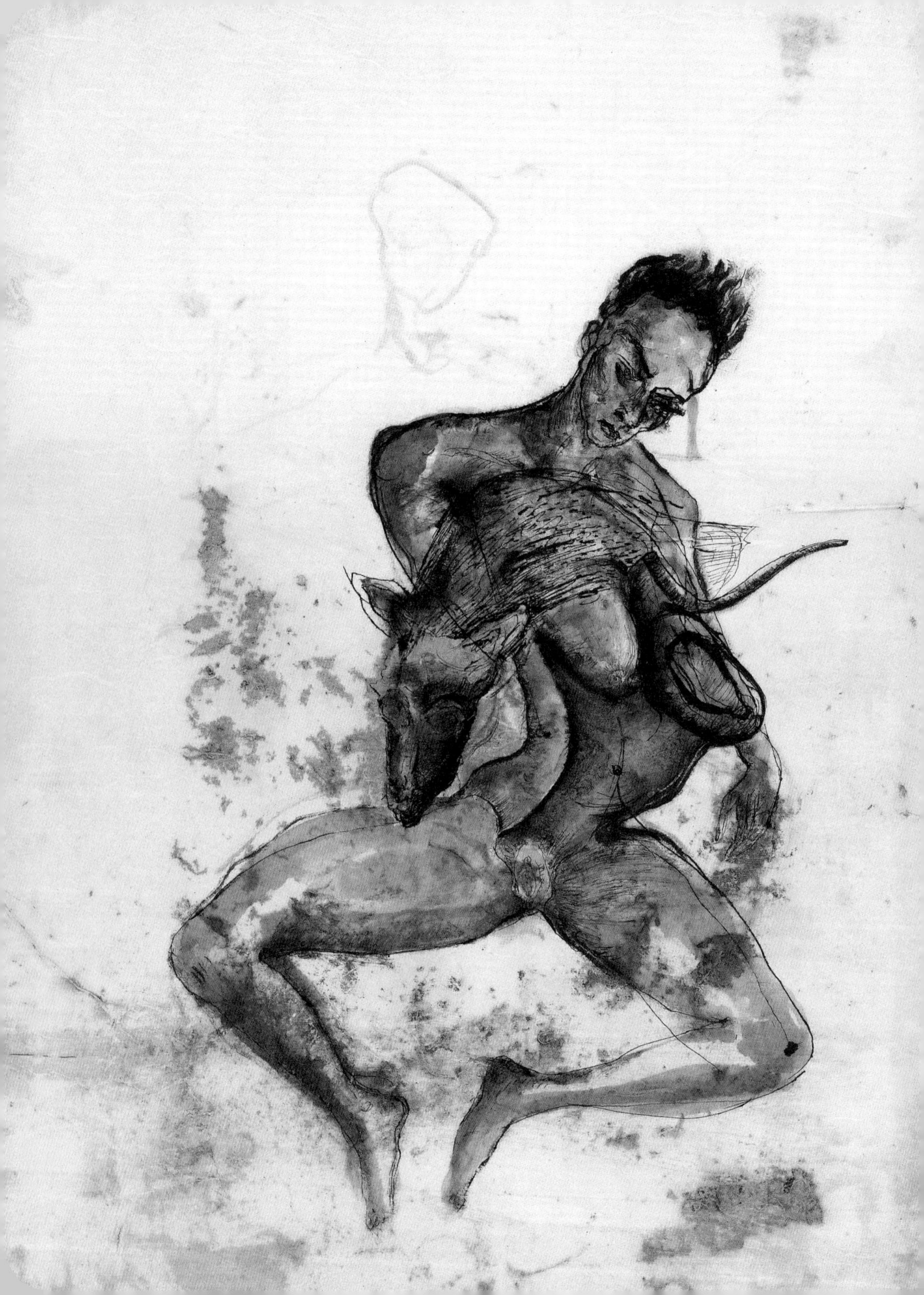

o.T. 1986
Japanpapier auf Vlies kaschiert & Tusche
Japan paper laminated on fleece & Indian ink
76 x 56 cm

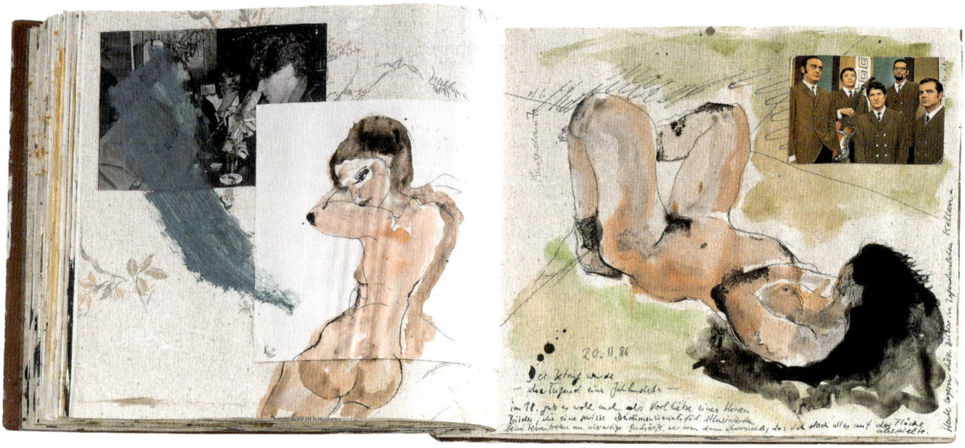

Tapeten-Tagebücher 1986-87
Collage & Tusche & Aquarell (Doppelseite)
Collage & Indian ink & watercolour (double page)
40 x 50 cm

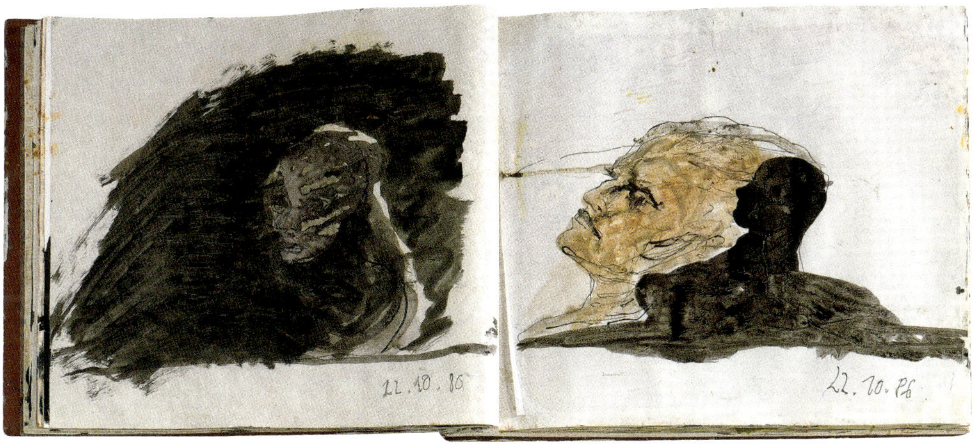

Tapeten-Tagebücher 1986-87
Collage & Tusche & Aquarell (Doppelseite)
Collage & Indian ink & watercolour (double page)
40 x 50 cm

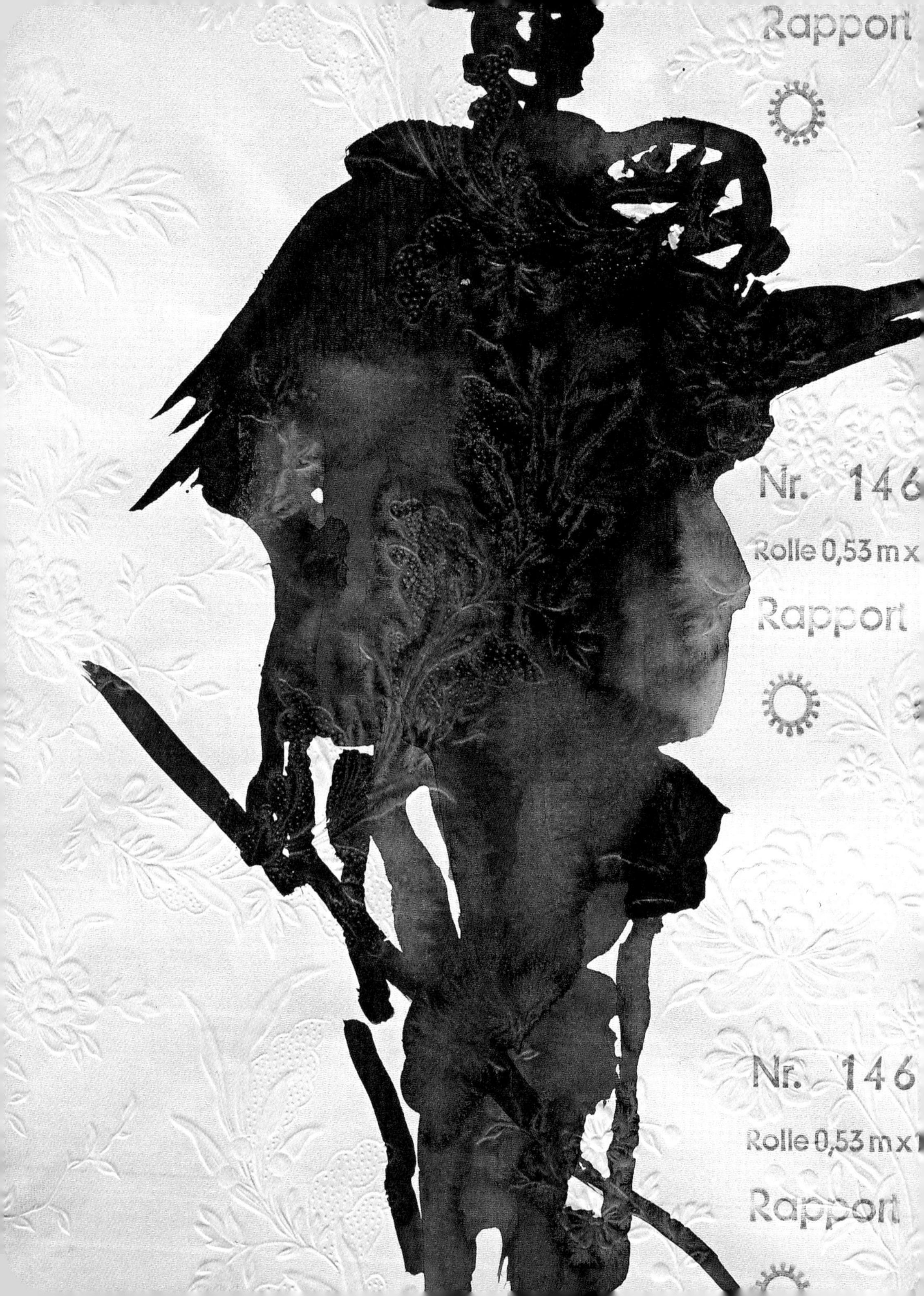
Rapport
Nr. 146
Rolle 0,53 m x
Rapport
Nr. 146
Rolle 0,53 m x
Rapport

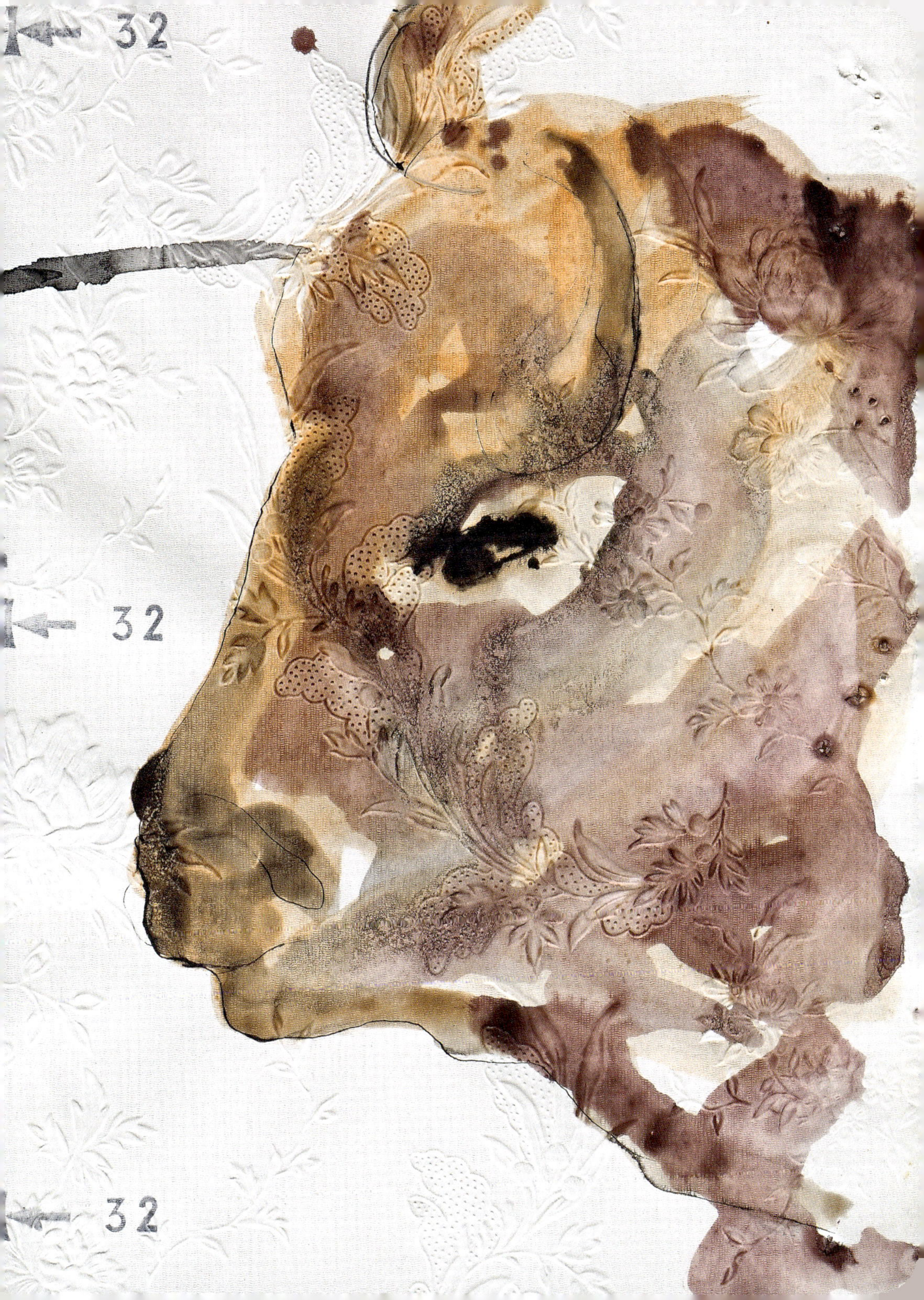
32
32
32

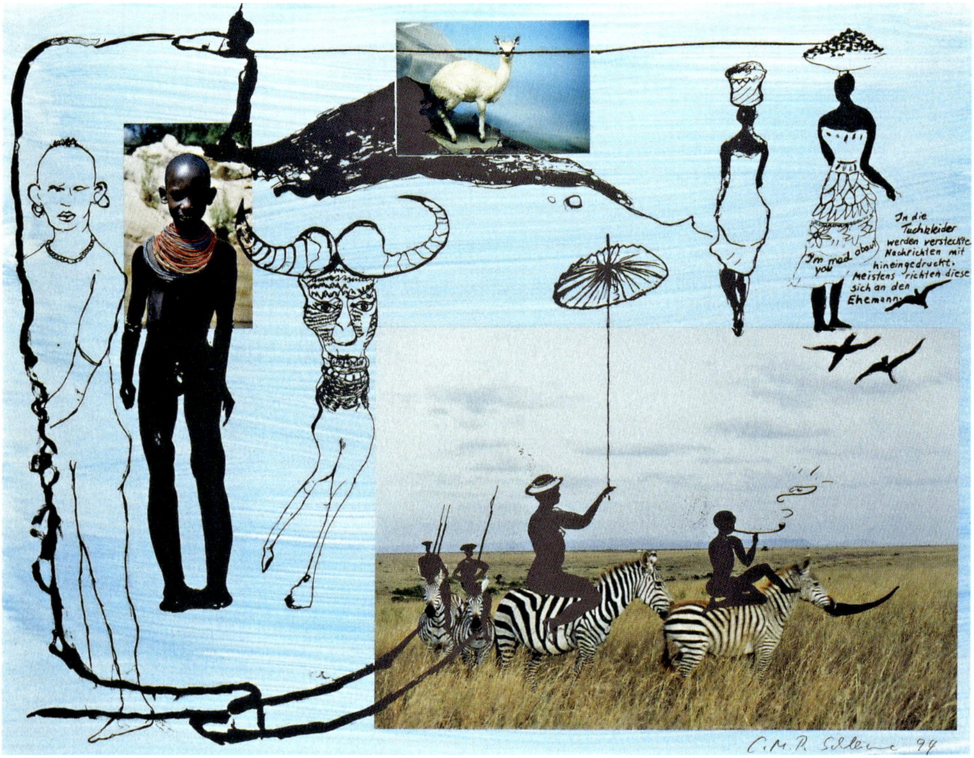

Afrika 1999
Foto & Siebdruck Photo & screen print
58 x 79 cm

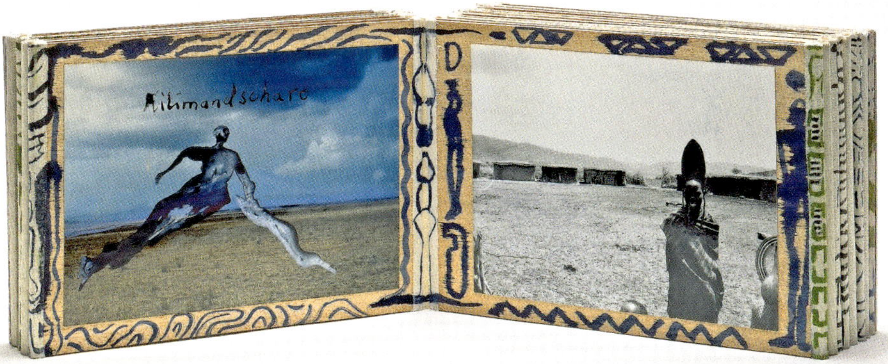

Kenia-Reise 1994/95
Leporello, Zeichnungen, Fotoübermalungen, Texte
Fanfold, drawings, photo overpainted, texts
21 x 31 cm

Drive through Canyon 1990

Foto & Gouache auf Hartfaser montiert Photo & gouache mounted on hardboard

215 x 180 cm

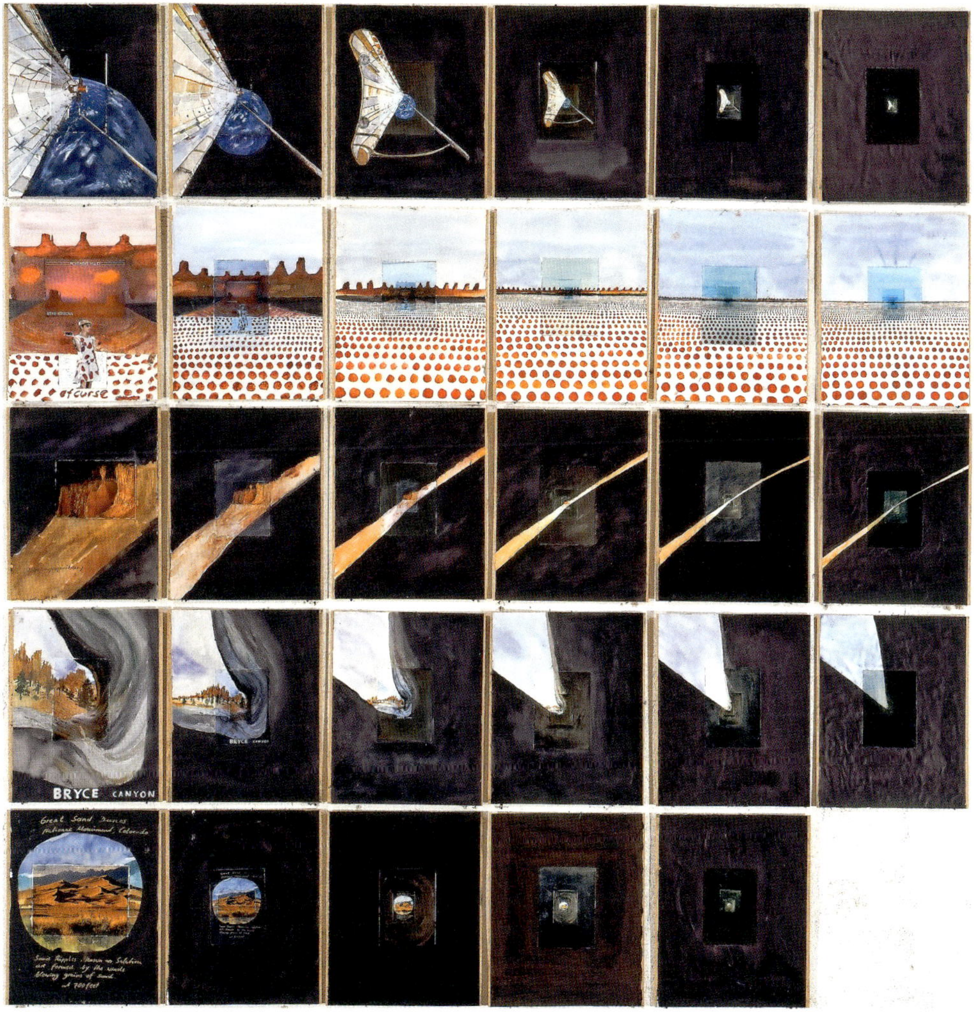
BRYCE CANYON
Great Sand Dunes

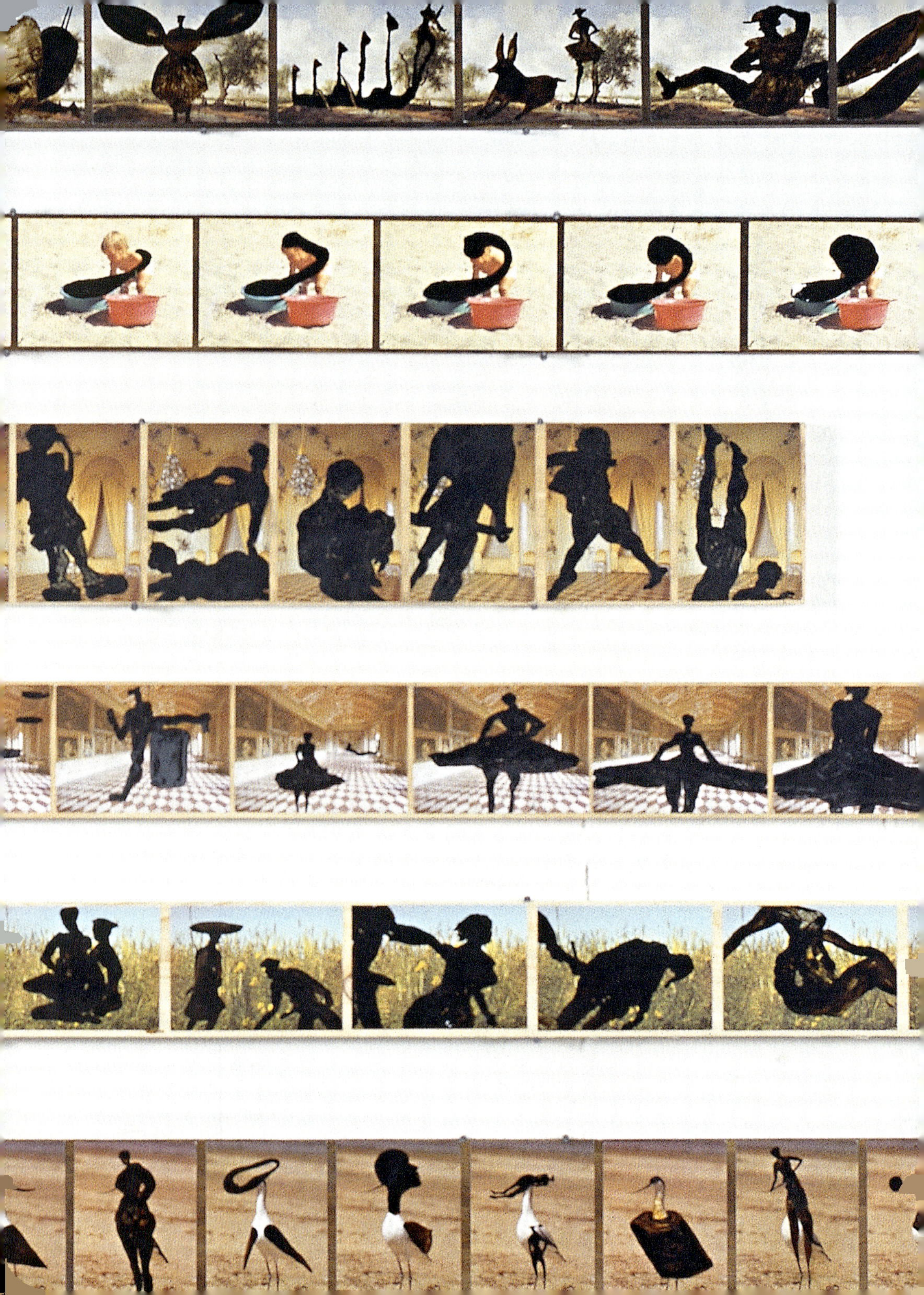

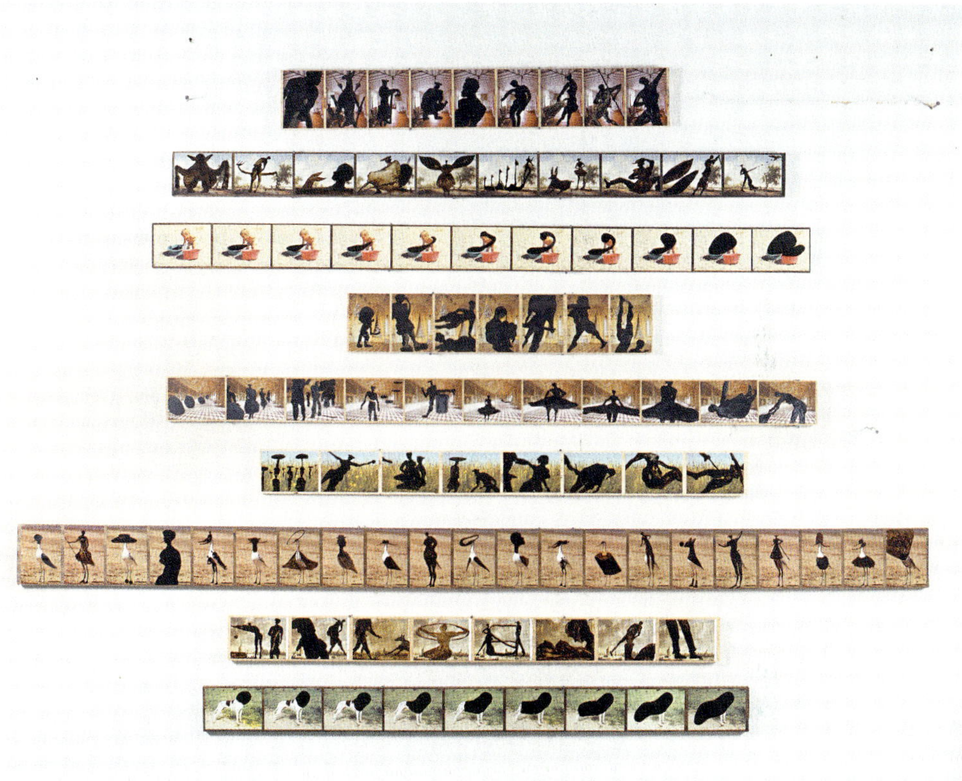

Postkartenübermalungen 1990

Leporello auf Sperrholzplatten montiert, Foto & Gouache

Fanfold mounted on plywood, Photo & Gouache

180 x 200 cm

Ich würde mir den in der Mitte nehmen 1991
Tusche auf Papier Indian ink on paper
100 x 70 cm

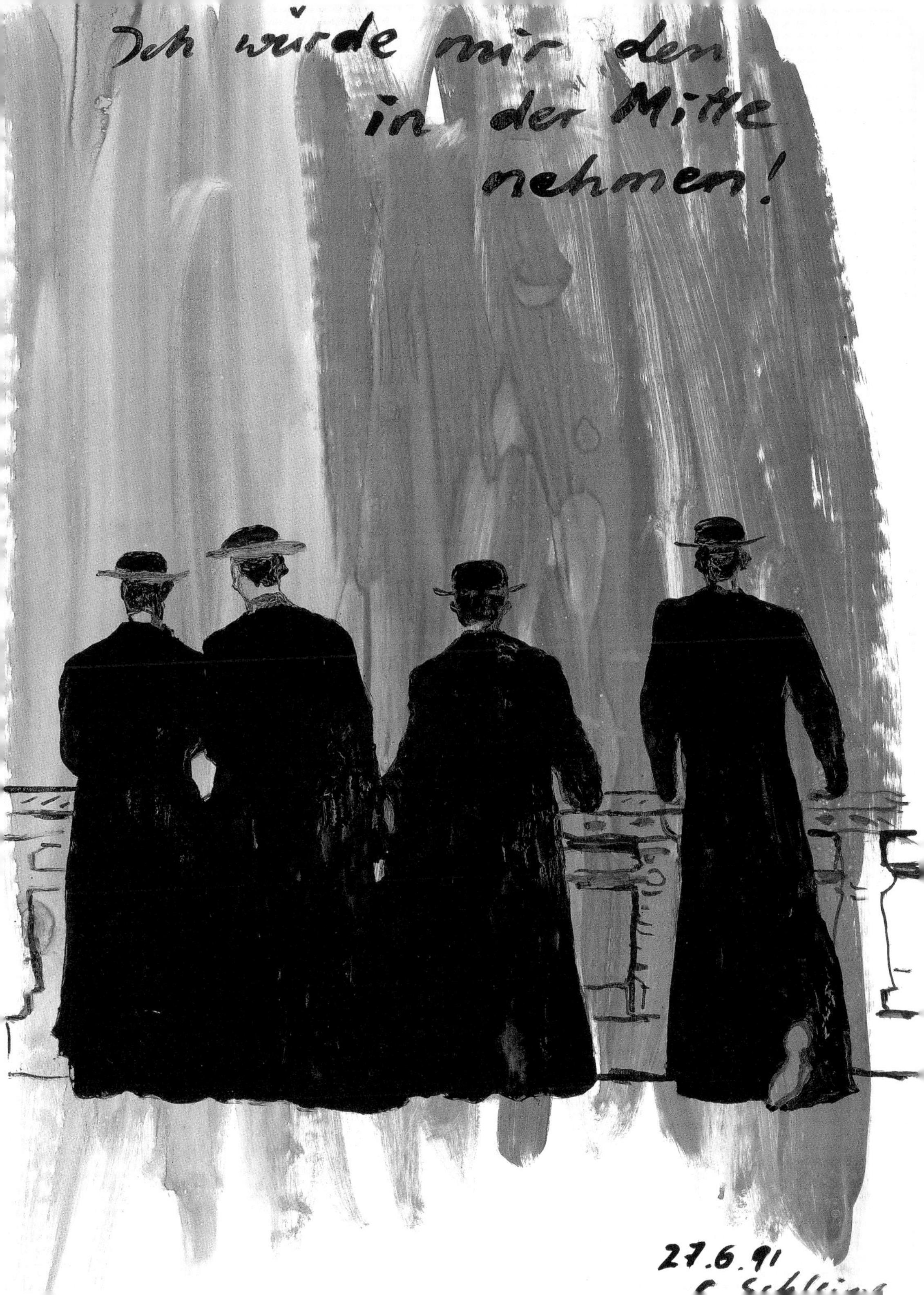
Ich würde mir den
in der Mitte
nehmen!
27.6.91

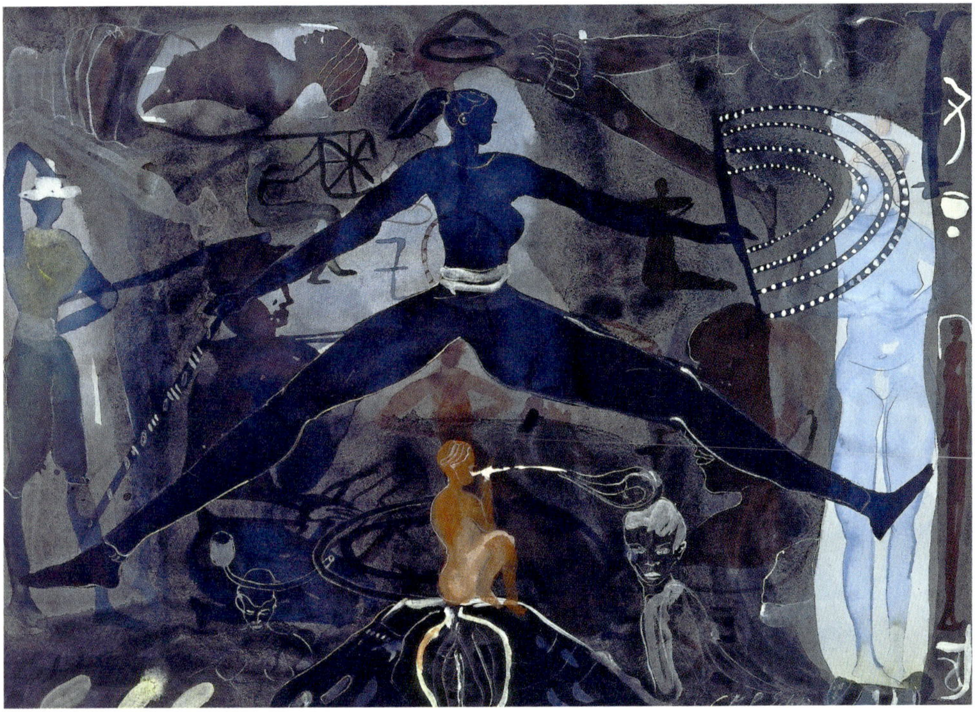

Nächtliche Verhältnisse 1995
Tusche auf Büttenpapier Indian ink on handmade paper
50 x 70 cm

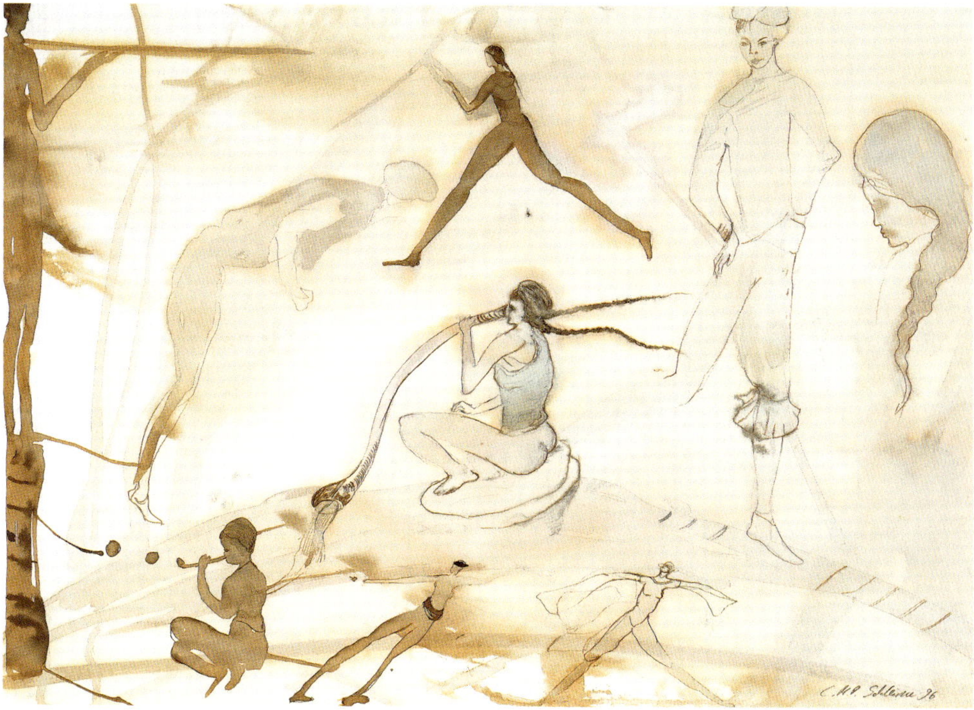

Ich sehe was, was Ihr nicht seht 1996
Tusche auf Papier Indian ink on paper
70 x 100 cm

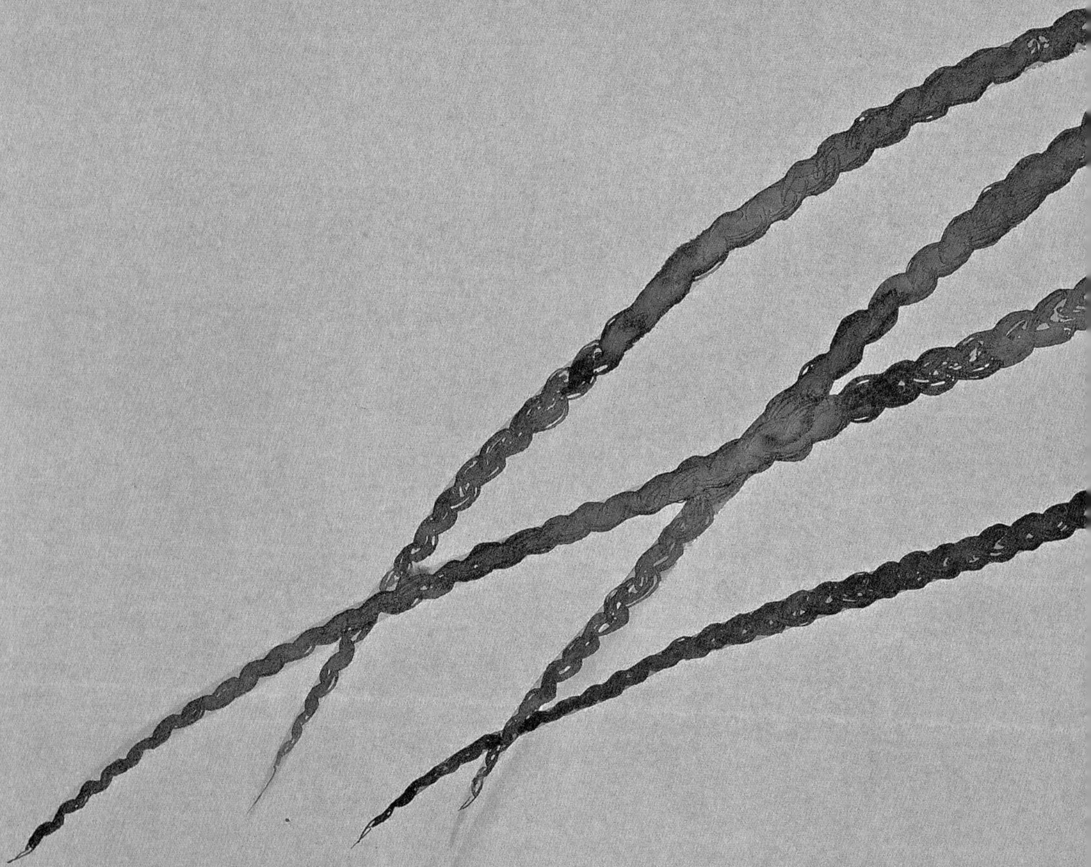

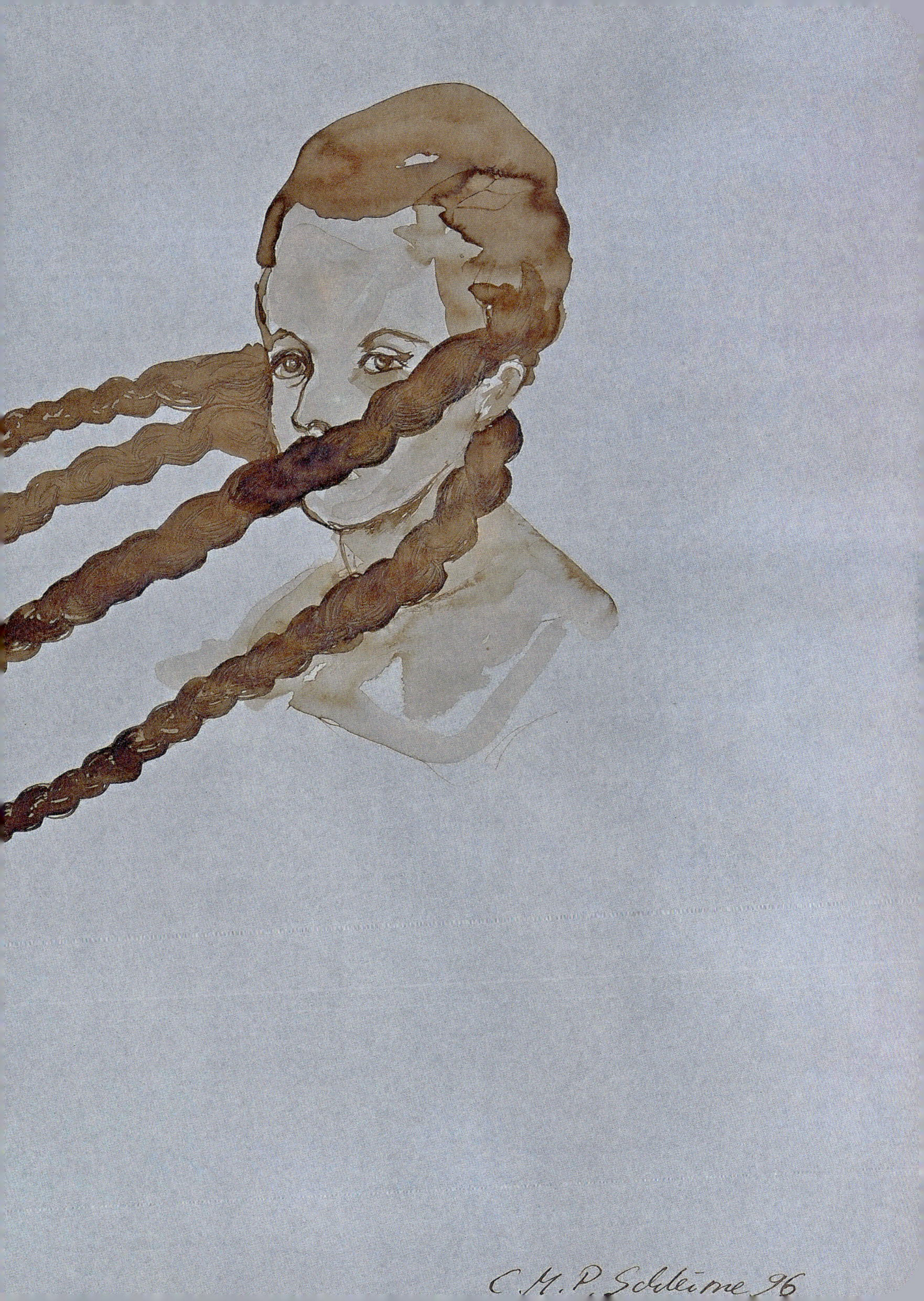
C.M.P. Schleime 96

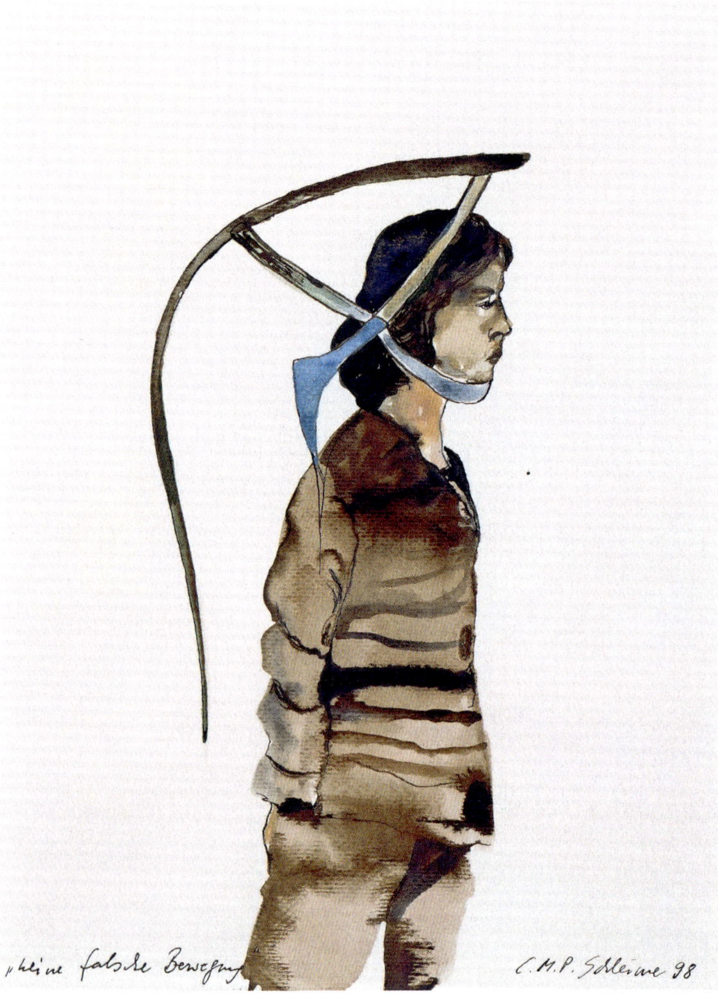

Keine falsche Bewegung 1998
Mischtecknik, Papier Mixed media on paper
33 x 27 cm

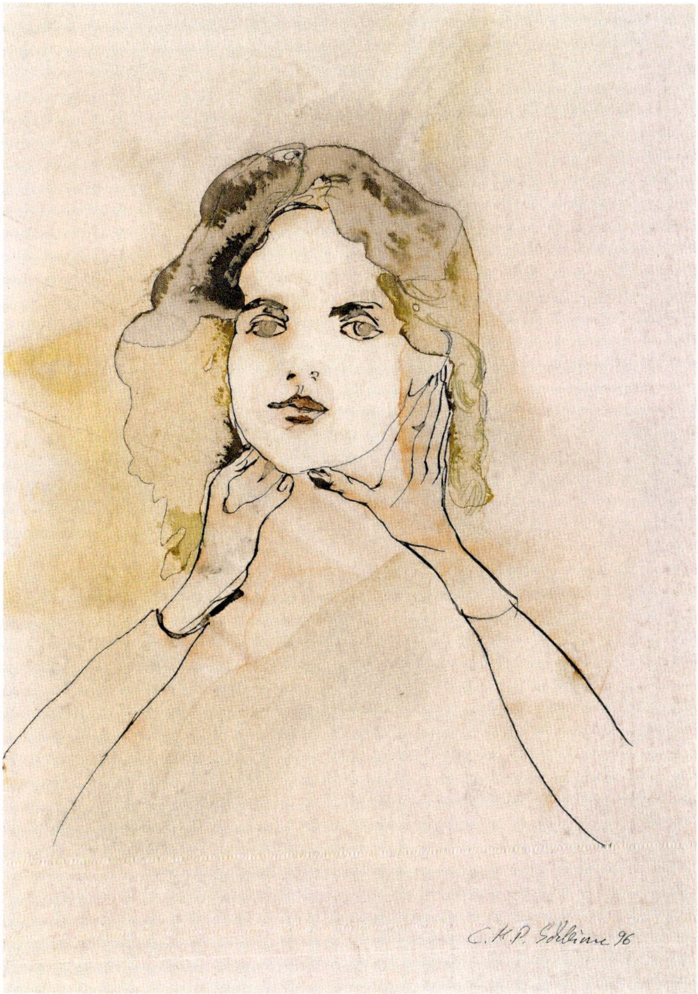

o.T. 1996
Tusche auf Papier Indian ink on paper
30 x 20 cm

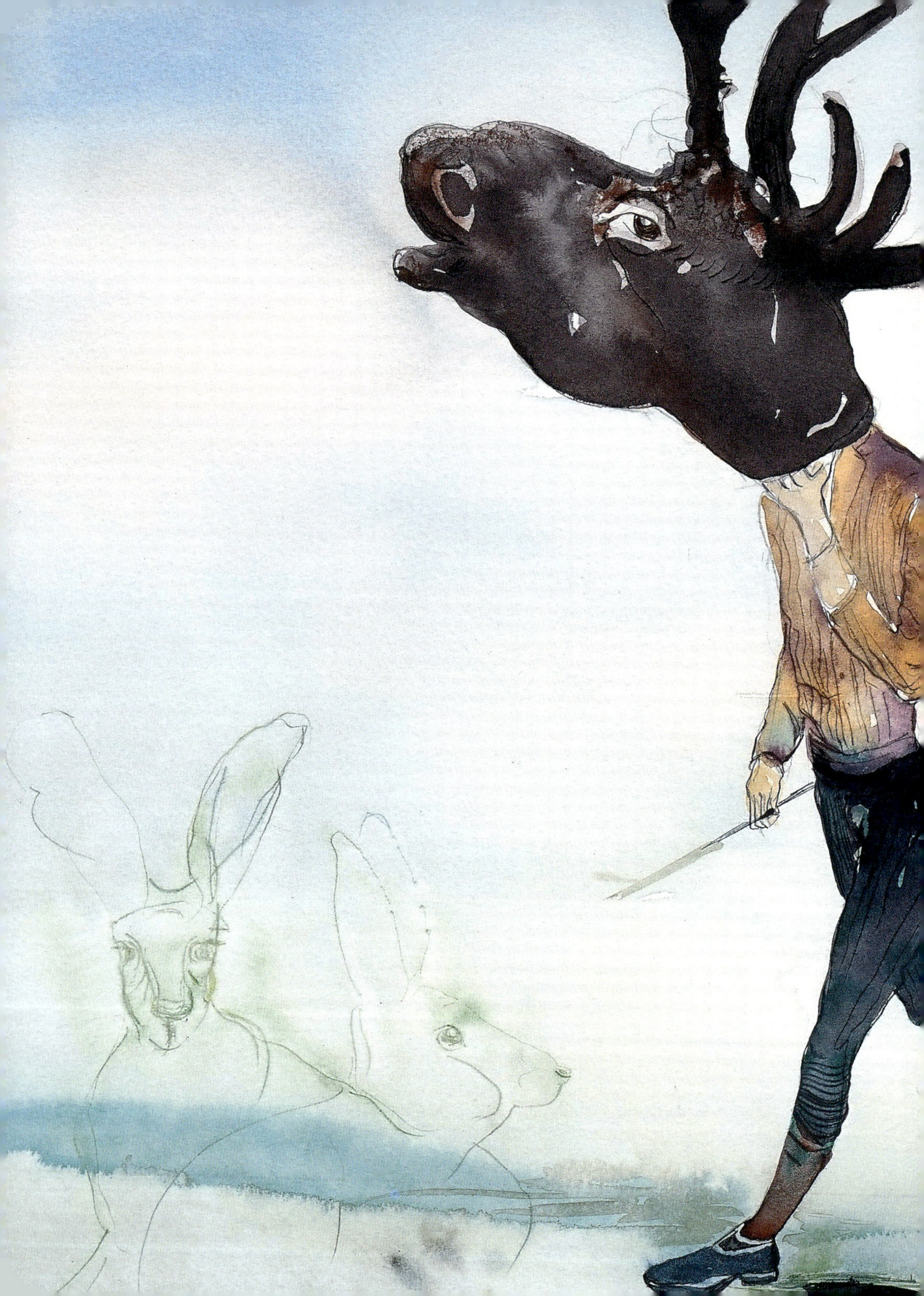

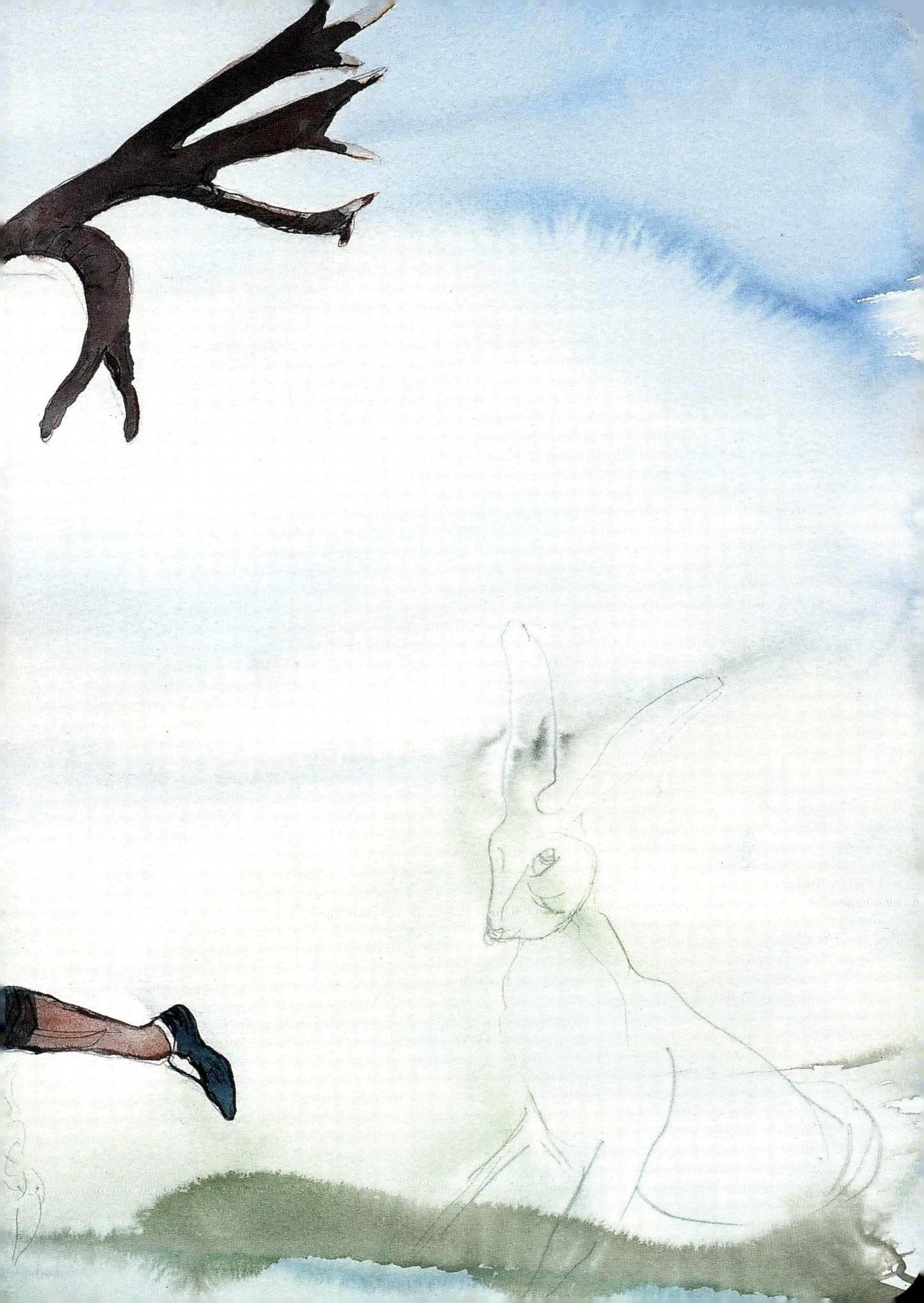

Wir werden immer weiter ziehen...

Christiane Bühling

Ein Theaterbesuch im Berliner Ensemble im Oktober 2011: Romeo und Julia in einer beeindruckenden Inszenierung von Mona Kraushaar. Gäbe es den Raum dafür, in der Enge einer ausverkauften Vorstellung vom Stuhl zu fallen, mir wäre es hier passiert. In dem Moment, als Peter, Diener bei den Capulets, in einem roten Anzug mit einem Eselskopf auf dem Haupt und ein paar bunten Luftballons in der Hand wortlos über die karge Bühne schreitet. Mein Herz rast: Eine lebendige Schleime-Zeichnung denke ich, und sie selbst sitzt neben mir. Wir kennen uns seit vielen Jahren, aber das ist unser erster gemeinsamer Theaterbesuch. Ich starre sie an, erst in der Pause können wir darüber reden, aber sie bleibt ganz ruhig. „Wahnsinn" sagt sie und strahlt mich an.

Die Tierköpfe haben sie in den Jahren 2008-2010 nicht nur in ihren großen Bildern beschäftigt, sondern bis heute auch in vielen Zeichnungen. Ihr Thema stand somit auf dieser Bühne.

Peter versinnbildlicht mir in der Kunst der Theaterwelt in wenigen Sekunden die Wirkung von Cornelia Schleimes Zeichnungen. Die Feindschaft zwischen den Familien der Capulets und Montaguse, die tragische Leidenschaft, die verzwickten Missverständnisse, die unglückselige Macht des Schicksals, all dies hebt Peter mit seinem bedächtigen und entrückten Gang über die Bühne auf. Seine

Keep on Moving ...

Christiane Bühling

An evening at the theatre, watching a performance by the Berliner Ensemble in October 2011: an impressive production of Romeo and Juliet directed by Mona Kraushaar. If it were possible to fall off your chair with excitement in a sold-out performance, it would have happened to me here.

It would have happened when Peter, a servant in the Capulet household, strode silently across the barren stage in a red suit with an ass's head on his shoulders and holding a few brightly coloured balloons. My heart raced and I thought to myself: a living Schleime drawing. In fact, the artist herself was sitting next to me. We have known each other for many years, but this was the first time that we watched a play together. I stared at her. We could not talk about it until the intermission, but she remained completely calm. "Wow," she said, and beamed at me.

She tackled the subject of animal heads in big paintings in the period between 2008 and 2010, and continues to do so to this day in many drawings. Her subject thus walked across the stage.

I felt that, for that short moment, Peter symbolised in the thespian idiom the effect of Cornelia Schleime's drawings. The enmity between the families of Capulet and Montague, the tragic passion, the intricate misunderstandings, the star-crossed power of fate: Peter overrode all of this as he walked across the stage, lost in thought. His social posi-

soziale Rolle zwischen den Gegnern ist eindeutig, er hat keine Macht, keine Entscheidungsgewalt, hat sich nicht einzumischen. Aber in dem Moment, in dem er sich einen Tierkopf anlegt, kann er der bitteren Realität für einen Moment entfliehen. Die Luftballons voller Träume, mit Leichtigkeit kann man sie fliegen lassen. Er geht nicht über den Boden Veronas, er stolziert durch seine eigene Vorstellungswelt, und vielleicht ist hier die glückliche Liebe der Protagonisten möglich.

Das ist die Magie der Zeichnungen von Cornelia Schleime, nicht nur bei denen aus der Reihe Camouflage (Abb. S. 132/33). Sie erschafft auf dem Papier diesen kurzen Augenblick, in dem der Mensch losgelöst in eine Zwischenwelt eintaucht, die uns als Betrachter wie Peter in andere Sphären entlässt. Die Sprache der Wörter ruht, im Zungenschlaf artikuliert sich die Sprache der Bilder und Träume. Lassen wir uns als Betrachter ebenfalls ein auf diesen Wachzustand des somnambulen Schweigens, dann fallen wir bei Cornelia Schleime manchmal vom Stuhl, meist aber in weiche Federn. Es gibt durchaus auch harte, fast aggressive Zeichnungen, aber im Gegensatz zu ihren mächtigen, herausfordernden Gemälden dominiert ein lyrischer Duktus die künstlerische Welt ihrer Aquarelle.

Der zeitgenössischen Arbeit auf Papier haftet längst nicht mehr nur das idealistische Konzept eines Mittels der Selbstoffenbarung an. In ihrer künstlerischen Praxis ist sie in den Raum expandiert und wird als Instrument

tion between the enemies is unambiguous, he has no power and no authority to make decisions, and is not supposed to become involved. But when he put on an animal's head, he was able to escape brutal reality for a moment. The balloons full of dreams can easily be set free so that they can fly away. He was not walking through the streets of Verona but strutting through his own, imagined world. Perhaps it is a world in which the protagonists can live their love in happiness.

This is the magic of Cornelia Schleime's drawings, and not just those in the Camouflage (pages 132/33) series. She creates this moment on paper, this instant in which humans are detached and able to dive into a twilight zone that removes us into other spheres, like Peter. The language of words pauses and while tongues rest, a language of images and dreams is articulated. If we the viewers also abandon ourselves to this waking-while-sleepwalking silence, we might well fall off our metaphorical chairs when looking at Cornelia Schleime's work, although the fall is usually cushioned by soft feathers. There certainly are harsh, almost aggressive drawings, too, but in contrast to her overwhelming and challenging paintings, a lyrical flow dominates the artistic world of her watercolours.

Contemporary work on paper is no longer associated only with the idealistic concept of a medium for self-revelation. In artistic practice, its scope has been expanded and it is used as an instrument for conceptual ideas. For Cornelia

für konzeptuelle Ideen benutzt. Für Cornelia Schleime bleibt sie jedoch ein sehr intimes Medium und sie steht dafür ein, „… dass sich in der Handzeichnung die Spontaneität, Originalität und Authentizität einer schöpferischen Subjektivität unmittelbar auszudrücken und zu artikulieren scheinen.“[1] Obwohl in der zeitgenössischen Kunst so viele unterschiedliche Herangehensweisen möglich sind, ein großes Repertoire an Ausdrucks- und Hilfsmitteln zur Verfügung steht, geht sie das Wagnis ein, sich gerade von der unerschöpflichen Zahl der Möglichkeiten zu befreien und vertraut nur ihrer Intuition. In ihren Zeichnungen ist sie – die mit großen Leinwandformaten kämpft, die auch installativ arbeitet – in ihrem künstlerischen Credo noch kompromissloser. Die äußere Welt scheint mir hier mit größerer Radikalität ausgeschlossen zu sein als in der Malerei.

Verweilen wir zunächst noch bei den Tier-Menschverwandlungen, der Reihe Camouflage. Frauen und Mädchen durchziehen ihr gesamtes künstlerisches Werk, hier nun verstecken, maskieren sie sich, zeigen sich mit Hasenköpfen und Hirschgeweihen. Viele Deutungsmöglichkeiten bieten sich hierfür an. Sie wollen sich nicht vollständig zeigen, suchen Schutz im Tierkörper. Das Tier ist gleichsam Antipode von Logik und Ratio. In diesem Sinne spielt es im zeichnerischen Werk von Beuys eine große Rolle: „Das Tier verkörpert Kräfte, über die der ‚vernünftig‘ gewordene Mensch seit langem schon nicht mehr

Schleime, however, it remains a very intimate medium, and she makes no excuses for the fact that: "... the spontaneity, originality and authenticity of a creative subjectivity appear to express and articulate themselves in a straightforward manner in drawings" [1]. While so many different approaches are possible in contemporary art and such a large repertoire of means of expression and mediums is available, her courage lies precisely in liberating herself from the inexhaustible possibilities and trusting her intuition. In her drawings, the artist – who also embraces the challenges of large-scale canvases and creates installations – is even more uncompromising with her artistic credo. It seems to me that the outer world is even more radically excluded here than in her painting.

Let us remain for a moment longer with the animal-human transformations of the *Camouflage* series. Women and girls pervade her entire artistic oeuvre. Here, they hide and put on masks, presenting themselves with rabbit heads and deer antlers. A wide range of possible interpretations presents itself. They do not want to show themselves in their entirety and seek protection in the bodies of animals. The animal is basically the polar opposite of logic and reason. In this sense, it plays a significant part in Beuys's drawings: "The animal embodies powers that humans, who have become 'reasonable', have long since forfeited, and even forgotten"[2]. The uncovering of these hidden powers may also play a part in Cornelia Schleime's drawings.

verfügt, die er gar vergessen hat."[2] Diese verborgenen Kräfte frei zu legen, könnte auch in den Zeichnungen von Cornelia Schleime eine Rolle spielen.

Einen anderen Deutungsakzent bietet uns Martin Hellmold an, der die Unterschiede zwischen Mensch und Tier überdenkt und das Erinnerungsvermögen als Besonderheit des Menschen hervorhebt. „Wer sich erinnern kann … kann also ‚Ich' sagen und dieses Ich mit Bedeutung füllen."[3] So gibt es im Leben und in der Kunst Momente, in denen und an die man sich nicht erinnern kann oder will, meist wenn sie besonders schmerzhaft waren. So bietet das Tier vielleicht die Möglichkeit, sich vorübergehend vom Ich zu lösen und sich somit von Erinnertem zu befreien. Der Mensch schlüpft in den Seinszustand des Tieres, so wie schon in der griechischen Mythologie, er kann sich erholen von den Tücken des Schicksals und Abstand dazu gewinnen. In einer anderen Haut lässt es sich vorübergehend leichter ruhen. Auch die Künstlerin schlüpft beim Kreieren ihrer Mischwesen in einen anderen Bewusstseinszustand, den Zungenschlaf. So eloquent sie manchmal ist, ist sie doch süchtig nach diesen kostbaren Momenten und bleibt ihnen in manischer Getriebenheit auf der Spur. Unglaubliche Wandlungsfähigkeit und Vielfältigkeit sind die Belohnung für den Mut, sich seit mehr als vier Jahrzehnten dem eigenen inneren Kosmos hinzugeben.

In der Reihe Mutationen (Abb. S. 138/39) ist dies ihr Thema, schöne Frauen schlüpfen aus Eidechsenschwänzen, Füße

Martin Hellmold provides another interpretive focus in considering the differences between humans and animals, highlighting the human capacity for remembering. "Anybody who can remember ... can therefore say 'I', and can imbue this with meaning"[3].

In both life and art, there are moments in which and that we no longer can, or do not want to, remember, usually because they were particularly painful. Animals perhaps provide the opportunity for a temporary release from the self, and thus allow us to free ourselves from that which is remembered. The human slips into the animal's state of being, as was already the case in Greek mythology, and can in this way find respite and gain distance from the twists and turns of fate. It is easier to relax in another's skin. The artist, too, slips into another state of consciousness when creating her composite creatures: one in which the tongue is still. As eloquent as she sometimes is, she is addicted to these precious moments and pursues them with manic single-mindedness. Remarkable mutability and multiplicity are the reward for her courage in abandoning herself to her inner cosmos for more than four decades.

In the series Mutations (pages 138/39), this is her subject. Beautiful women hatch from lizard tails, feet are embedded in snail shells, women are attached to aquatic plants as if to umbilical cords, which smultaneously strangle them. An irrepressible imagination emerges from this series, creatures are connected to everything the story of creation has to offer.

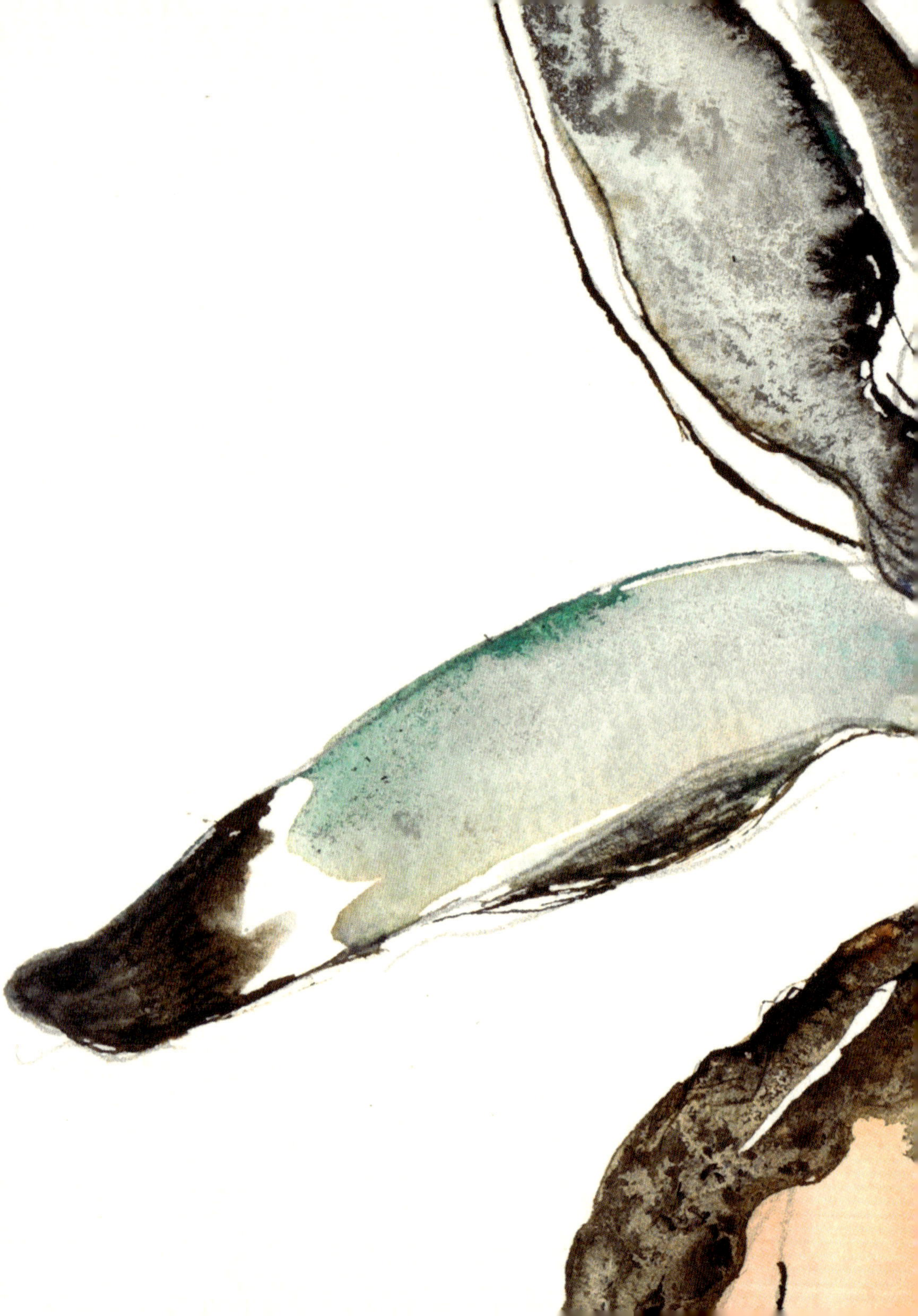

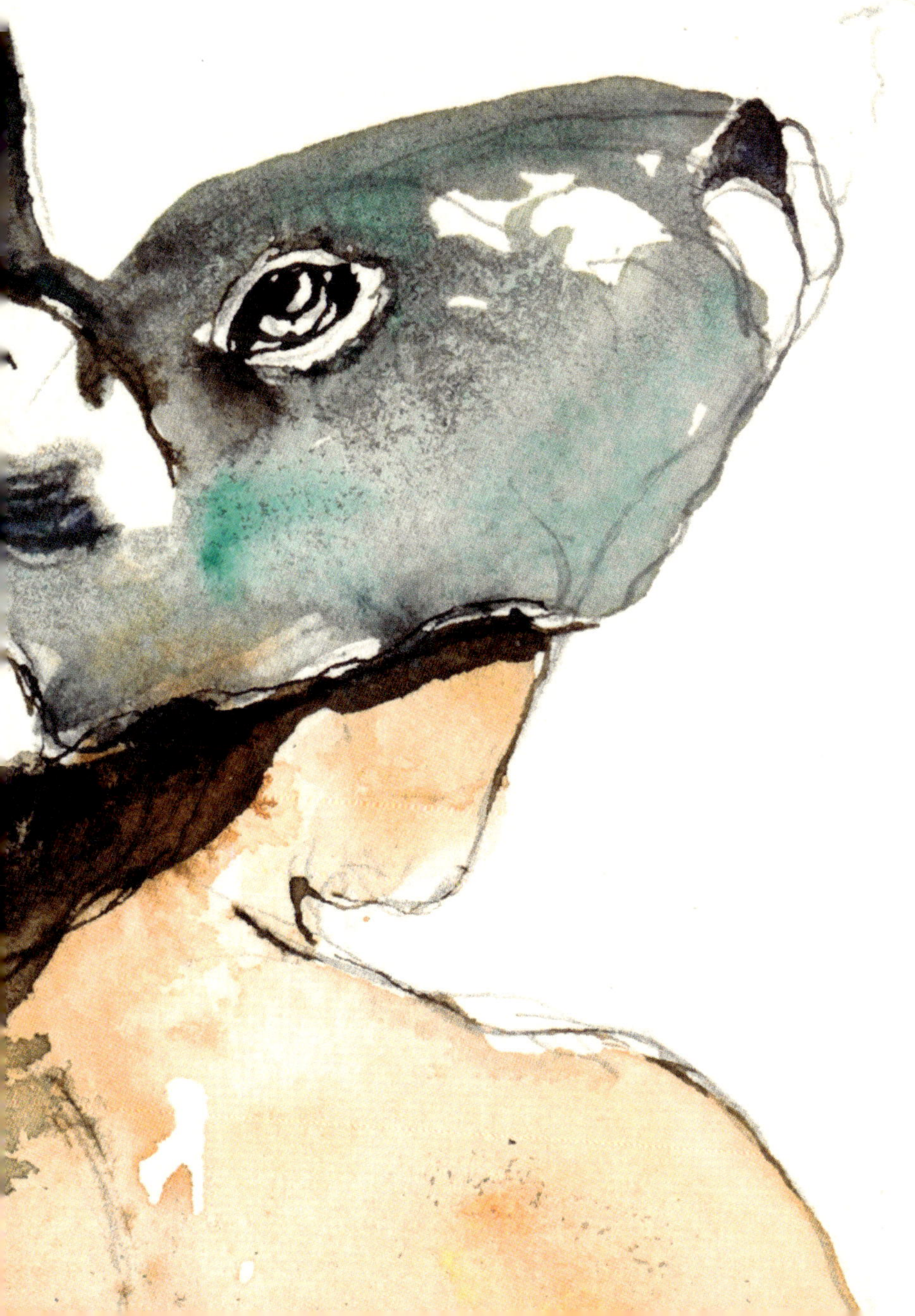

stecken in Schneckengehäusen, Frauen hängen an Wasserpflanzen wie an Nabelschnüren, an denen sie sich auch erwürgen. Eine unbändige Phantasie spricht aus dieser Serie, Kreaturen verbinden sich mit allem, was die Schöpfungsgeschichte hergibt. Die Künstlerin schreibt diese gewissermaßen neu. Es gibt keinerlei Beschränkung, alles ist möglich. Eine eigenwillige Alchimistin ist hier am Werk, die Wasserpflanzen, Fische, Kröten mit Totenköpfen, Paradiesvögeln und zarten Frauenkörpern zu neuen anmutig-bedrohlichen Kreaturen erschöpft.
Viele dieser Arbeiten sind auf dem Boot entstanden. Auf dem Wasser zu sein, bedeutet einen Teil der Alltagswirklichkeit verlassen zu haben. Ich sehe die Künstlerin vor mir auf ihrem Boot, sie hat den Anker gelegt und schaut auf das Wasser. Sie setzt sich an den kleinen Zeichentisch an Deck, den ihr damaliger Gefährte extra für sie eingebaut hat. Sie ist nun ganz ruhig geworden, sieht ein Seerosenblatt treiben und beginnt zu tuschen. Schon ist sie den Brandenburger Gewässern entrückt und ist in ihrer eigenen Welt. Sie verbindet das Blatt mit ihren imaginären Figurinen und Träumen, die nach oben drängen. Die Pinsel fließen mit dem gleichen Duktus der Ewigkeit über das Blatt wie die stetigen Bewegungen des Wassers, von dem sie umgeben sind. Man könnte auch annehmen, die Künstlerin ist tief hinab getaucht auf den Grund des Sees oder des Flusses, da wo noch nie ein Mensch gewesen ist. Sie berichtet nun von dem Unglaublichen, das sie dort unten gesehen hat.

And this is essentially rewritten by the artist. There are no limitations and anything is possible. A headstrong alchemist is at work here who creates new, graceful-yet-threatening creatures from aquatic plants, fish, toads with death's heads and birds of paradise with delicate women's bodies.

A large proportion of these artworks were created on a boat. Being on a body of water means abandoning part of the realities of everyday life. In my mind's eye, I see the artist in her boat. She has dropped the anchor and looks out across the water. She sits down at the little drawing table on deck, which a former partner built specially for her. She has become quite calm, watches a water-lily leaf drift by, and starts to paint using watercolours. In no time, she has distanced herself from the rivers and lakes of the Brandenburg area in Germany and entered her own world. She connects the sheet of paper with her imaginary figures and dreams, which float up to the surface. The eternal flow with which the brushes move across the paper is like that with which the water surrounding them undulates. One could equally assume that the artist has dived deep down to the bottom of the lake or river, where no human has ever been. And then she reports the unbelievable things she has seen while she was down there.

These creatures from the underwater world are captured on papyrus, a material not defined by straight edges, but which carries with it the flair of the natural and of old traditions.

Festgehalten werden diese Kreaturen der Tiefe auf Papyrus, einem nicht von geraden Kanten bestimmten Material, das das Flair von Naturbelassenheit und alter Tradition in sich trägt.

Auf demselben Malgrund finden wir die Reihe Leibeslust (Abb. S. 140/41), die uns auf eine ganz andere Fährte führt. Wie geht das zusammen, mag man sich fragen: Die schüchternen fragilen Mädchen und die selbstbewussten extrovertierten Frauen dieser orgiastischen Zeichnungen. Was fließt da Unterschiedliches aus der Hand derselben Künstlerin? Sie lässt die eine sich unter einem Hasenkopf verstecken und die andere ihre Schamlippen für mehr als tiefe Blicke spreizen. Schaulust und Schutzsuche als Extreme einer künstlerischen Palette bilden bei Cornelia Schleime keinen unauflöslichen Widerspruch. Sie bedingen sich gegenseitig. Die weibliche Sinnlichkeit artikuliert sich sowohl unbefleckt-mädchenhaft als auch wolllüstig begehrend.

Die Leibeslust bleibt eine heftige Serie mit gigantischen Penissen und Riesenbrüsten. Hier wird kein Blatt vor den Mund genommen, sondern lieber ein fester Schwanz in den Mund. Sexualität in ihrer direkten Spielart erweitert das Thema des Nicht-Rationalen ihrer Zeichnungen.

Das formale Prinzip der Übertreibung, das aus ihren Zopfarbeiten bekannt ist und das sie in vielerlei Schattierungen anwendet, kommt auch hier zum Tragen. Wie sehr sie

The same medium is used for the *Leibeslust* ("bodily pleasures") (pages 140/41) series, although this takes us in an entirely different direction. One may wonder what they have in common: the timid, fragile girls and the confident, extroverted women of these orgiastic drawings. How can such different artworks have been created by the same artist's hand? She makes one hide behind a rabbit's head and makes another open her labia for more than just penetrating gazes. Curiosity and the search for protection as two extremes of an artistic palette are not an irreconcilable contradiction in Cornelia Schleime's work. They determine one another. Female sensuality articulates itself as both unsullied girlishness and as salacious desire.

Leibeslust is undoubtedly a provocative series, with gigantic penises and enormous breasts. The women are not silenced, although their mouths are stopped with erect penises. Sexuality at its most direct expands the subject of the non-rational in her drawings.

The formal principle of exaggeration that is well known from her plait works and which she deploys in many variations is relevant in this context, too. Her propensity for continuing to use old motifs, modifying and quite casually placing them in new contexts is becoming increasingly visible. In *Die Zopfbläserin* ("the plait-blower") (page 141), the girlish fantasy of long plaits that develop a will of their own and act independently is combined with the unrestrained sexuality of *Leibeslust*. The delicate plait grows into a penis, or the big, hard penis dissolves into a long, slender

ältere Motive und Kunstgriffe ihres Schaffens weiter verwendet, modifiziert und fast beiläufig in andere neue Zusammenhänge setzt, lässt sich zunehmend beobachten. In der Arbeit Die Zopfbläserin (Abb. S. 141) vereint sich die Mädchenpoesie der langen Zöpfe, die sich verselbstständigen können und teilweise zu eigenen Akteurinnen werden, mit der prallen Sexualität der Leibeslust. Der zarte Zopf wächst sich zu einem Penis aus oder der kräftige pralle Penis löst sich im feingliedrigen langen Zopf auf. Die Extreme sind in dieser Zeichnung in einem gemeinsamen Glied vereinigt.

Besonders wagemutig erscheinen die Leibeslust-Arbeiten auch in formaler Hinsicht. Hier werden Extremperspektiven austariert, die den voyeuristischen Blick des Betrachters noch verstärken. Überhaupt scheint der Betrachter in diesen Arbeiten viel mehr herausgefordert zu sein als bei den übrigen Zeichnungen. Die Introvertiertheit weicht der ausdrücklichen Extrovertiertheit.

Im überwiegenden Teil ihrer Zeichnungen sind die Figuren sehr für sich, sie räkeln sich in ihrem eigenen Kosmos, sind wie in einen Kokon eingesponnen und scheinen gar kein Gegenüber zu benötigen. Sie fragen nicht, schauen uns nicht so geradewegs und provozierend ins Auge wie viele ihrer großen malerischen Porträts. Die Leibeslust-Frauen hingegen wollen gesehen werden, exhibitionistisch preisen sie ihre Geschlechtsteile an.

Würde man die Zeichenkunst von Cornelia Schleime mit

plait. The extremes are brought together in a single element in this drawing.

The *Leibeslust* drawings also appear very daring from a formal point of view: the artist balances out extreme perspectives that further amplify the viewer's voyeuristic gaze. Overall, the challenge to the viewer is more pronounced in these artworks than in the other drawings. Introversion gives way to explicit extroversion.

In most of her drawings, the people depicted are very focused on themselves, luxuriating in their own worlds, as though wrapped up in a cocoon, and do not appear to require a counterpart. They ask no questions, do not look at us in as immediate a provocative way as many of those in the large, painterly portraits. The *Leibeslust* women, on the other hand, want to be looked at, exhibitionistically flaunting their genitals.

If one were to describe Cornelia Schleime's drawings using literary tools – which is legitimate, considering her work as a writer of novels and poems and poetic texts – one would use the term *écriture automatique*, a form of writing from the unconscious. Her artworks from the 1980s are very narrative and, in contrast to the artworks described above, make use of all of the available pictorial space. Here, we can see more complex compositional structures featuring several figurines, surrounded by decorations and writing. She illustrates entire dream worlds with a variety of actors. Over the course of time, Cornelia Schleime has carried out a process of reduction and

dem Handwerkszeug der Literatur beschreiben – was bei ihr als Romanautorin und Verfasserin von Gedichten und poetischen Texten legitim ist – so käme man auf die écriture automatique, jenes Schreiben aus dem Unbewussten heraus. Sehr narrativ sind ihre Arbeiten aus den 80er Jahren, die im Gegensatz zu den bisher beschriebenen Blättern bildfüllend angelegt sind. Hier finden wir noch komplexere Kompositionsstrukturen mit mehreren Figurinen, die mit Ornamenten und Schriftzügen umrankt werden. Sie illustriert eine ganze Traumwelt mit unterschiedlichen Akteurinnen. Über die Jahre geht Cornelia Schleime in die Reduktion, die Konsequenz. Der Bildgrund bleibt nun auf einer hellen offenen Fläche bestehen und das Motiv, meist nur noch aus einer Figur bestehend, wird ins Blatt gesetzt. Aber auch dies gilt nicht apodiktisch, denn Cornelia Schleime unterwirft sich keinen statischen Gesetzen und kommt in manchen Schildkrötenzeichnungen der letzten Jahre wieder auf das durchgängige Aquarellieren der kompletten Bildfläche zurück.

Das Selbstvergessene ihrer Frauen und Mädchen zieht sich durch alle Jahrzehnte ihres zeichnerischen Werks, es gilt der Rückzug in die innere Welt. Der Titel einer Ausstellung mit Gemälden im Jahr 2011 lautete „Die sind nicht von hier". Dies könnte auch als Leitfaden über Cornelia Schleimes Zeichnungen stehen. In ihnen wird das Konzentrat des Einfangens eines flüchtigen Moments besonders spürbar. Unwiederholbare Momente, mit eleganter Leichtig-

consequence. The grounding now remains a light, open surface, and the subject, which usually consists of just one figure, is positioned on the paper. But this, too, is not apodictic, for Cornelia Schleime does not submit to static laws and has returned in some of her turtle-drawings of recent years to the application of water-colours to the entire surface of the painting. The ob-liviousness of her women and girls, the withdrawal into one's inner world, is a feature of her drawings through-out the decades. An exhibition of her paintings in 2011 was entitled "Die sind nicht von hier" ("they aren't from around here"). This could also be a motto for Cor-nelia Schleime's drawings. It is here that the intensity of capturing a fleeting moment becomes particularly tangible. Unrepeatable moments, painted on paper in watercolours with beautiful lightness, often wordlessly release the viewer into dream worlds and imaginary spheres. We, too, can confidently abandon ourselves to a wordless world when we allow ourselves to be touched by her work. Throughout the years during which I have accompanied and viewed Cor-nelia's work, I have looked into countless delicate faces of women and girls. They never become boring, do not repeat themselves, are transformed and never static. They are all united by a fascinating paradox: their independence and strength increases in proportion to the degree of their fragility. In this instant, everything stops. The artist achieves an essence that makes further questions and additional explanations unnecessary. In this respect, her

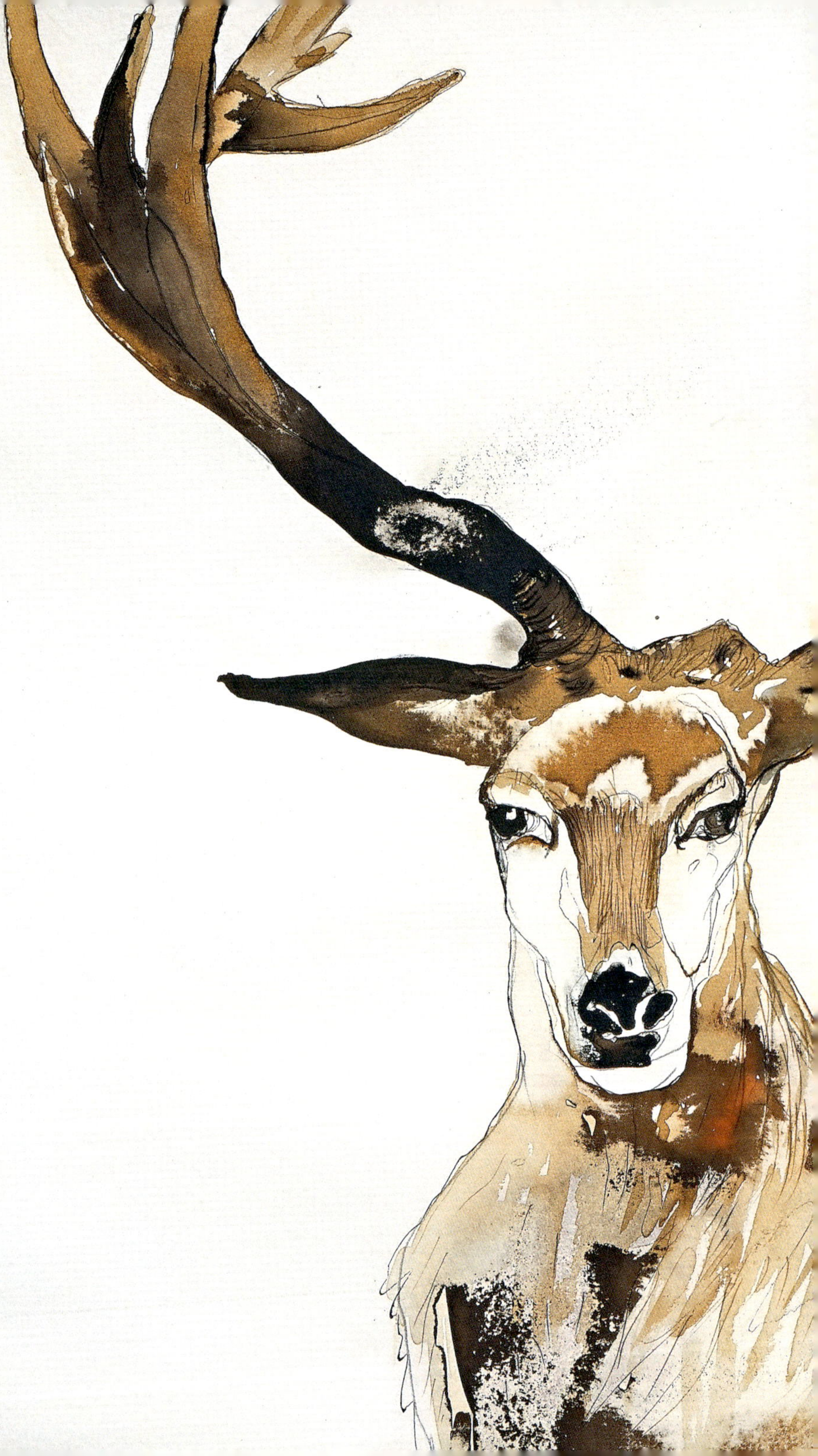

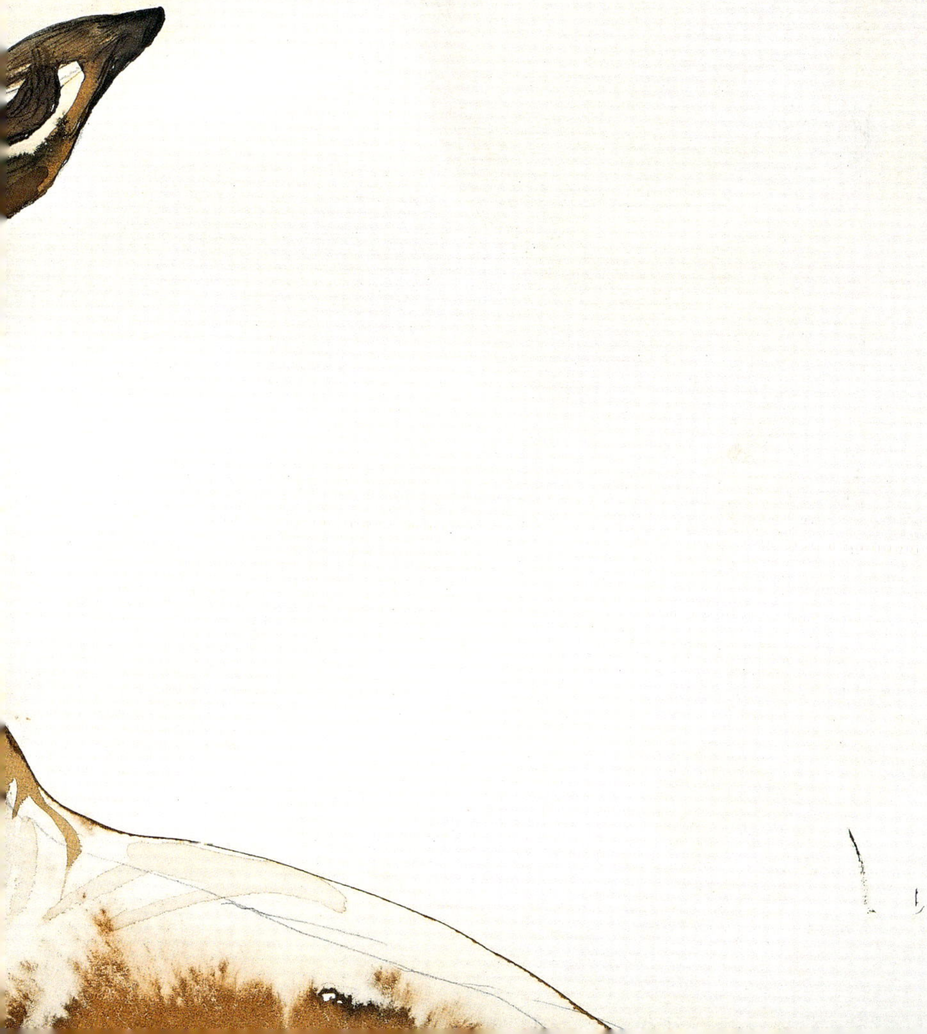

keit auf das Papier getuscht, entlassen die Betrachter häufig sprachlos in Traumwelten und imaginäre Sphären. Auch wir können getrost in den Zungenschlaf verfallen, wenn wir uns von ihren Arbeiten berühren lassen. In wie viele unterschiedliche zarte Frauen- und Mädchengesichter habe ich schon geschaut über die Jahre der Begleitung und Betrachtung von Cornelias Arbeit? Sie werden nie langweilig, wiederholen sich nicht, sind in Wandlung begriffen, stehen nicht still. Ein Faszinosum verbindet sie alle miteinander: Auf dem Grat ihrer Zerbrechlichkeit gewinnen sie ihre Souveränität und Stärke. In diesem Moment steht alles still. Der Künstlerin gelingt eine Essenz, die Nachfragen oder weitere Erklärungen unnötig macht. Ihre Zeichnungen erscheinen mir in dieser Hinsicht wie Lyrik. Das Selbstverständnis der Lyrikerin Hilde Domin ist daher übertragbar auf die Zeichenkunst Cornelia Schleimes: „Sie verbindet uns wieder mit dem Teil unseres Seins, der nicht angetastet ist von den Kompromissen, mit unsrer Kindheit, mit der Frische unsrer Reaktionen … Die Mitteilung des nicht – oder doch kaum – Mittelbaren: das ist also die Aufgabe des Lyrikers.“[4]

Die Subjektivität als einzigartige und immer sprudelnde Quelle des schöpferischen Prozesses zu erklären, ist ein Wagnis oder sogar eine zwingende Notwendigkeit, der sich die Künstlerin aussetzt. Dies öffnet ihr die Tür für eine spielerische Offenheit, die sic Geschichten erzählen

drawings strike me as akin to poetry. The selfconception of the lyricist Hilde Domin can therefore be applied to Cornelia Schleime's drawing: "She reconnects us with a part of our being that is not touched by compromises, with our childhood, the freshness of our reactions ... The communication of that which cannot – or can only just – be communicated: this, then, is the lyricist's challenge"[4]. The artist exposes herself to the risk, or even the necessity, of explaining subjectivity as the unique and constantly replenishing source of the creative process. This opens the door to a playful openness that allows her to tell stories that can only come into being within the unfettered space created created by art. Here, one can be partially transformed into an animal and abandon oneself to erotic seduction, one can be timid and lascivious. Childlike games in the garden of paradise are possible, as are bad games such as those in Animationen ("animation") and Ertüchtigungen ("toughening up") (pages 123-127). The dark sides, too, are part of this opening up to the unconscious. In his quality assessment of good art, Hanno Rauterberg writes: "Here, actions can be executed, demonstrations made and words uttered, without there being any direct consequences – neither positive nor negative. Only because it remains temporary, in limbo, can it manage to eschew the constraints and laws of reality and to explore the world without restraint"[5]. Cornelia Schleime's drawings pass this test with flying colours. She also confronts experiences with curiosity on her travels, transforming these

lässt, wie sie nur im Freiraum der Kunst entstehen können. Da kann man halb zum Tier werden, da kann man sich erotischer Verführung hingeben, da kann man schüchtern oder lasziv sein. Kindliche Spiele im Paradiesgarten sind ebenso möglich wie böse Spiele, zum B in den Animationen und Ertüchtigungen (Abb. S. 123-127). Auch die Schattenseiten gehören zu dieser Öffnung für das Unbewusste hinzu.

In seiner Qualitätsprüfung über gute Kunst schreibt Hanno Rauterberg: „Hier kann gehandelt, gezeigt, gesprochen werden, ohne dass es direkte Konsequenzen hätte – weder positive noch negative. Nur weil sie vorläufig bleibt, in der Schwebe, kann es ihr gelingen, von den Zwängen und Gesetzen der Wirklichkeit abzusehen, die Welt unbegrenzt erkunden zu dürfen."[5] Dieser Prüfung halten die Zeichnungen der Künstlerin mit Bravour stand. Neugierig greift sie auch auf allen ihren Reisen Eindrücke auf, die sie dann zu eigenen Geschichten macht, in denen sie das bereiste Land in ihrer Gedankenwelt wieder verlässt, um in ihr inneres Land zu reisen. In ihren Reisetagebüchern, auf ihren Postkartenübermalungen (Abb. S. 76-81) finden wir diese Fabulierlust, die die Fremdheit und das Neue aufnehmen, um sie sich auf ganz andere Art einzuverleiben, Sie werden mit dem Selbst verbunden, um letztlich wieder im Niemandsland Kunst anzukommen. Ihre Phantasie ist gerade in diesen Arbeiten zügellos. Das Reisen als Aufbruch in eine Freiheit, das Hintersichlassen von ba-

impressions into her own stories when she mentally leaves the country she is visiting in order to travel to her inner world. In her travel diaries and the drawings she superimposes on postcards (pages 76–81), we bear witness to this love of spinning tales in which the foreign and the new are absorbed and incorporated in entirely new ways. They are connected to the self only to arrive again in the no man's land of art. Her imagination knows no bounds in these works. Travelling as a departure to freedom, as an abandonment of banal everyday realities and as the experience of opening one's eyes to see what is new, provides the artist with a great reservoir for inner journeys to other worlds. Again and again, her drawings also capture impressions from journeys in the real world, such as the turtles from Zanzibar. She has created an impressive cornucopia of drawings, and replenishes it with her most recent works, executed in the course of this year. In these, she fuses the old and the new in a conspicuously muted colour palette and with even greater openness and lightness. She appears to forsake clear contours, and many works feature nebulous conditions and blurring. She conducts formal experiments with the opportunities offered by watercolours, mixes wine and coffee grounds into her paints. The concept of the ephemeral has become increasingly dominant, possibly the consequence of an even greater artistic freedom. Her entire oeuvre appears here: the composite beings, centaurs, rabbit heads and antlers, as well as the erotic nudes, the plaits and figurines from the beginnings of her artistic career.

naler Alltäglichkeit und das Öffnen der Augen für Neues bieten der Künstlerin ein großes Reservoir für den inneren Aufbruch in andere Welten. Immer wieder halten in ihre Zeichnungen auch Eindrücke von Reisen Einzug, wie zum Beispiel die Schildkröten aus Sansibar.

Ein beachtliches Füllhorn an Zeichnungen hat sie geschaffen und mit den aktuellsten Arbeiten aus diesem Jahr wird es weiter gespeist. In einer auffällig gedämpften Farbigkeit und einer noch größeren Offenheit und Leichtigkeit verbindet sie hier Neues mit Altem. Sie scheint die klaren Konturen zu verlassen, in vielen dieser Arbeiten finden wir nebulöse Zustände, Verwischungen. Sie experimentiert formal mit den Möglichkeiten des Aquarells, mischt Wein und Kaffeesatz in ihre Tuschen. Der Gedanke der Flüchtigkeit wird dominanter, vielleicht die Konsequenz einer noch größeren künstlerischen Freiheit. Ihr gesamtes Werk taucht hier auf, die Mischwesen, Zentauren, Hasenköpfe und Geweihe, auch die erotischen Akte, die Zöpfe und Figurinen aus den künstlerischen Anfängen. Letztere finden wir auf dem unteren Teil des Blattes, wie ein Fundament, das den neuen Geschöpfen den Halt bietet.

„Wir werden immer weiter ziehen …" hat Cornelia mir als Widmung auf eine Fotoinszenierung geschrieben. Das Foto zeigt das bekannte Motiv, bei dem sie ihre Zöpfe an einen alten Kinderwagen bindet und hinter sich her zieht. In dieser aktuellen Inszenierung geht sie in einem

The latter can be seen in the lower section of the paper, like a foundation that provides the new creatures with secure footing.

"We will always keep moving ..." reads Cornelia's dedication to me on a staged photograph. The photograph features the well-known image of her tying her plaits to an old pram, and pulling it along behind herself. In this current version, she walks barefoot across a field in Brandenburg, wearing a gold sequin dress. We can read whatever we like into this photograph: one should preserve one's childhood, or one always remains attached to one's past. Art provides the artist with the strength and meaning that allow her to keep moving. Ideally without shoes, free of ballast, so that contact to the original levels of consciousness can be made even more directly.

It is a beautiful thing when we, too, keep moving, both with her and with ourselves; carrying as little baggage as possible, free and open to experience wordless worlds.

(1) Johannes Meinhardt, "Spätmoderne Zeichnung", in *Gegen den Strich. Neue Formen der Zeichnung*, Markus Heinzelmann, Matthias Winzen (eds), p. 33, Nuremberg, 2004

(2) Rolf Wedewer, "Joseph Beuys – Die Zeichnungen", in: *Künstler · Kritisches Lexikon der Gegenwartskunst*, Munich, 1993, p. 10

(3) Martin Hellmold, *Wer aus mir trinkt, wird ein Reh*, Bielefeld, Leipzig, Berlin, 2010, p. 9

(4) Hilde Domin, "Wozu Lyrik heute", in *Abel steht auf*, Stuttgart, 1979 p. 79-80

(5) Hanno Rauterberg, Und das ist Kunst?!, Frankfurt/Main, 2007, p. 143

goldenen Paillettenkleid barfuß über ein Brandenburger Feld. Was immer uns dieses Bild sagen mag: Man möge sich die Kindheit bewahren oder man bleibt immer an seine Vergangenheit geknüpft. Die Kunst gibt der Künstlerin die Kraft und den Sinn, immer weiter zu ziehen. Am besten ohne Schuhe, ballastfrei, damit der Kontakt zu ursprünglichen Bewusstseinsschichten noch direkter aufgenommen werden kann.

Wunderbar ist es, wenn auch wir weiter ziehen, mit ihr und mit uns, mit möglichst leichtem Gepäck, wenn wir frei und offen bleiben für den Zungenschlaf.

[1] Johannes Meinhardt, Spätmoderne Zeichnung, in: Gegen den Strich. Neue Formen der Zeichnung. Hrsg. Von Markus Heinzelmann, Matthias Winzen, S. 33, Nürnberg, 2004

[2] Rolf Wedewer, Joseph Beuys – Die Zeichnungen, in: Künstler · Kritisches Lexikon der Gegenwartskunst, München, 1993, S. 10

[3] Martin Hellmold, Wer aus mir trinkt, wird ein Reh, Bielefeld, Leipzig, Berlin, 2010, S. 9

[4] Hilde Domin, Wozu Lyrik heute, in: Abel steht auf, Stuttgart, 1979 S. 79/80

[5] Hanno Rauterberg Und das ist Kunst?!, Frankfurt/Main, 2007, S. 143

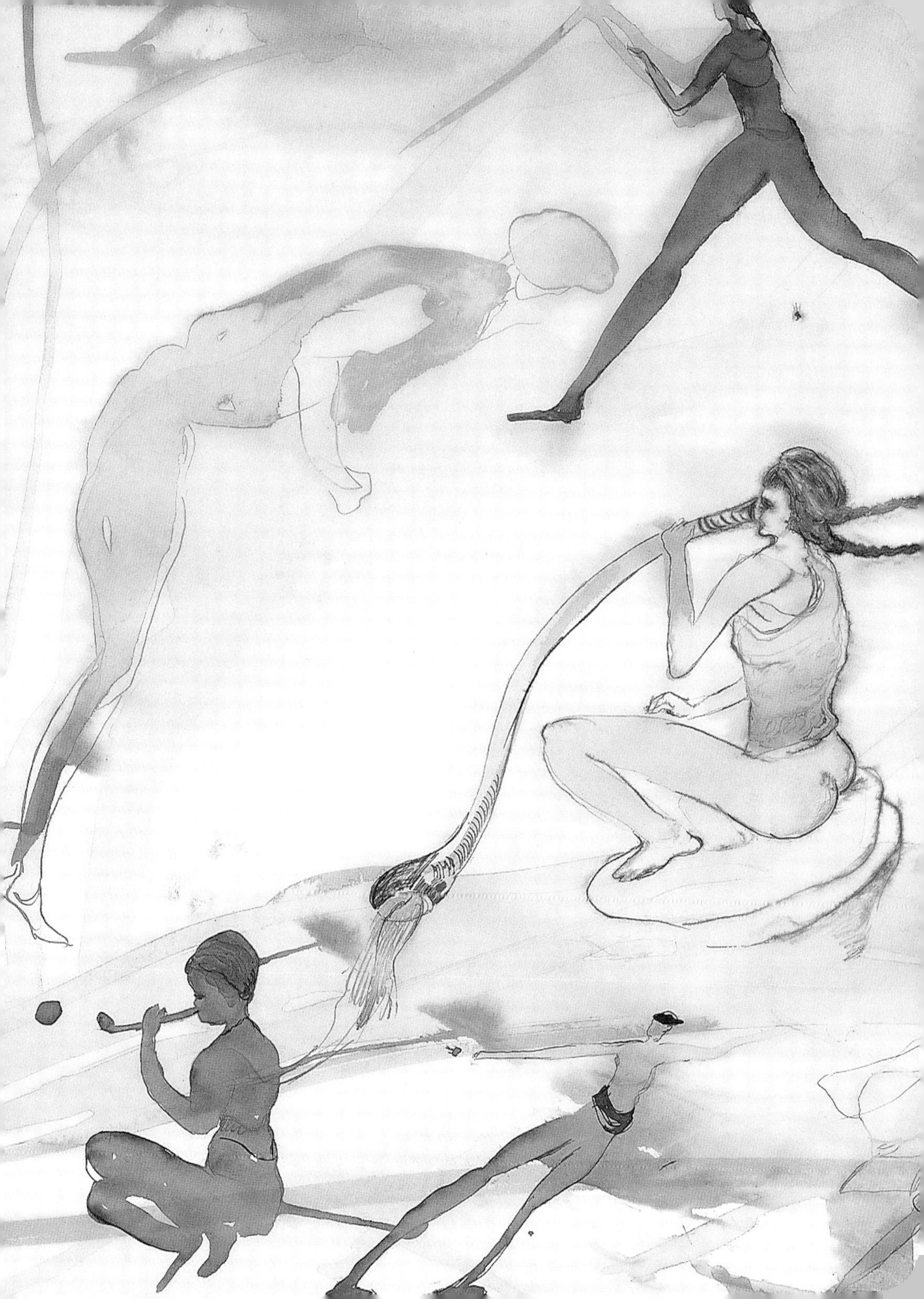

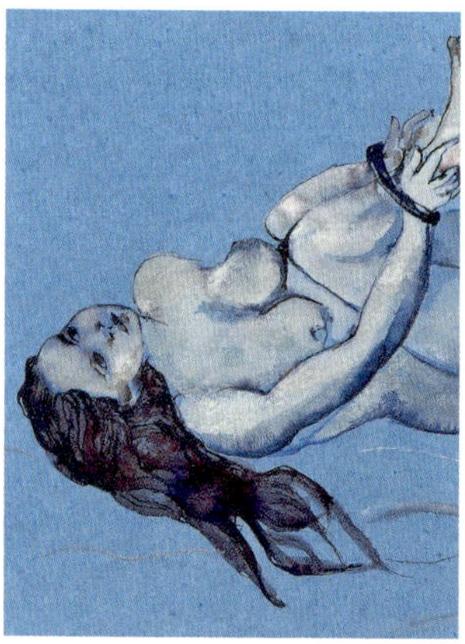

1999–2009

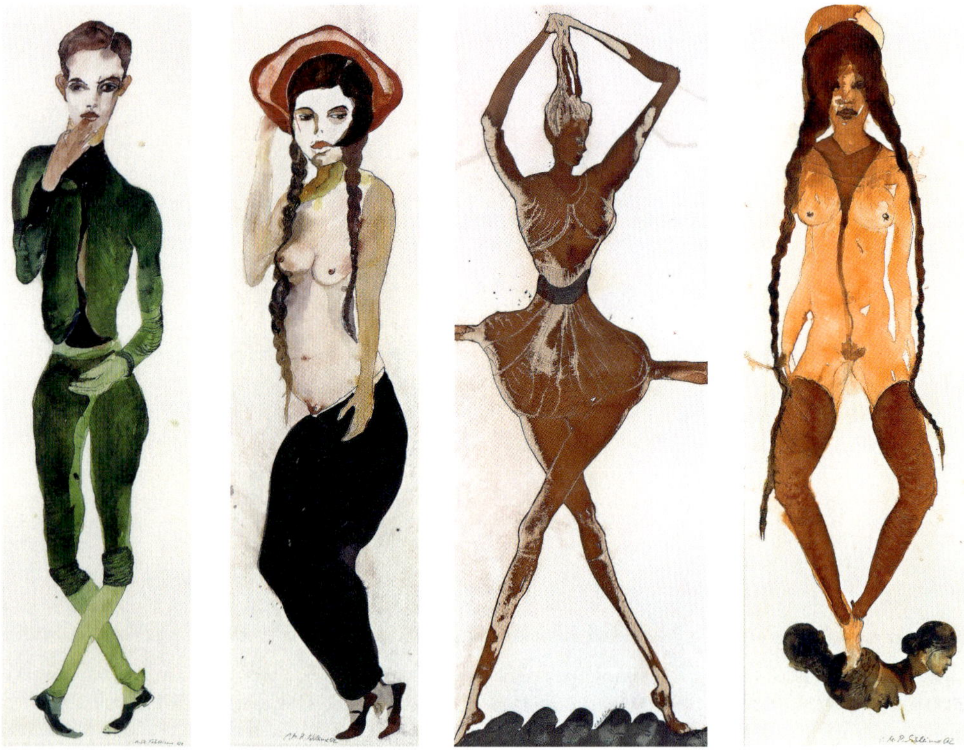

Stelen 2002

Tusche, Passepartoutkarton Indian ink, matboard

101 x 27 cm, 100 x 28 cm, 101 x 35 cm, 100 x 32 cm

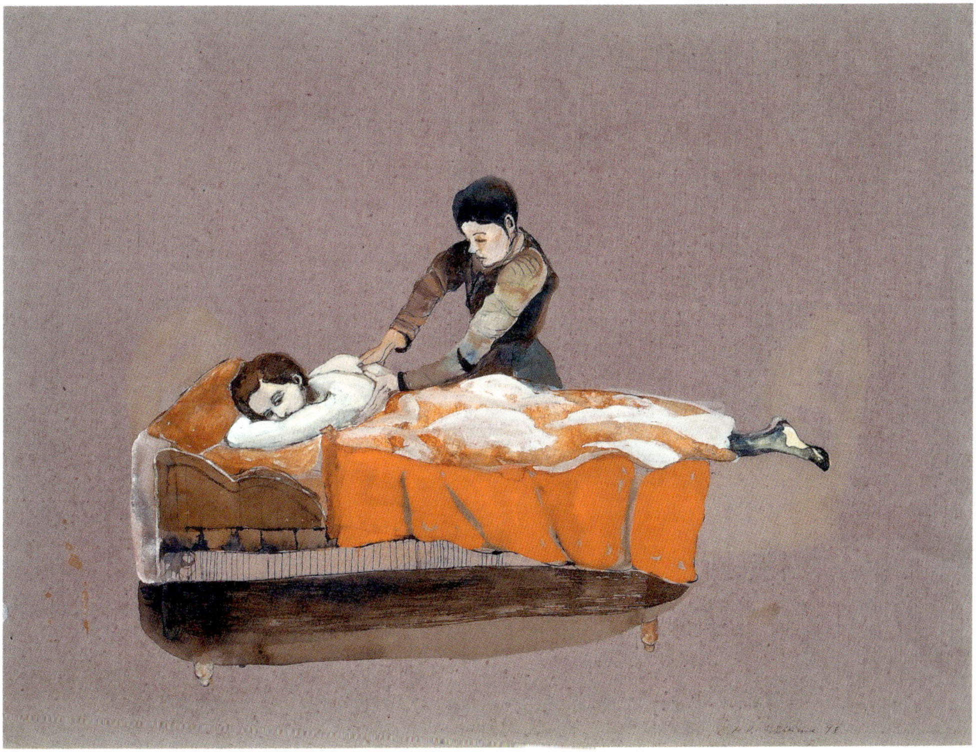

aus der Reihe „Ertüchtigungen" 1996-1998
Aquarell & Tusche auf farbigem Papier Watercolour & Indian ink on coloured paper
56 x 76 cm

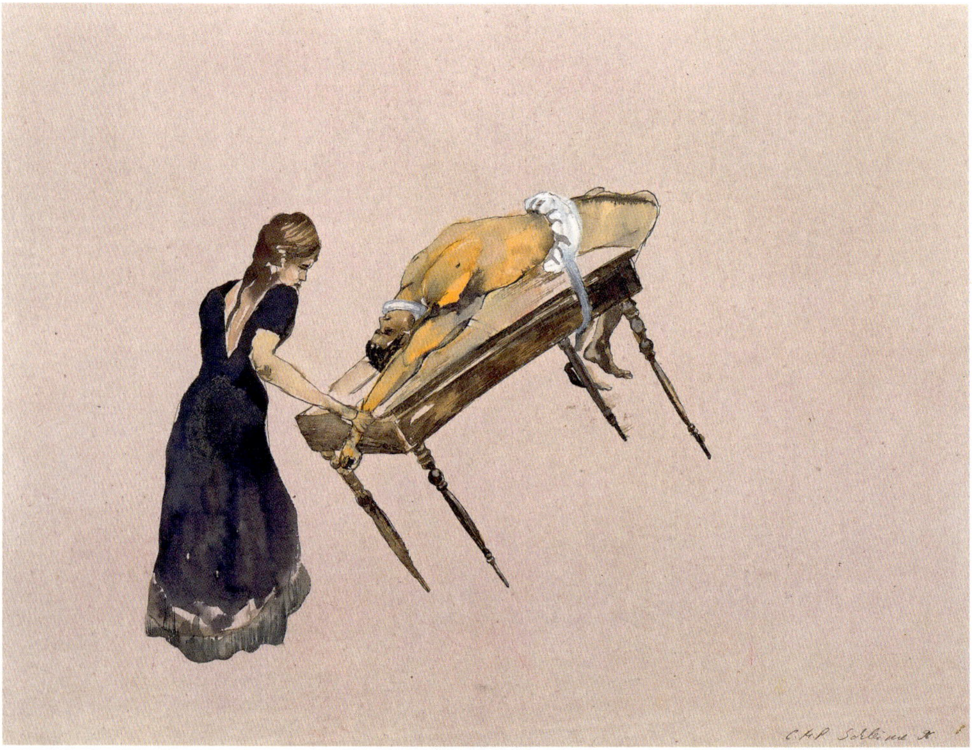

aus der Reihe „Ertüchtigungen" 1996–1998
Aquarell & Tusche auf farbigem Papier Watercolour & Indian ink on coloured paper
56 x 76 cm

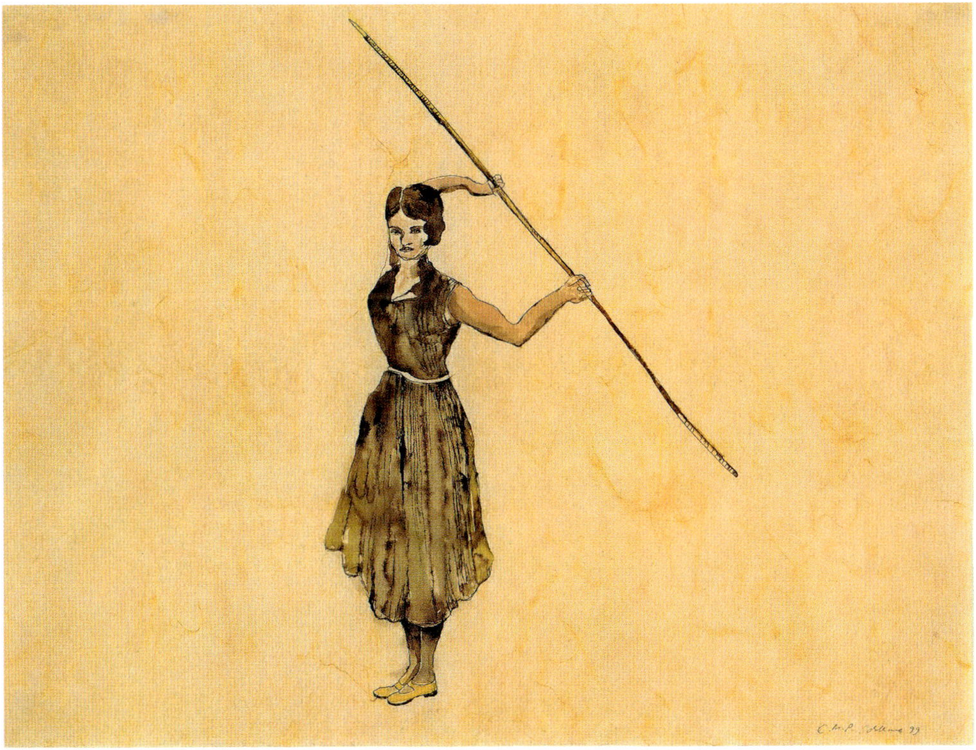

aus der Reihe „Ertüchtigungen" 1996–1998
Aquarell & Tusche auf farbigem Papier Watercolour & Indian ink on coloured paper
56 x 76 cm

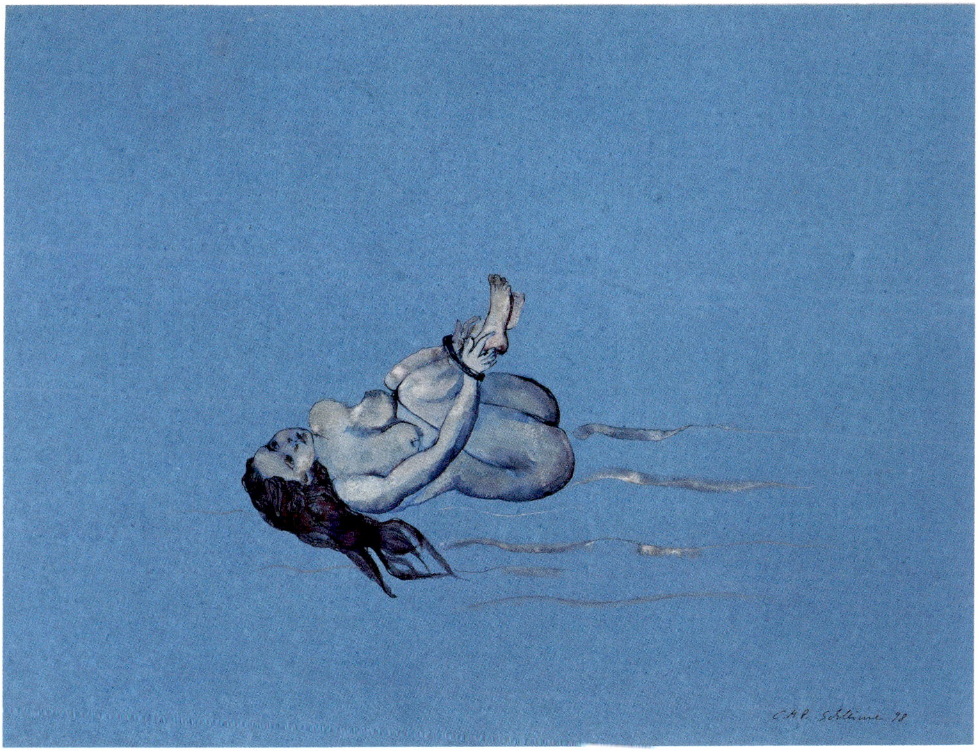

aus der Reihe „Ertüchtigungen" 1996-1998
Aquarell & Tusche auf farbigem Papier Watercolour & Indian ink on coloured paper
56 x 76 cm

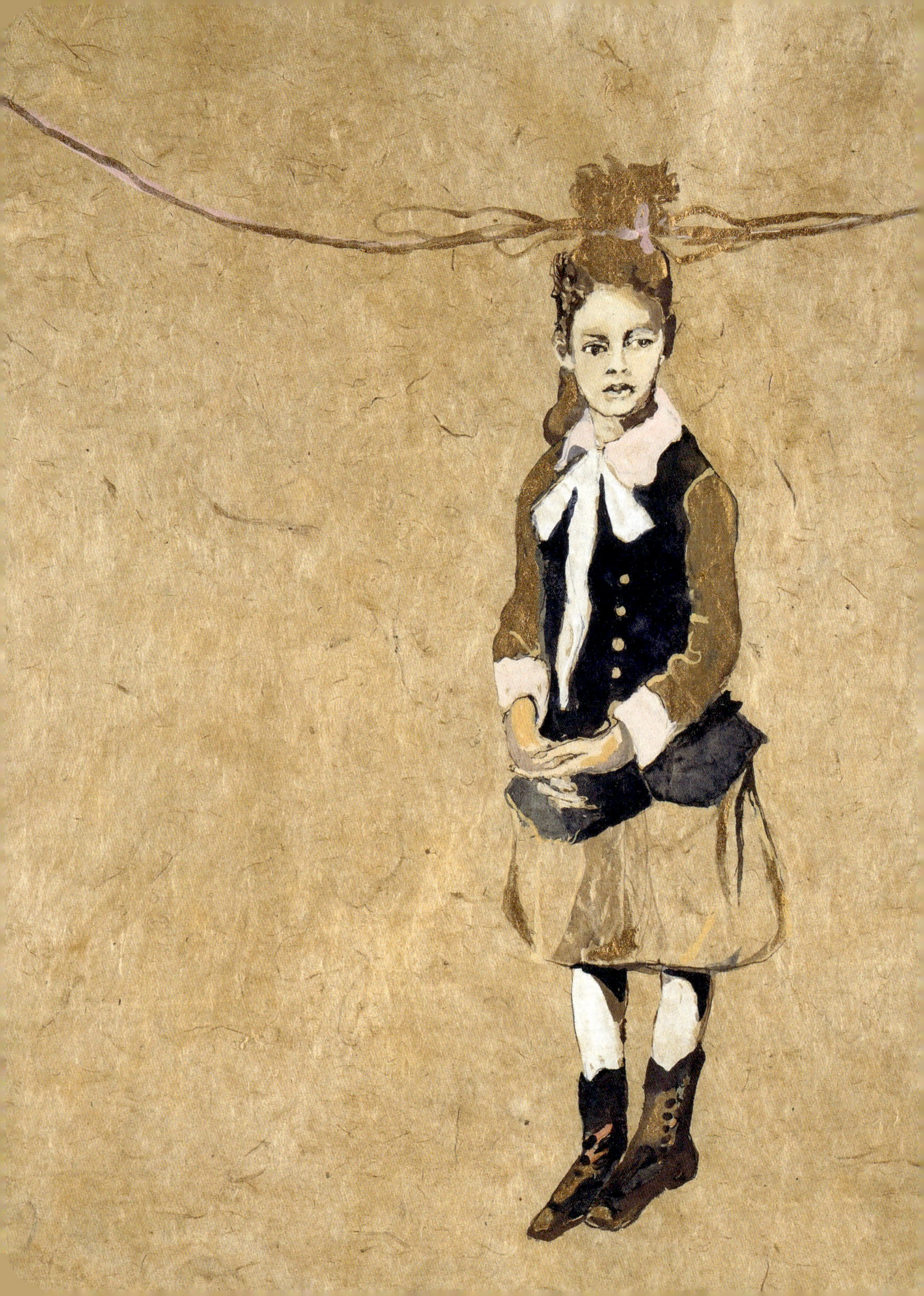

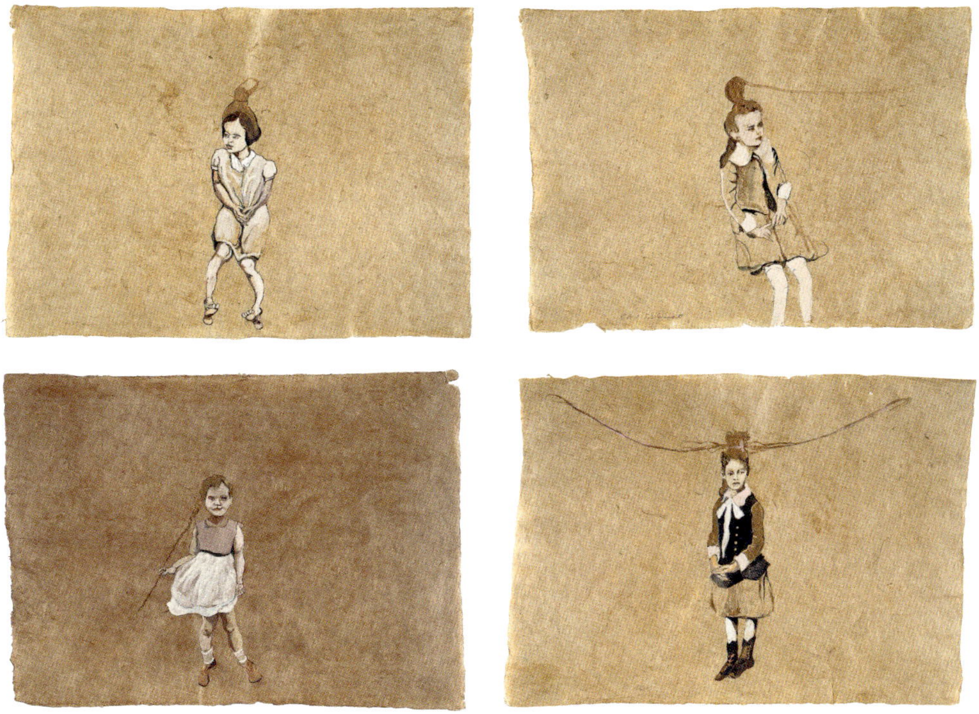

o.T. 1999
Aquarell & Tusche auf Reispapier
Watercolour & Indian ink on rice paper
68 x 48 cm

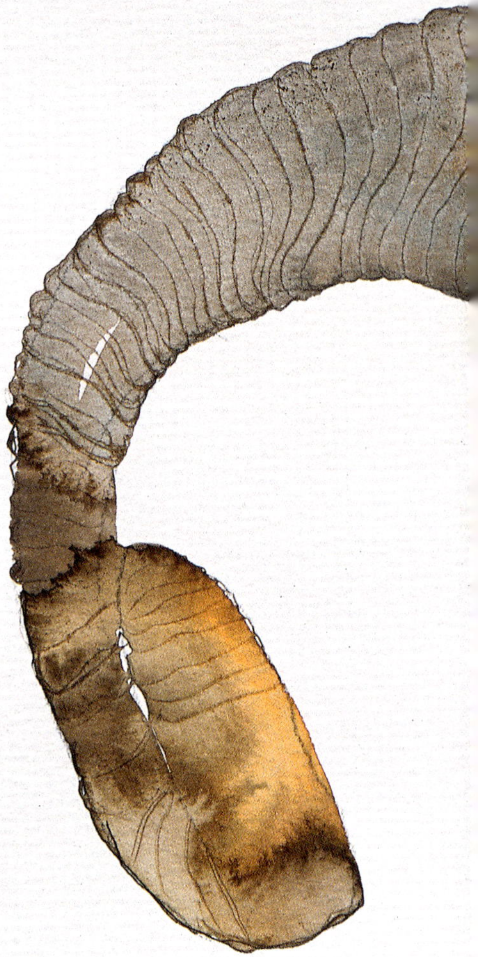

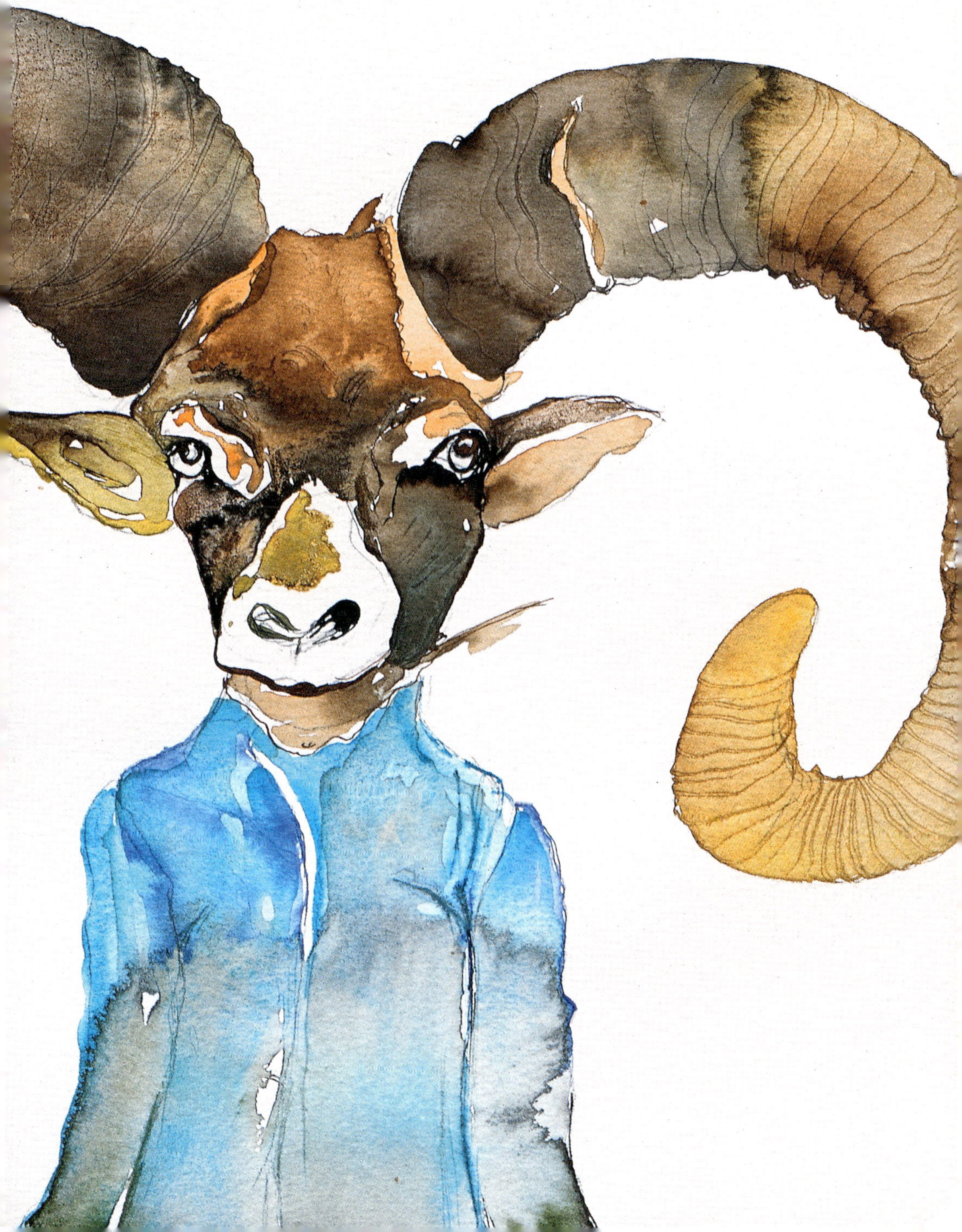

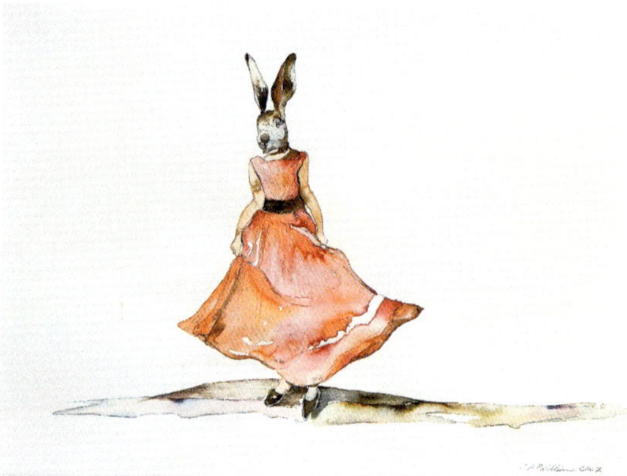

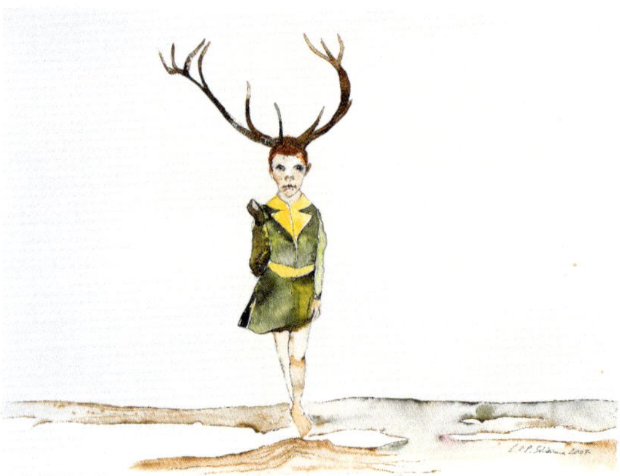

aus der Reihe „Camouflage" 2008
Aquarell & Tusche auf Papier Watercolour & Indian ink on paper
57 x 76 cm

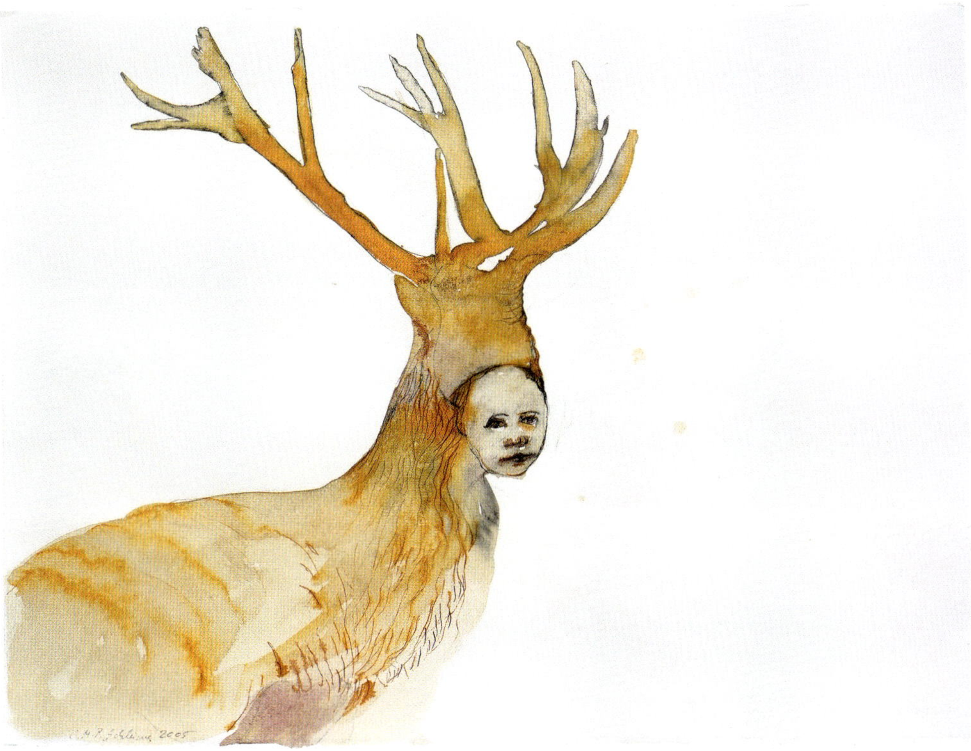

aus der Reihe „Camouflage" 2008
Aquarell & Tusche auf Papier Watercolour & Indian ink on paper
57 x 76 cm

Marlene B. kauft bei Prada, Gucchi & Co. Sie ist eine gute Kundin.
Die Türsteher verneigen sich vor ihr. Die Verkäuferinnen bieten ihr Champania an.
Noch nie verließ sie ein Geschäft, ohne etwas zu erwerben, auch wenn ihr die aktuelle Kollektion nicht immer gefiel. Sie redet dann kaum. Seit einigen Monaten verweilt die exklusive Garderobe nicht lange bei ihr. Höchstens ein bis zwei Stunden. Die Neuerwerbungen, für die sie einige hundert Euro hinblätterte, bringt sie schnurstracks nach Haus. Dort reißt sie das seidene Papier auf, faltet es sorgfältig zusammen, legt es in die Schublade.
Die neuen Sachen lässt sie in einer Plastiktüte verschwinden, meistens eine von Kaisers, Edeka und Co.
Augenblicklich bringt sie diese in den An- & Verkauf. Dort lässt sie sich Zeit.
Mehr Zeit, als für das Einkaufen. Sehr umständlich verhandelt sie den Second-Hand-Preis. Lobt Schnitt und Qualität, weist auf die gute Pflege hin. Betont, dass die Ware wie neu aussieht. Anschließend fährt sie zurück in ihre Wohnung.

Marlene B. ist ein gutes Beispiel für die Wirtschaftsförderung.

Cornelia Schleime

Marlene B. shops at Prada, Gucci & Co. She is a good customer. The door staff bow to her. The shop assistants offer her champagne. She has never left a shop without purchasing something, even if she does not always like the current collection. She does not talk much then. For the last few months, the exclusive garments have never been in her possession for long. One or two hours at most. She takes the new acquisitions, for which she has shelled out several hundred euros, straight home. She tears open the wrapping tissue, folds it carefully and places it in the drawer.

She tucks the new things away in plastic bags, often from run-of-the-mill supermarkets.

She then immediately takes them to the second-hand shops. She takes her time there.

More time than she spent shopping. Laboriously, she negotiates the second-hand price.

Vaunts the cut and the quality, points out their good condition. Fmphasises that the items look like new. Finally, she drives back to her flat.

Marlenc B is a good example of the promotion uf ecnnomic development.

Cornelia Schleime

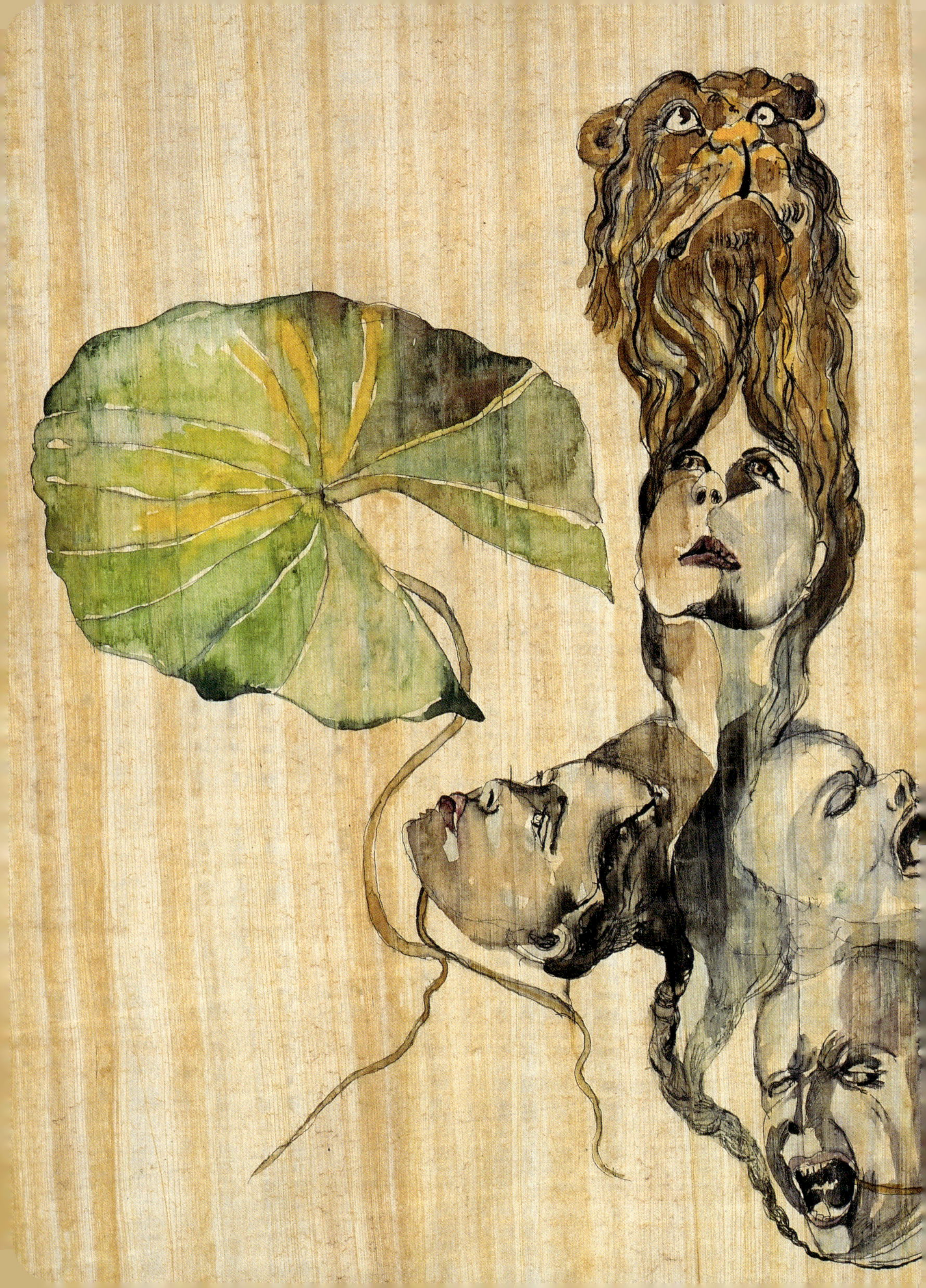

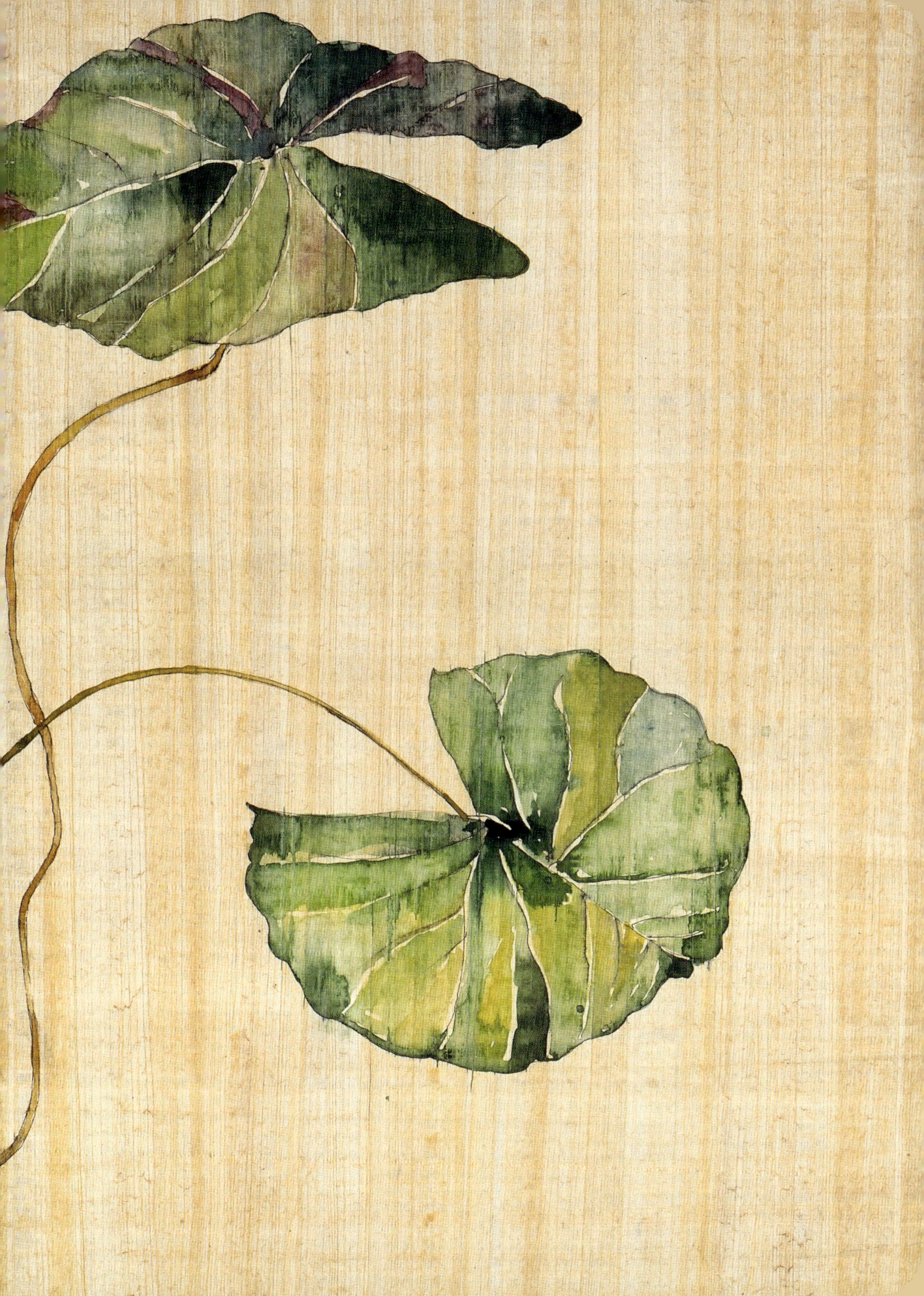

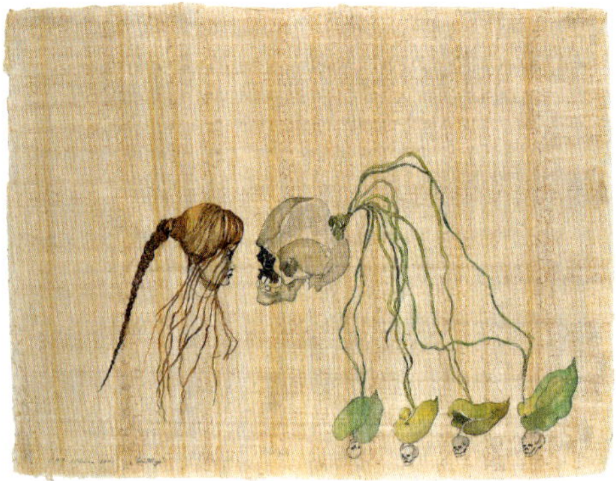
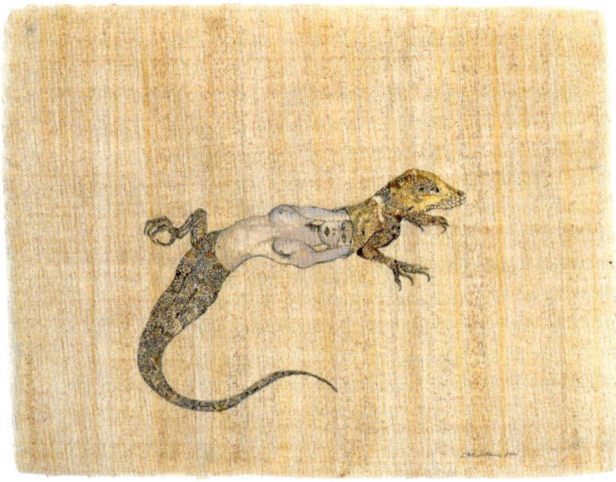
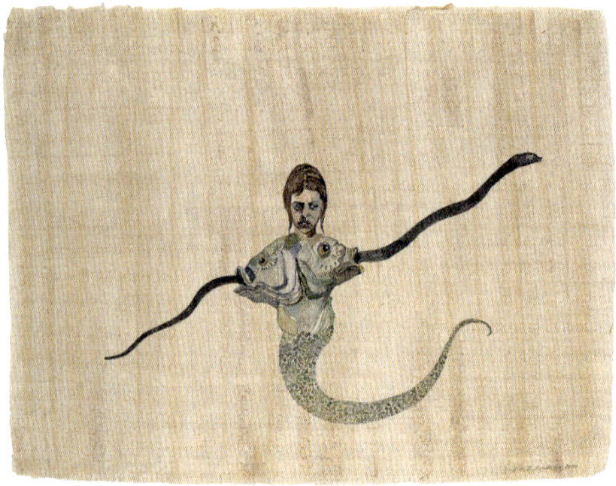
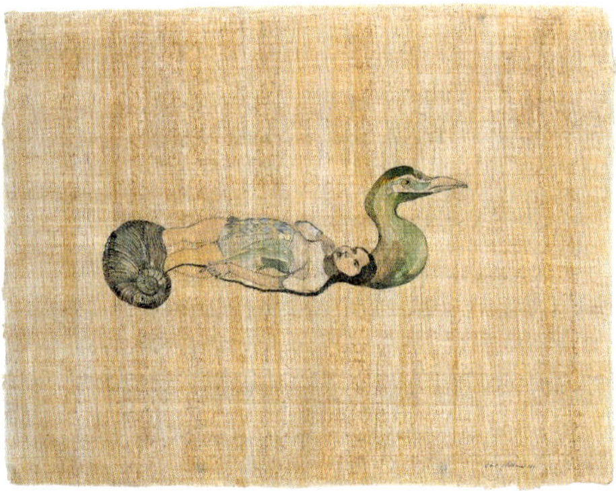

aus der Reihe „Mutationen“ 2001
Aquarell & Tusche auf Papyrus Watercolour & Indian ink on papyrus
60 x 80 cm

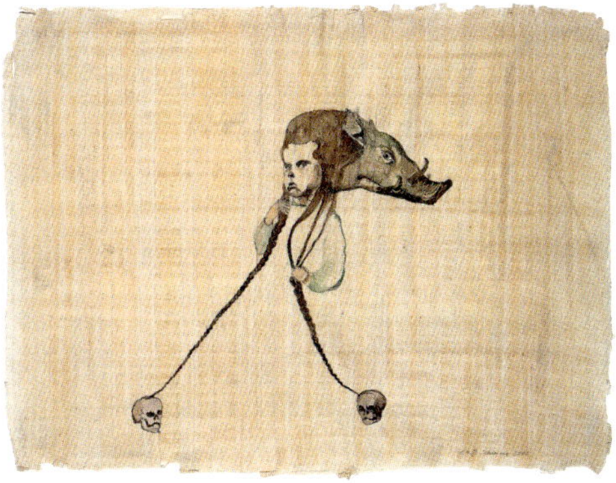

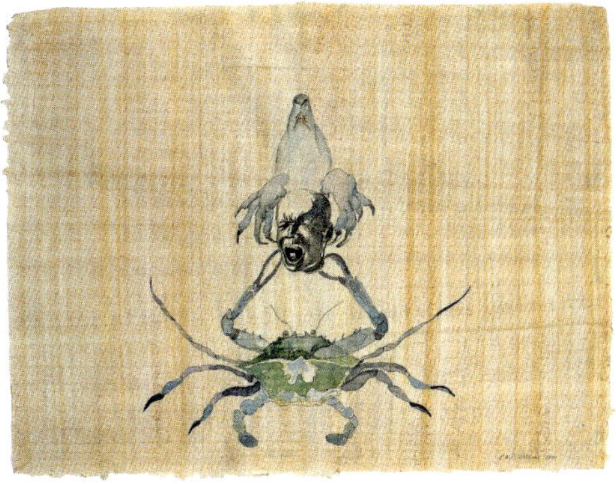

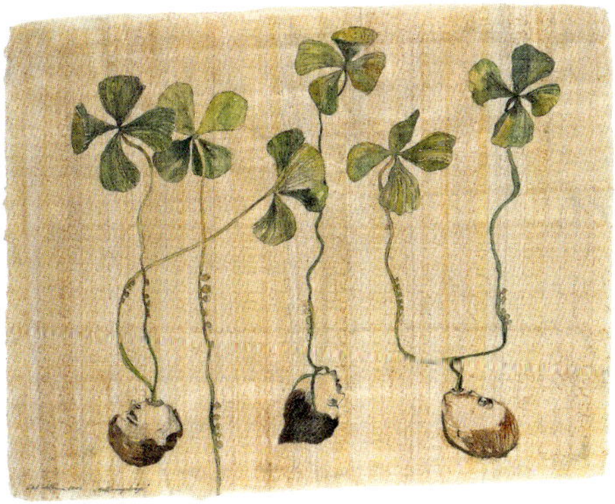

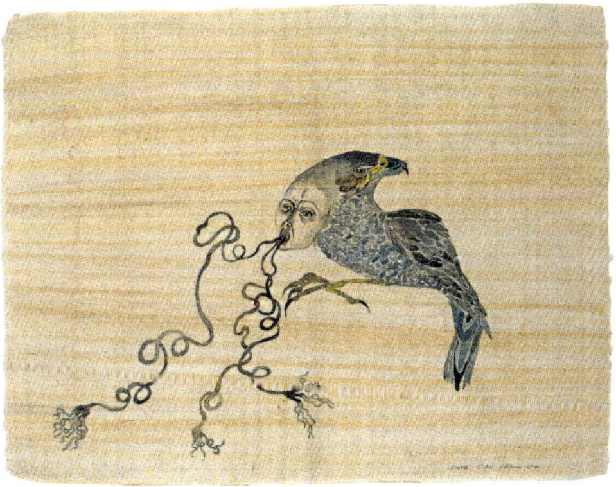

aus der Reihe „Mutationen" 2001
Aquarell & Tusche auf Papyrus Watercolour & Indian ink on papyrus
60 x 80 cm

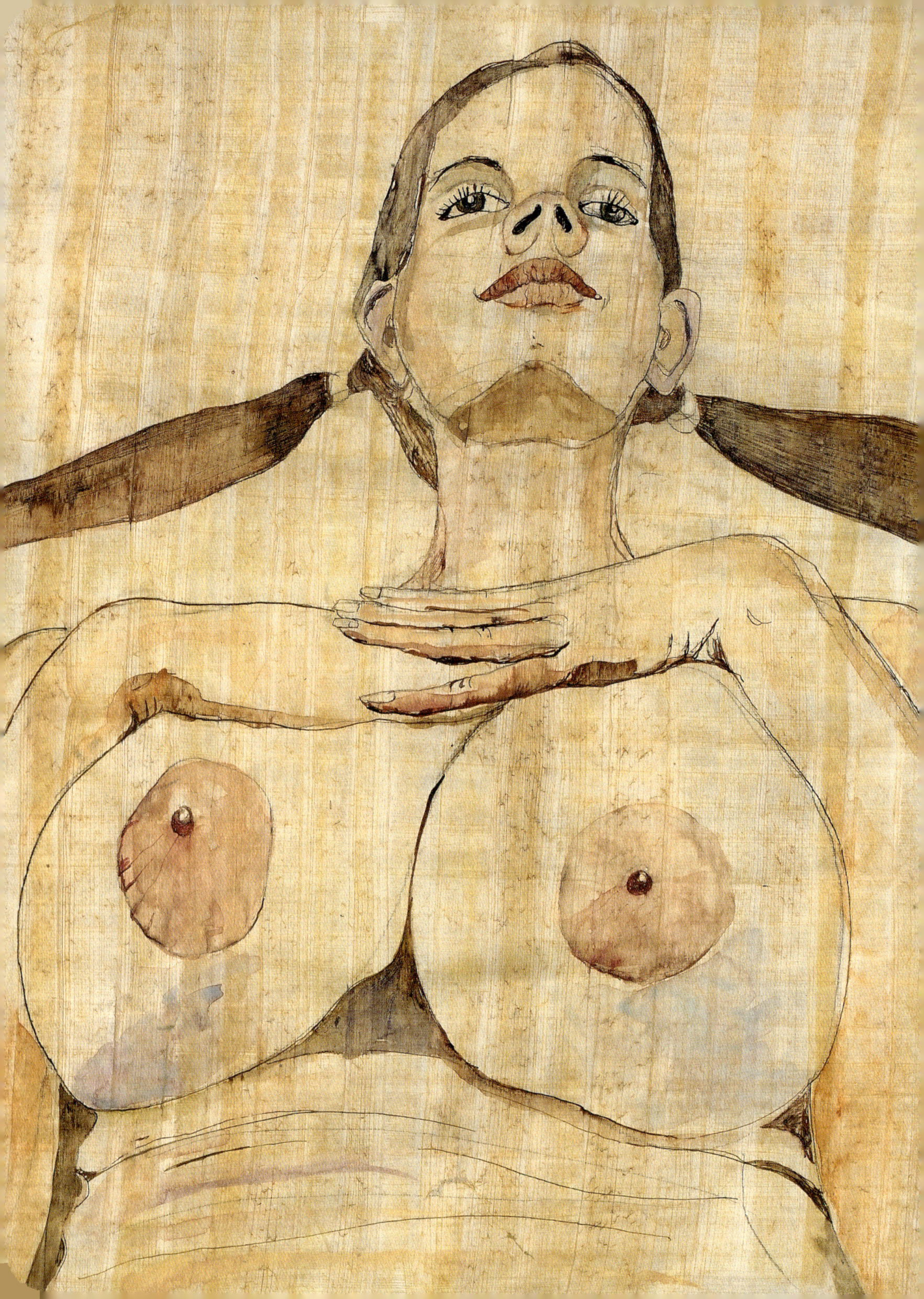

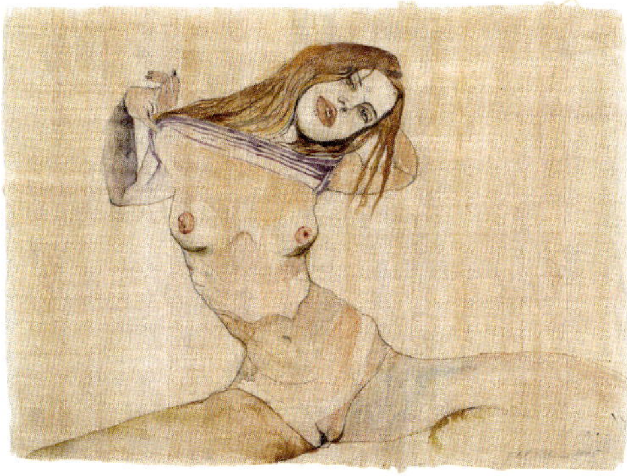

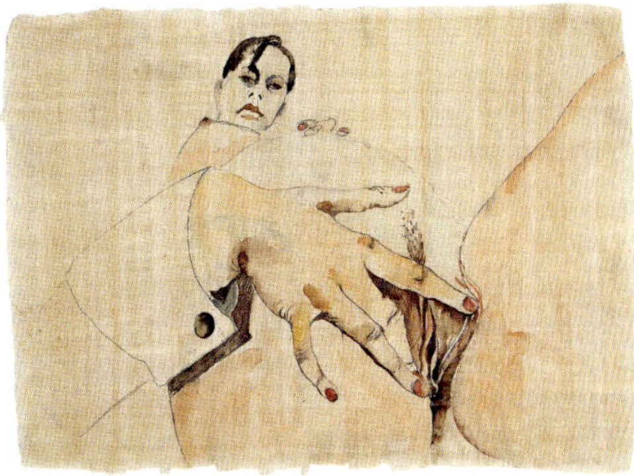

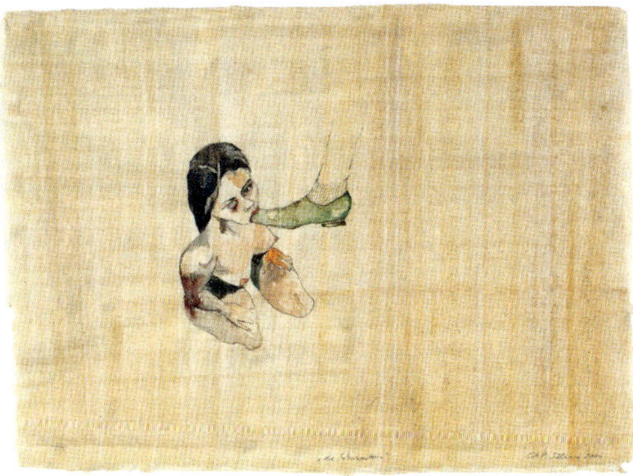

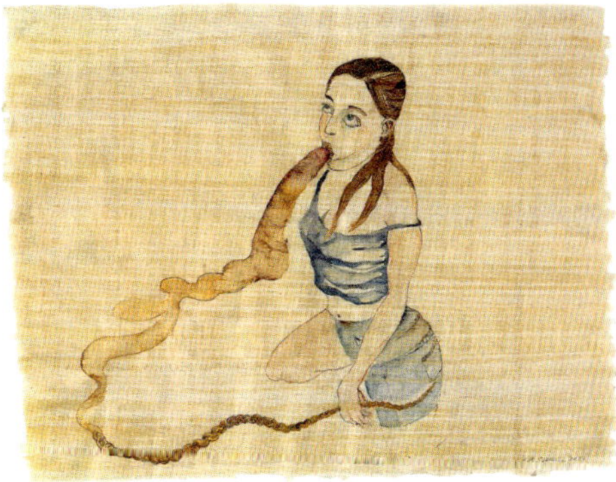

aus der Reihe „Leibeslust“ 2007
Abb. 1 o.T. Abb. 2 Sesam öffne Dich,
Abb. 3 Die Schuhputzerin, Abb. 4 Die Zopfbläserin
Mischtechnik auf Papyrus Mixed media on papyrus
53 x 70 cm

Mondscheinsonate 2005

Aquarell & Tusche auf Papier Watercolour & Indian ink on paper 58 x 76 cm

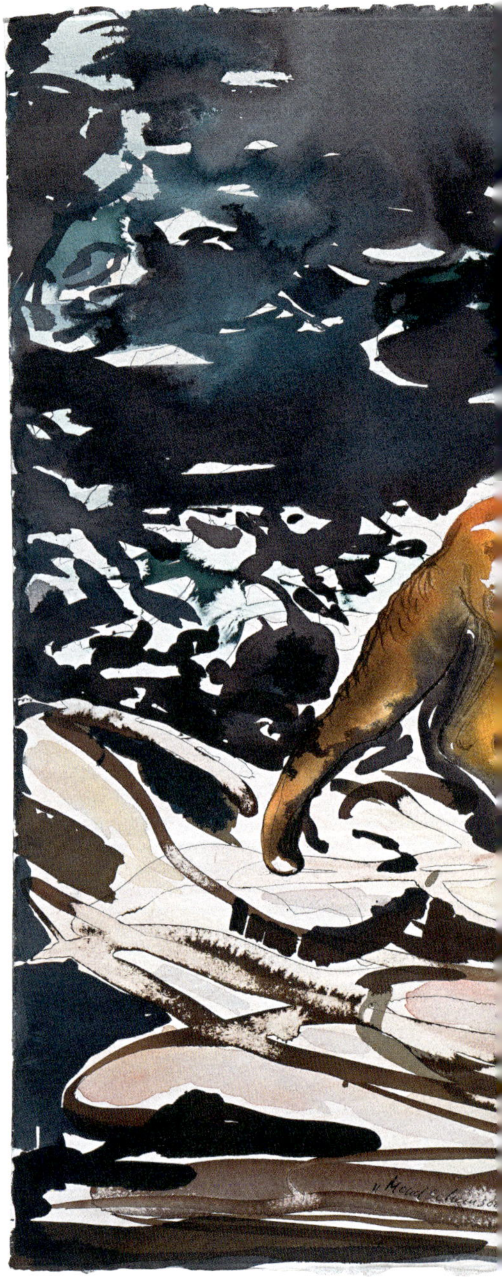

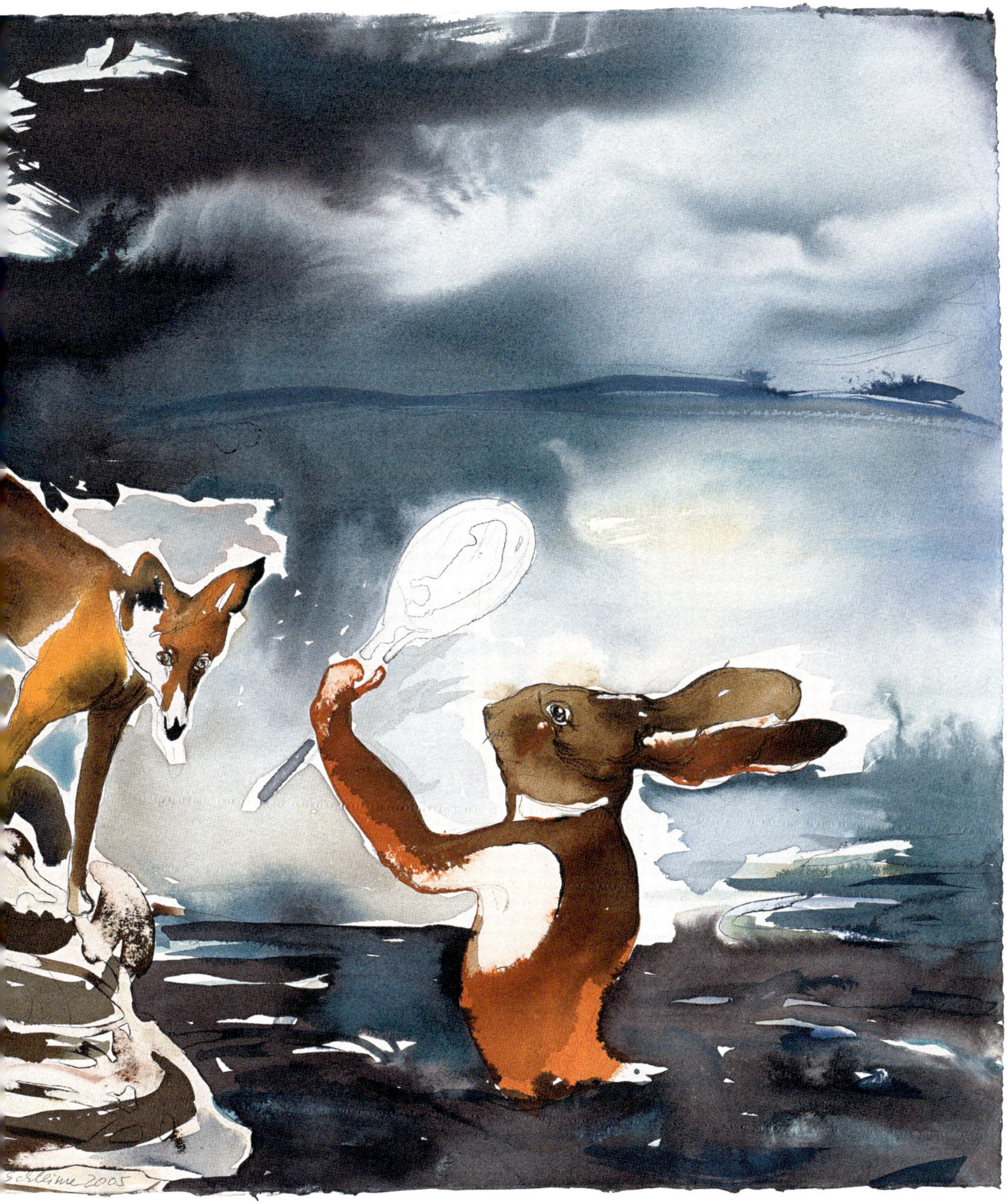

Das Kind liegt im Bett
und hat Fieber.
Das Fenster geöffnet
kein Baum, kein Schatten
ein Hof. Absätze knallen.
Stimmen.
Das Kind liegt im Bett und hat Fieber.
Nur Nase und Ohren.
Alles Gegenstandslos.
Bis die Mutter es
zudeckt.
Sie hat Gräten
auf den Lippen
als sie spricht.

Cornelia Schleime

The child lies in bed
and has a fever.
The window ajar
not a tree, not a shadow
a courtyard. Heels bang.
Voices.
The child lies in bed and has a fever.
All nose and ears.
All meaningless.
Until the mother
covers the child.
There are fishbones
on her lips
as she speaks.

Cornelia Schleime

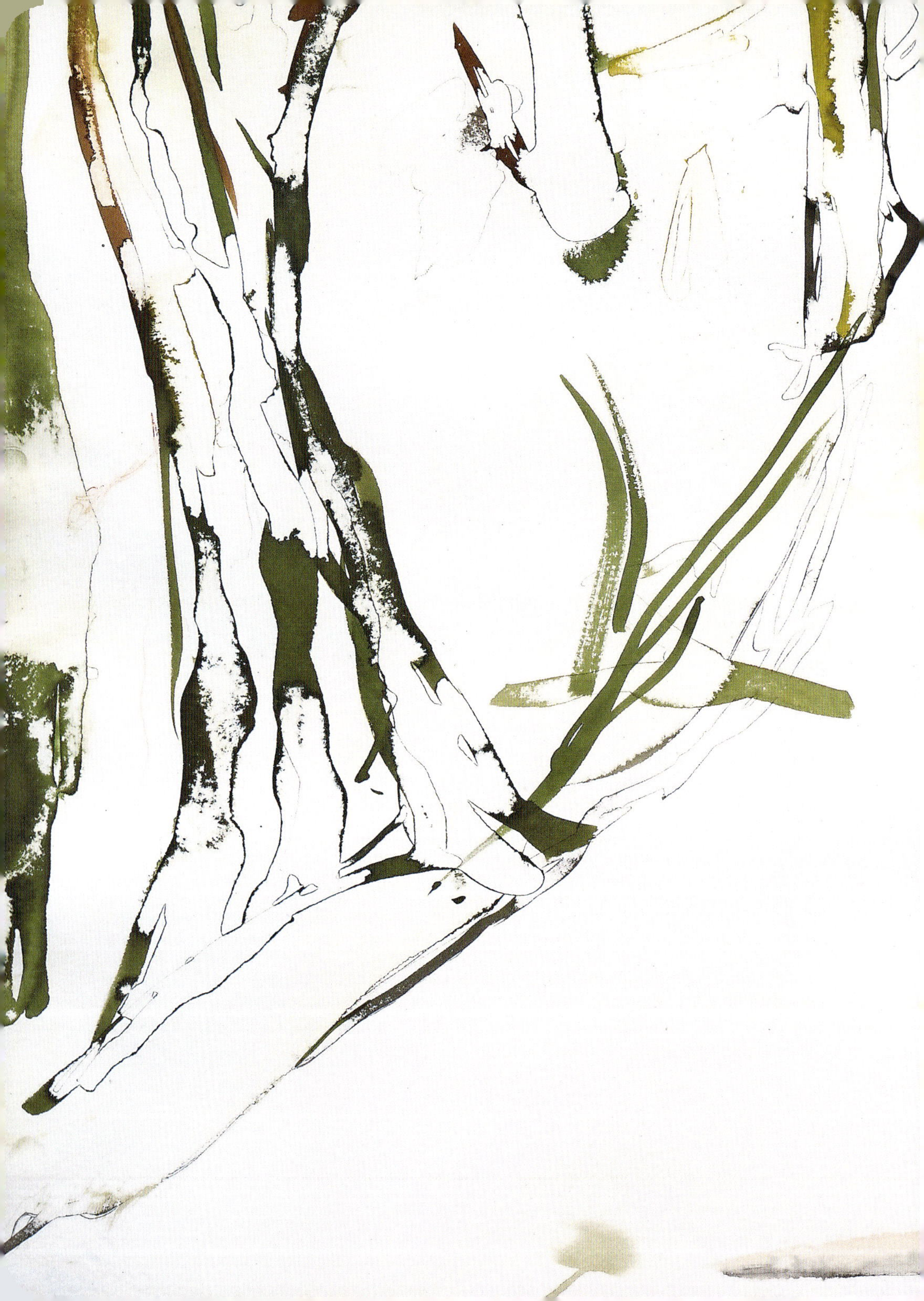

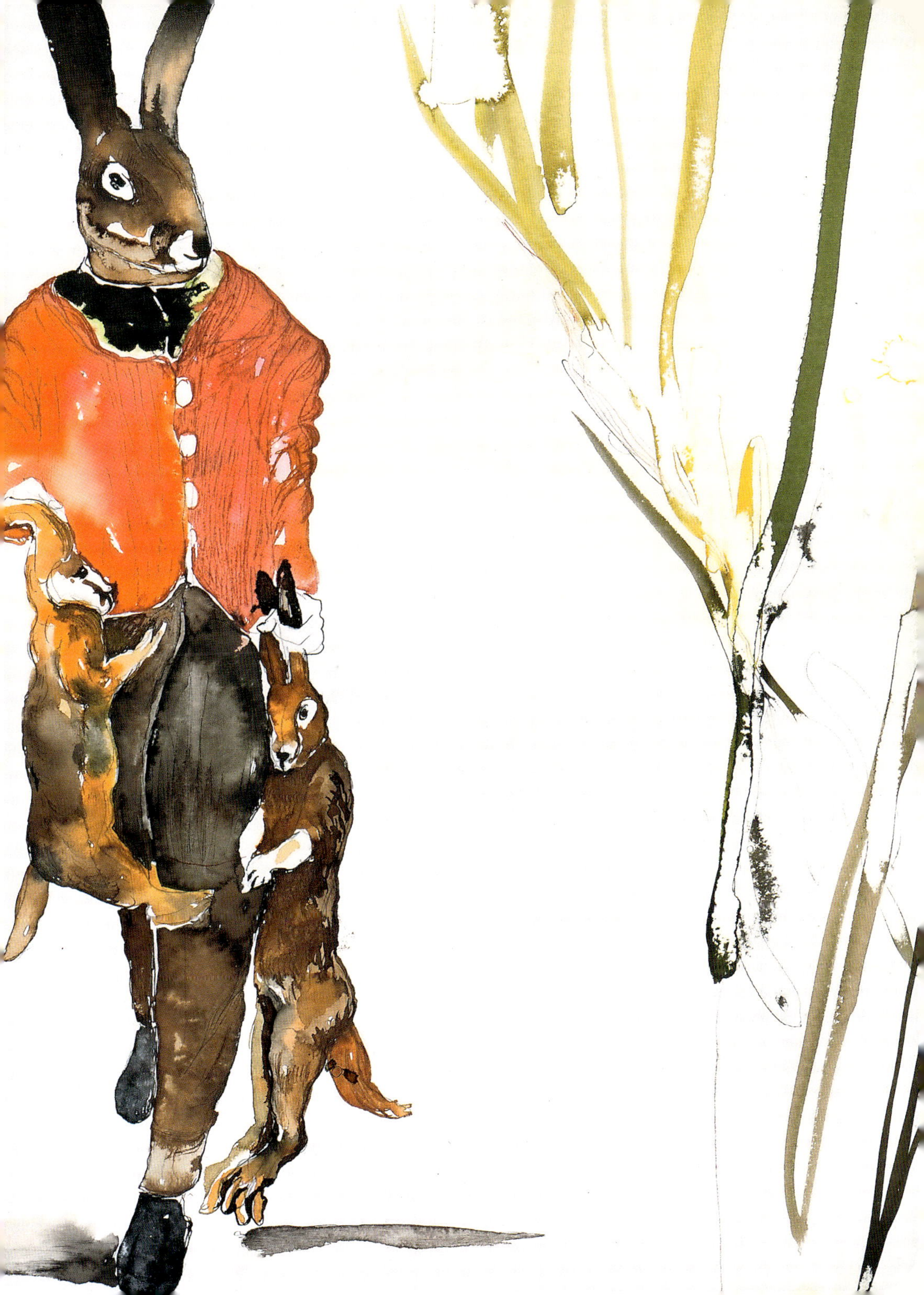

Vergessen & Erinnern
Cornelia Schleime

Lieber O.

Weißt Du noch, wie wir eine Ausstellung in Italien sahen, ich kam von einer winzigen Zeichnung Leonardo da Vincis nicht mehr los. Es war kaum etwas auf dem Blatt drauf. In der oberen linken Ecke des Papiers war eine kleine Hand gezeichnet, sie schien aus dem Nichts zu kommen. In der rechten unteren sah man schemenhaft einen kleinen Kopf, aber er war wegradiert, so dass man ihn nur erahnen konnte. Ein Studienblatt, wie gesagt winzig. In dieser Zeichnung war alles drin, was mich von da an bewegte und in Staunen versetzt.

Mehr will ich von der Kunst nicht, als in Staunen versetzt werden. Diese kleine Zeichnung hat dazu beigetragen, dass es immer um etwas anderes geht, als das, was sich auf vier Ecken etablieren lässt. Die Zeichnung ist für mich der Fahrstuhl in den Raum, der vom Realen abhebt. „Sie trägt ein himmelblaues Kleid und auch der Himmel war blau" Ist dies nicht eine Zeile von der Kaschnitz? Auch so ein Satz, der mir nicht mehr aus dem Kopf geht. Genau wie eine Zeile von Peter Orlowsky „er winkte zum Abschied & verlor den Arm im Schnee". Ich habe über die Jahre hinweg daraus meine eigene Zeile gemacht „Er winkte zum Abschied und ich verlor meinen Arm im Schnee",

Forgetting & Remembering

Cornelia Schleime

Dear O.

Do you remember when we saw an exhibition in Italy and I was so fascinated by a tiny drawing by Leonardo da Vinci? There was hardly anything on the sheet of paper. In the top left-hand corner a little hand had been drawn: it seemed to come from nowhere. In the bottom right-hand corner you could just make out a little head, but it had been erased so that you could only guess at its presence. It was a study, and tiny as I said. But this drawing contained everything which moved me and filled me with wonder.

That is all I want of art: to be filled with wonder. This tiny drawing contributed to the idea that it is always a question of something else beyond what you can create within the rectangular space. For me a drawing is a lift into a room which is set apart from reality.
"She is wearing a sky-blue dress, and the sky was also blue." Isn't that a line by [the poetess Marie Luise] Kaschnitz? That's another sentence which I can't get out of my head. Just like that line by Peter Orlowsky "He waved farewell and his arm was lost in the snow." For years I made of it my own version "He waved farewell and my arm was lost in the snow." Because I couldn't remember the original. I hope Orlowsky will forgive me!

weil ich mich an die Originalzeile nicht mehr richtig erinnern konnte. Orlowsky mag es mir verzeihen!
Und dann? Dann fühle ich meinen Arm erst wieder, wenn ich beginne zu zeichnen. Nur so kann ich mich von Trennungen erholen, das war schon immer so. Nur das Papier hilft, nicht die Leinwand und gut gemeinte Ratschläge helfen schon gar nicht.

Meine Zeichnungen, Aquarelle sind mein Stock, mit dem ich durchs Leben gehe. An ihm halte ich mich fest, mache mir den Weg frei und vertreibe lästige Fliegen. Wenn man mich einsperren würde, könnte ich den Knast überstehen, falls es Papier und Bleistift gäbe. Im Osten hatte ich davor Angst.
Wenn ich jetzt meine Zeichenschrankschubladen öffne, denn irgendwann musste ich mal Ordnung schaffen, fallen mir Mappen auf, die ich seit über zwanzig Jahren nicht mehr berührt habe. Und jede Mappe steht für einen speziellen Lebenszusammenhang. Sieben Leben hat die Katze oder neun? So fühle ich mich jetzt. Unterschiedliche Länder, Bezugspersonen, Eroberungen und Verluste, unterschiedliche Schwingungen und Stimmungen. Ich war glücklich, oder war es gerade nicht, an alles kann ich mich punktgenau erinnern, wenn ich ein Blatt in der Hand halte. Obwohl ich oft nur flüchtige Momente einfing, ist alles wieder da. Meine Papierarbeiten sind die Vergewisserung, dass es mich gibt.

And then? Then I only begin to feel my arm again when I start drawing. That is the only way I can recover from separations; that is how it has always been. Only paper helps; not canvas, and most definitely not well-meaning advice.

My drawings and watercolours are like a stick with which I go through life. I cling to it, use it to clear a path and to drive away the flies which annoy me. If I were to be locked away I would be able to endure being in prison if I had paper and pencil. That is what I was afraid of in the East.

If I open the drawers of my drawing cabinet now, because at some point I had to tidy them up, I notice folders which I haven't touched for more than twenty years. And each folder stands for a particular aspect of my life. A cat has seven lives, or is it nine? That's how I feel now. Different countries, different companions, conquests and losses, different vibrations and moods. I was happy, or maybe I wasn't at that time; I can remember precisely how it all was when I hold a sheet of paper in my hand. Although I often only captured fleeting moments it is all present once again. My works on paper are the confirmation that I exist. Do you remember when we were in Arezzo? Moritz was nine years old at the time. You had taught him how to play chess. He even managed to beat you once. Maybe you just let him win; anyway,it strengthened his self-confidence. I drew you at that time and now I found that drawing again in the

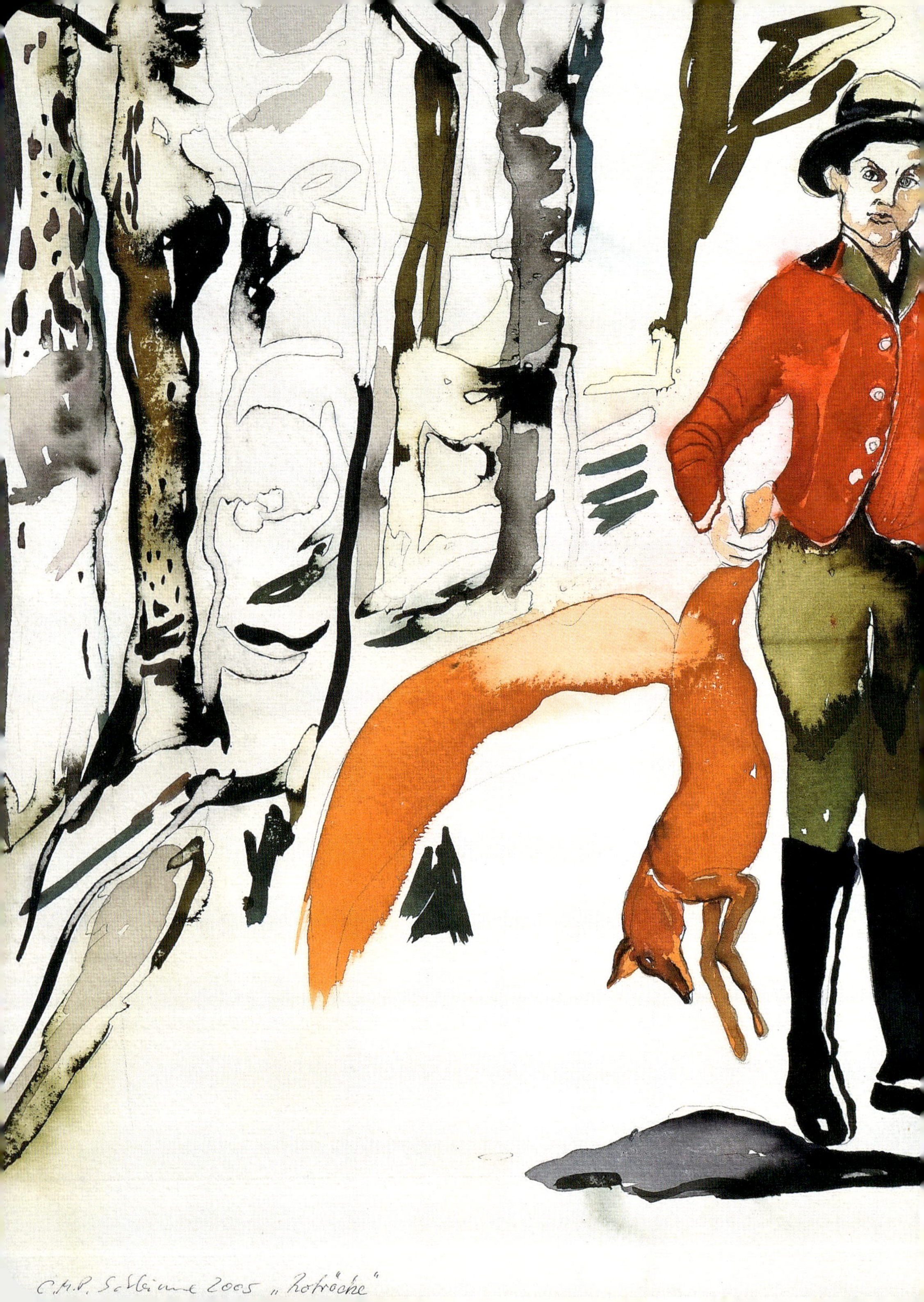
C.M.P. Schleime 2005 „Rotröcke"

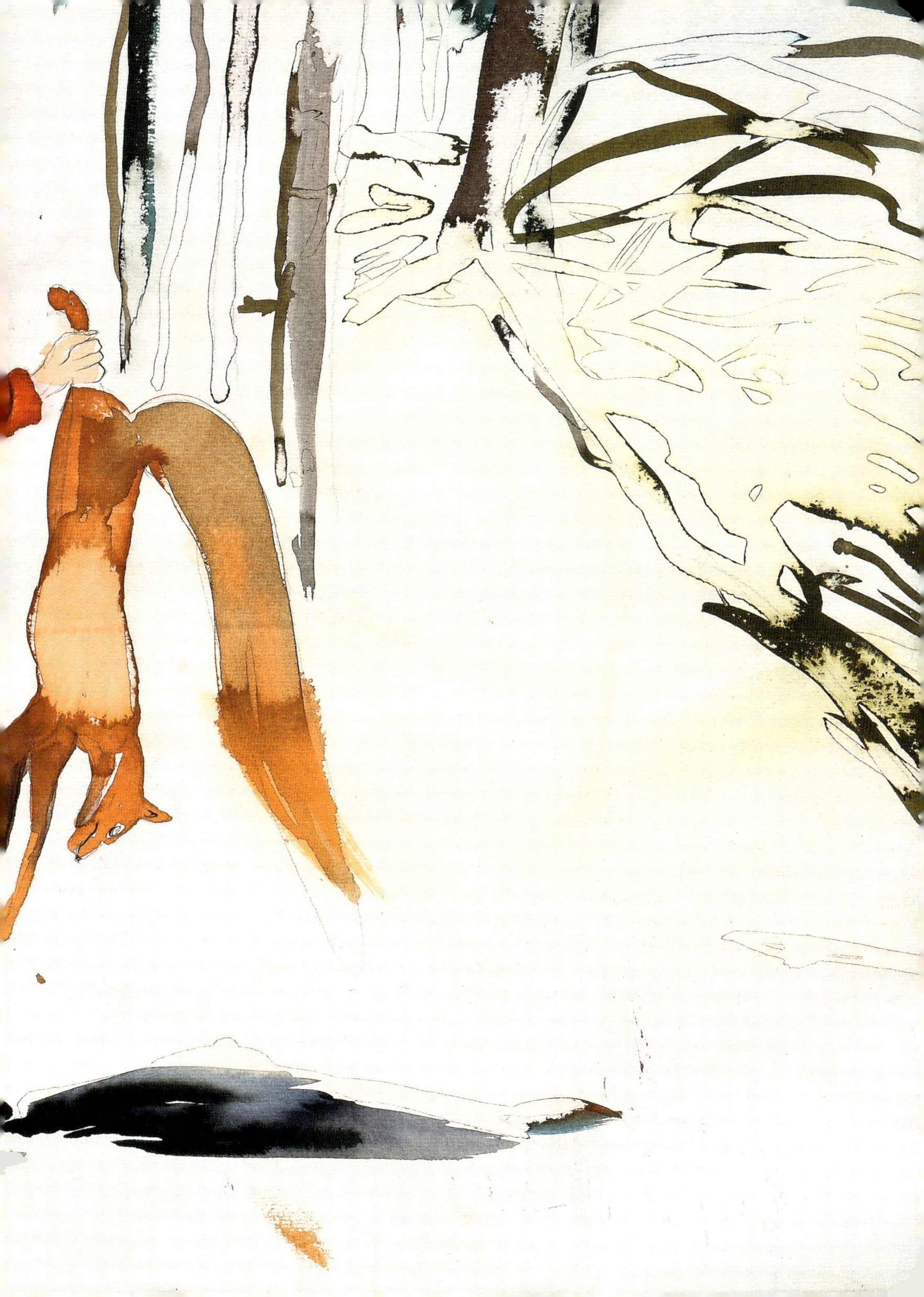

Weißt Du noch wie wir in Arezzo waren? Moritz war damals neun Jahre. Du hattest ihm dort das Schachspielen beigebracht. Er gelang ihm sogar einmal, dich zu schlagen. Vielleicht hast Du ihn nur gewinnen lassen, jedenfalls stärkte es sein Selbstvertrauen. Ich zeichnete Euch dabei und fand jetzt diese Zeichnung in der unteren Schublade, zweimal gefaltet war sie. Darunter eine andere, wo Moritz eine Zwiebel auf dem Kopf hat, er hatte Sonnenbrand und schälte sich. So einfach finden die Dinge mitunter auf einer Zeichnung zusammen: eine Zwiebel, die zufällig auf dem Tisch liegt, ein Kind, das Sonnenbrand hat.

Ich hänge noch immer an der unteren Schublade fest. Wir waren bei deiner Ex zum Essen eingeladen und es gab wunderschöne rote Krebse. Es war das erste Mal, dass ich so etwas aß. Sie gab mir einen Krebs mit nach Haus, damit ich ihn malen und zeichnen könnte. Im Atelier angekommen, setzte ich ihn überall hin und aquarellierte ihn. Mal legte ich ihn auf meine Kaffeekanne, mal aufs Telefon und dann ging die Phantasie mit mir durch und ich packte ihn in eine Kutsche, die mir gerade durch den Kopf ging. „Krebskutsche“. Stell Dir vor, vier Blätter davon sind noch da. Damals hätte ich gern ein Blatt verkauft, heute will ich es nicht mehr, weil sie ein Stück Erinnerung an unser Leben sind, was wir damals teilten. Genau wie “Drive through the canyon country ”, das fand

bottom drawer; it was folded twice. And then there was another one beneath it where Moritz has an onion on his head; he had sunburn and his skin was peeling. It's as simple as that when things suddenly appear together on a drawing: an onion which just happened to be lying on the table, and a child with sunburn. Was it a year later? I can't remember – that I started on my "Finger of God" series. We had very little money and even stole some cheese from the supermarket; and because I wanted to sell the series of silk-screen prints for more money I produced original sheets which I then overprinted with the motif of the Creation of Adam. Always nine works in a portfolio. They were cheaper than the original drawings but more expensive than the silk-screen prints. I charged DM 1,100 for a portfolio with nine overprinted originals. I hoped that someone would take one. I had hardly any collectors or purchasers. It was only many years later that the Deutsche Bank and the Federal Government and a Kupferstichkabinett bought them. They paid many times the original sum. I could never have dreamt of that at the time.

I am still stuck on the bottom drawer. We had been invited to your ex-wife's for dinner and there were these lovely red crabs. It was the first time I had ever eaten anything like it. She gave me a crab to take home with me so that I could paint and draw it. Having arrived in the studio I put it down all over the place and painted it in watercolours. First I put it on my coffee pot; then on the telephone; and then my imagination began to run riot and I put it in a coach which

ich in einem anderen Zeichenschrank ganz weit oben. Die Schublade ließ sich kaum öffnen, ich hatte die Arbeiten auf Hartfaser kaschiert und das blockierte nun, so dass ich mit einem Schraubenzieher zwischen gehen musste, um sie aufzubekommen.
Sofort dachte ich an Deinen kleinen gelben Honda Civic, mit dem wir von Los Angeles nach New York kutschierten. Zuvor waren wir mit ihm in Mexiko gewesen und ich hatte mir dort auf einem Markt ein Stück Stoff gekauft, mir ein langes Kleid daraus genäht, mit der Hand. Zurück in den USA, hatte ich es dann überm Knie abgeschnitten, weil ich auf unserem Trip braune Beine bekommen hatte und sie zeigen wollte. Du hast ein Foto von mir gemacht, wie ich vor den Canyonbergen stehe. Das Foto habe ich auf ein DIN A4 Blatt geklebt und die Landschaft auf dem Foto weiter auslaufend aufs Papier gemalt. Davon habe ich wieder ein Foto gemacht und wieder auf ein Blatt geklebt und diesen Vorgang ein paar Mal wiederholt. Auf dem letzten Blatt sieht man mich dann nur noch als winzigen Punkt. Es ist kein Klischee, dass der Mensch in Anbetracht überwältigender Natur immer kleiner wird, sondern es ist ein befreiendes Empfinden.
Nichtdestotrotz war dies meine erste konzeptuelle Arbeit und ich freue mich, diese Arbeit wieder zu sehen. Zwanzig Jahre sind seitdem vergangen und meine Zeichenschubladen lesen sich wie Ringe eines alten Baumes. Kaum zu glauben, wie alt ich schon bin.

suddenly occurred to me. "Krebskutsche" (Crab Coach). Just imagine – four of the sheets are still there. At the time I should have been pleased to sell a sheet; nowadays I don't want to anymore because they are a piece of remembrance of our life together and what we shared at that time. Just like "Drive thru Canyonland", which I found near the top in another drawing cabinet. The drawer was almost impossible to open; I had mounted the works on hardboard and it had got jammed, so that I had to use a screwdriver to prise it open.
I immediately thought of your little yellow Honda Civic, in which we drove from Los Angeles to New York. Before that we had been with it in Mexico and while we were there I had bought a length of fabric at a market and made myself a dress with it which I had stitched by hand. Returning to the States I had then cut it off above the knee because during our trip I had got brown legs which I wanted to show off. You took a photo of me standing in front of the Canyon mountains. I stuck the photo onto a sheet of A4 paper and then painted the continuation of the landscape on the paper. Then I took a photo of the result and stuck it onto another sheet of paper and repeated this process a few more times. On the last sheet all you can see of me is a tiny dot. It's not a cliché to say that Man becomes smaller and smaller when contemplating the overwhelming majesty of Nature; it results in a feeling of release.
Nonetheless this was my first conceptual work and I was pleased to see it again.

Und mit dreißig hat mein Leben erst angefangen, denn von der Zeit davor gibt´s nichts mehr in meinen Schubladen, die Ostzeit ist ausgelöscht, weil ich bei der Übersiedlung nichts mitnehmen konnte und alles verschwand. Nur eine dicke Fototüte mit Übermalungen hab ich bei meiner Ausbürgerung untern Arm geklemmt, die ist noch da von meinem Ostleben.

Aber soweit ich mich erinnere, war es da auch schon so: Ich möchte mit meinen Papierarbeiten nicht im Jetzt sein; ich möchte abdriften oder aufsteigen und mich leer machen, damit ich von irgendwoher was empfange. Inspiration sagt man dazu, aber ich kann mit dem Wort gar nichts anfangen.
Reisen möchte ich im Nirgendwo und wenn es für mich überhaupt Zeit gibt, dann nur Wolken- und Luftzeit. Andere würden sagen Auszeit, aber die gibt es für mich nicht.

Mein Papier, das auf den Knien, dem Tisch oder dem Boden liegt, ist überhaupt nicht geduldig, will sich nicht überstrapazieren lassen, eine Dusche in der Badewanne erträgt es, aber nur kurz und kalt. Es will nicht bearbeitet werden, als sei es ein Acker. Das Papier ist eine Diva, mal launisch, mal spröde. Diven brauchen auch viel Schlaf und so schläft es bei mir im Zeichenschrank. Es gibt die guten Schubladen, es gibt die mit einem Fragezeichen, so hatte ich es gerade noch gedacht.

Twenty years have passed since then and my drawers full of drawings can be read like the rings of an old tree. It's almost incredible how old I am.
And my life did not begin until I was thirty, because before that time there is nothing in my drawers; the time I spent in the East has been eradicated, because when I crossed over I couldn't take anything with me and everything disappeared. All I had when I was expatriated was a thick photo folder with overpaintings which I tucked under my arm; that is still left from my life in the East.

But as far as I can remember that is how it was there too: I don't want to be in the HERE & NOW with my works on paper; I want to drift away or climb upwards and empty myself, so that I can receive something from somewhere; that's what people call inspiration, but it's a word which means nothing to me.
I should like to travel through Nowhere-Land, and if time exists for me, then only as cloud and air time. Others would say time out, but for me that doesn't exist.

My paper, lying on my knee or on the table or the floor, is not in the least long-suffering and will not allow itself to be pushed too far. It will put up with a shower in the bath, but only briefly and only with cold water. It does not like to be worked as if it were a field. Paper is a diva, sometimes moody, sometimes aloof. Divas need plenty of sleep and so it sleeps in my drawing cabinet.

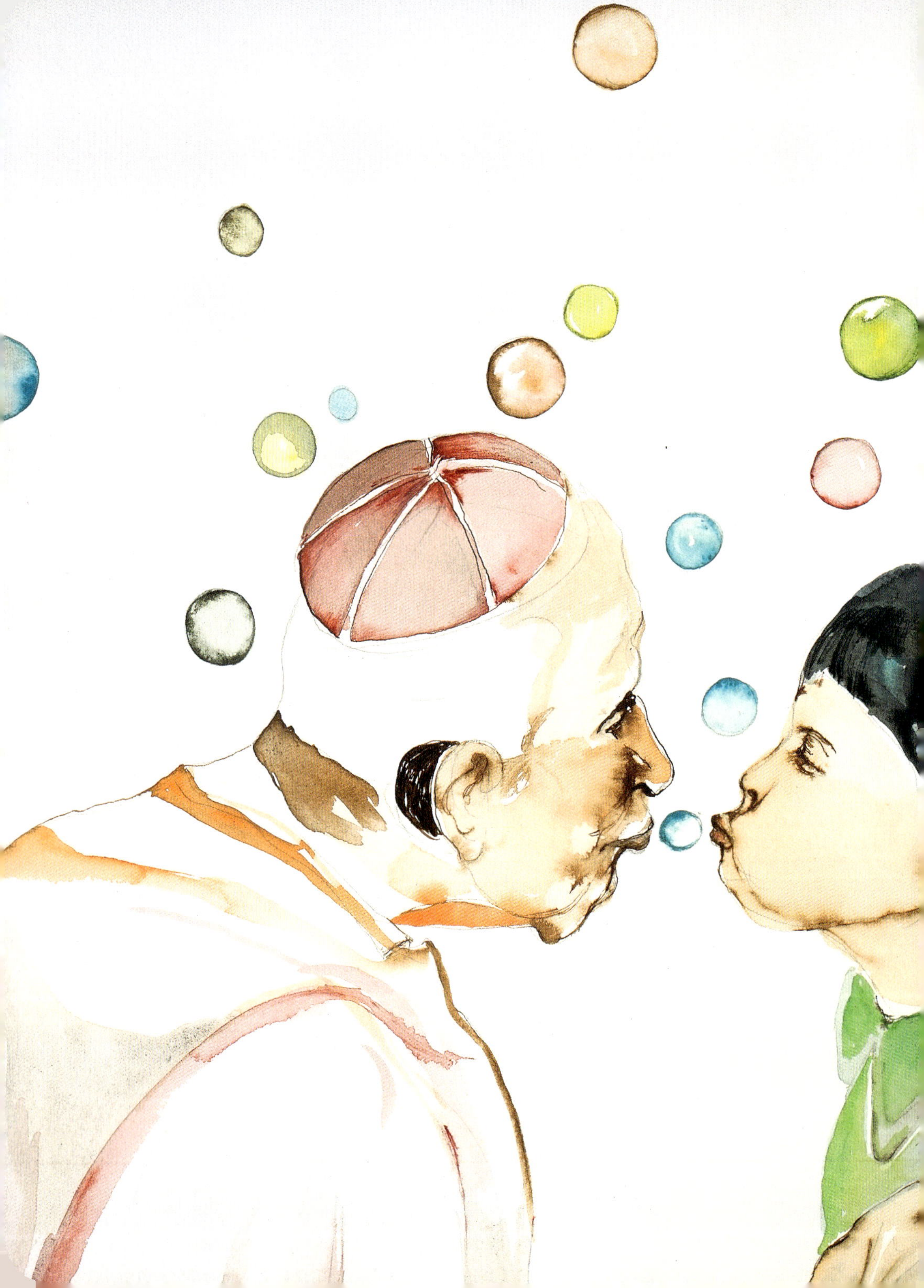

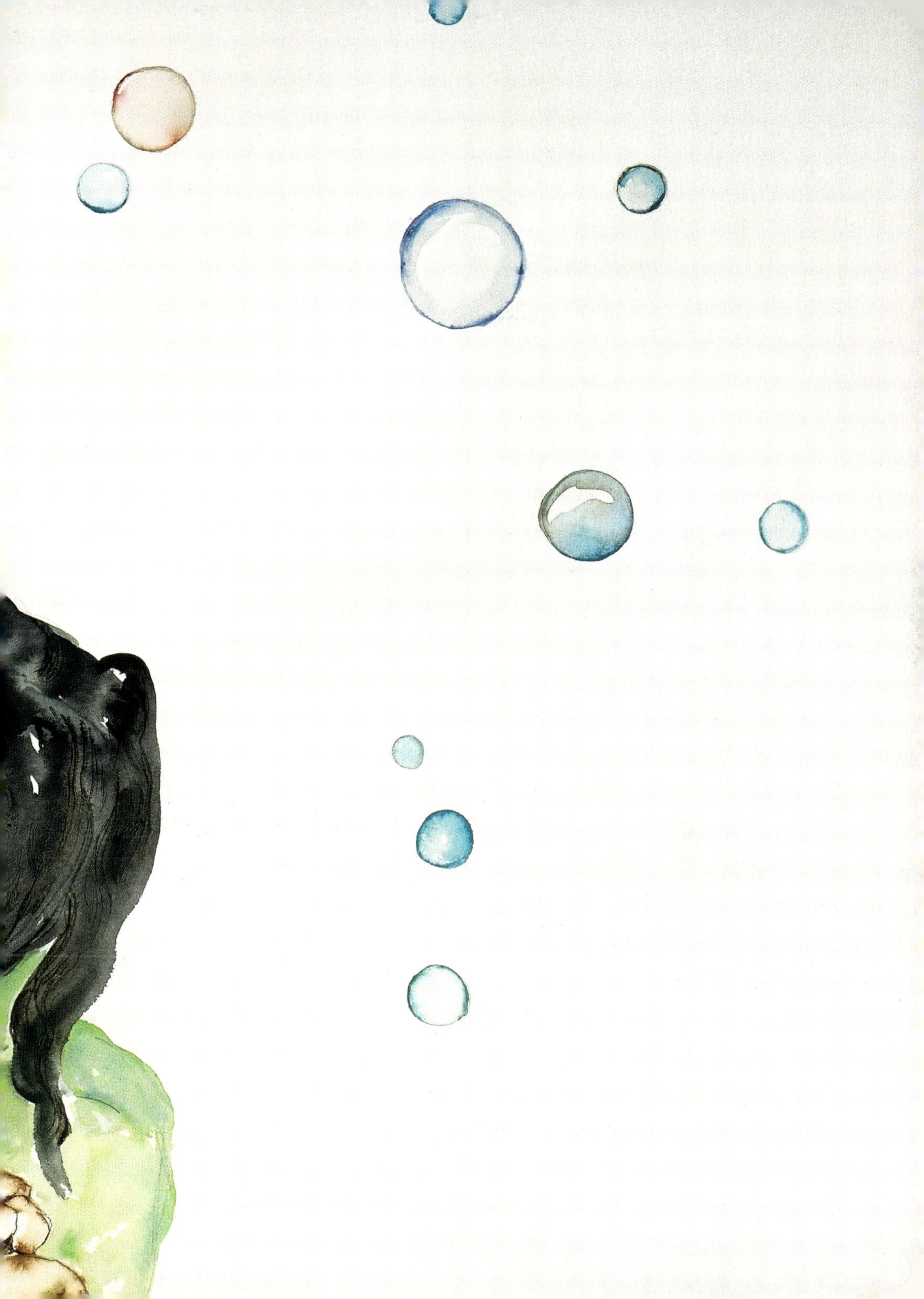

Aber siehe da, kaum vergehen ein paar Jahre, ist es manchmal andersrum. Im abgelegten Schubladenleben warten Überraschungen. Jetzt finde ich in der Fragezeichenschublade Zeichnungen, die so schlecht nicht sind, und unter den guten gibt es auch einigen Mist. In diesem Zusammenhang akzeptiere ich die Realzeit, da sie Distanz schafft und ich die Dinge mit anderem Auge betrachten kann.

Eines bleibt aber beständig: Zeichnungen, die für mich existenziell waren und sind und die ich deshalb niemals verkaufe, sind, wie sie sind, Zeugnisse einer Situation, die ausgedrückt werden musste, egal, ob sie nun gelungen oder misslungen sind, denn diese Kriterien zählen hierbei nicht. Ich behalte von jeder Serie immer ein, zwei Blätter zurück, auch aus den vielen Einzelblättern, die ich zwischendurch mache, picke ich mir immer eins oder zwei heraus, jene, wo ich die Poesie schramme, wie ich sie suche, oder wo die Ironie ohne Absicht geschah und sich gerade deshalb einstellte, Zeichnungen, wo ich ohne Gedanken bin und es von allein geschah. Vielleicht ist es auch das Trauma des Verlustes meines Frühwerks, ich weiß es nicht, aber vielleicht kann ich deshalb nicht alles weggeben und verkaufen. Dennoch vergesse ich die Arbeiten wieder, wenn sie erst im Schrank liegen.

Jetzt schreib ich schon wieder für mich und werde den Brief sicher nicht in den Kasten werfen, wie etliche

There are good drawers and there are those with too few question marks; that was how I had thought of it. But just imagine; once a few years have passed it is sometimes the other way round. Surprises lie in wait in the abandoned life within the drawers. Now I have found drawings in the drawer with question marks which really aren't that bad, and in the good ones there is rubbish as well. In this context I accept real time because it has created distance and I can see things in a different light.

But one thing remains constant: for me, drawings which were existential and which I therefore didn't sell, are as they are, bearing witness to a situation which had to be expressed, regardless of whether they were successful or not, because these criteria don't count here. I always retain one or two sheets from each series, and also from the numerous single sheets I produce in between I always select one or two: the ones where I scratch the poetry, where I search for it and where the irony was unintentional and I therefore put an end to it, drawing where there were no thoughts behind them and they happened of their own accord. Perhaps it is the trauma of losing my early works, I don't know, that I don't give everything away and sell it. And yet I forget the works again once they are lying in the cabinet.

Now I am writing for myself again and I will certainly not post the letter, like countless letters which I glued

Briefe, die ich auf die letzte Seite meiner Reisetagebücher geklebt hab, versiegelt mit Klebeband. Mit einer Briefmarke darauf, doch nie abgeschickt. Abschiedsbriefe an den einen oder den anderen geliebten Freund. Ich werde sie erst wieder öffnen, wenn ich uralt bin. Zeichnen und Abschied nehmen wollen; zeichnen und verlassen worden sein, das ist ein Seil, was sich durch mein Leben zieht, ein Ankerseil. Und schon öffnet sich die zweite Schublade des dritten Zeichenschranks von unten.

Wasserwege statt Wolken oder Abschiedswege. Mit fünfzig habe ich noch die Bootsprüfung gemacht und in Rostock ein hochseetaugliches Motorboot gekauft, um auf den Havelwegen zu schippern. Was für schöne Sommer hab ich dabei erlebt! Drei Dinge habe ich von dieser Zeit zurückbehalten: die Papierarbeiten von den Fischen, die Texte, die ich zu ihnen schrieb und der Pigmentfleck auf meiner rechten Wange. Ich hatte die Sonnenschutzcreme vergessen, jetzt geht der Fleck nicht mehr weg. Ich weiß auch noch, dass es ein anderes Malen und Zeichnen war, wenn 30 Meter Wasser unter einem lagen, wenn es schaukelt und das Boot mitten auf dem See liegt. Mit einem anderen Mann hab ich mein Wasserleben geteilt, es war in den vielen Jahren mit ihm unsere schönste Zeit. Er hatte mir auf dem Achterschiff einen Tisch gebaut, hatte mich gefragt, wie groß mein Papier sein wird, mit dem ich dort zeichnen möchte, genau berechnet hatte er die Größe, damit noch die Tuschegläser und die Aquarelltuschkästen Platz fänden.

to the last page of my travel diaries, sealed with adhesive tape. With a stamp stuck on but never actually posted. Letters of farewell to some beloved friend or other. I shall only open them again when I'm really old. Drawing and wanting to take one's leave; drawing and being abandoned, that is a thread running through my life, like a rope with an anchor attached. And already the second drawer of this third drawing cabinet from the bottom is being opened.
Waterways instead of clouds or paths of farewell. At the age of 50 I took the yachting certificate and bought a motorboat in Rostock that was seaworthy for the high seas, so that I could chug up and down the Havel routes. What a lovely summer I had! I kept two things from this period:

The works on paper with the fish, the texts I wrote to accompany them, and the pigmented spot on my right cheek. I had forgotten the suntan lotion and now the spot won't go away. But I still remember that painting and drawing was quite different with 30 metres of water beneath you, when the boat is rocking and you are lying at anchor surrounded by sea. I shared my life on the water with another man; it was the best time of all the many years I spent with him. He had built me a table in the stern; he asked me how big the paper would be that I wanted to draw on there, and he calculated the size exactly so that there was even space for the bottles of Indian ink and the box of watercolours.

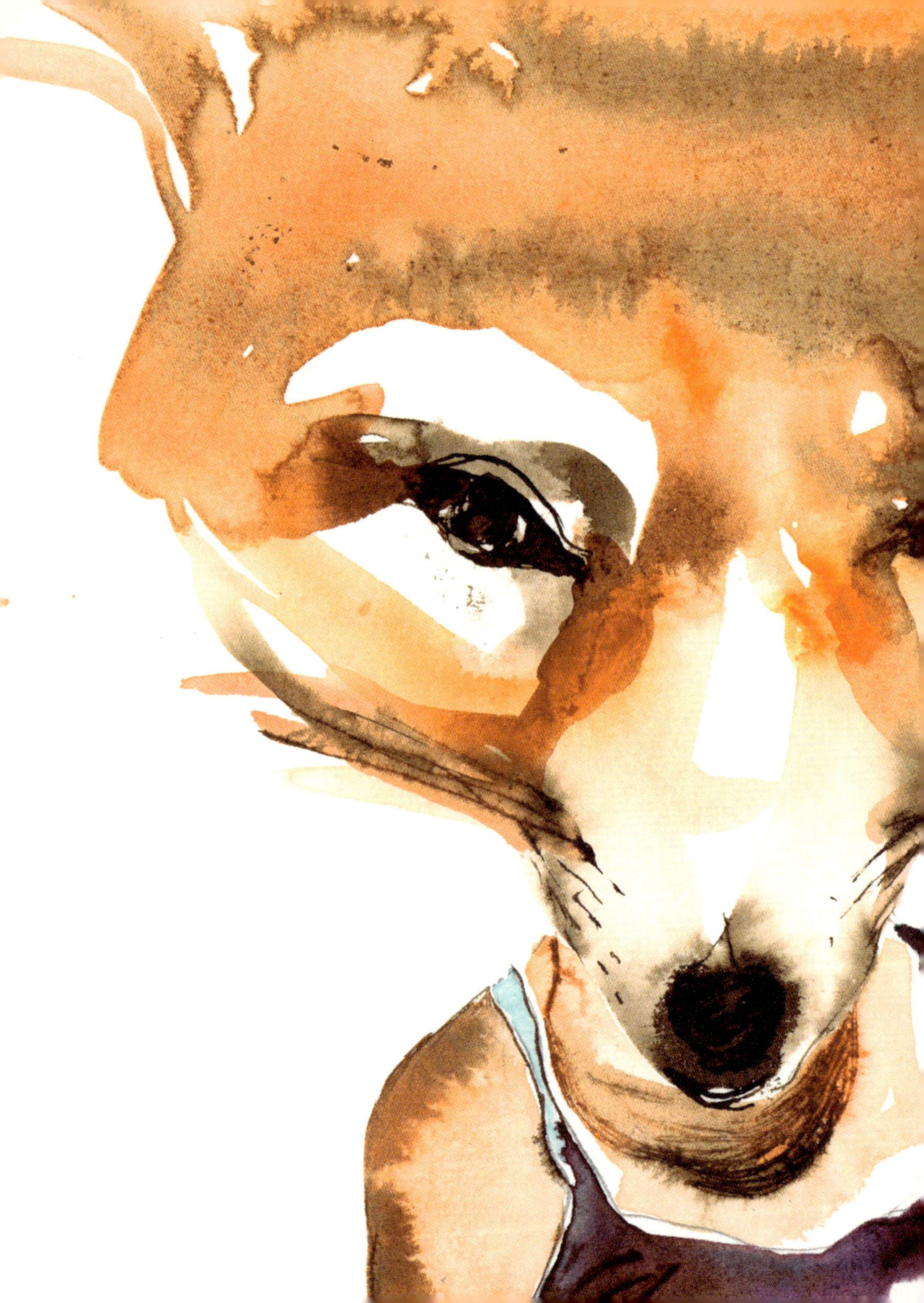

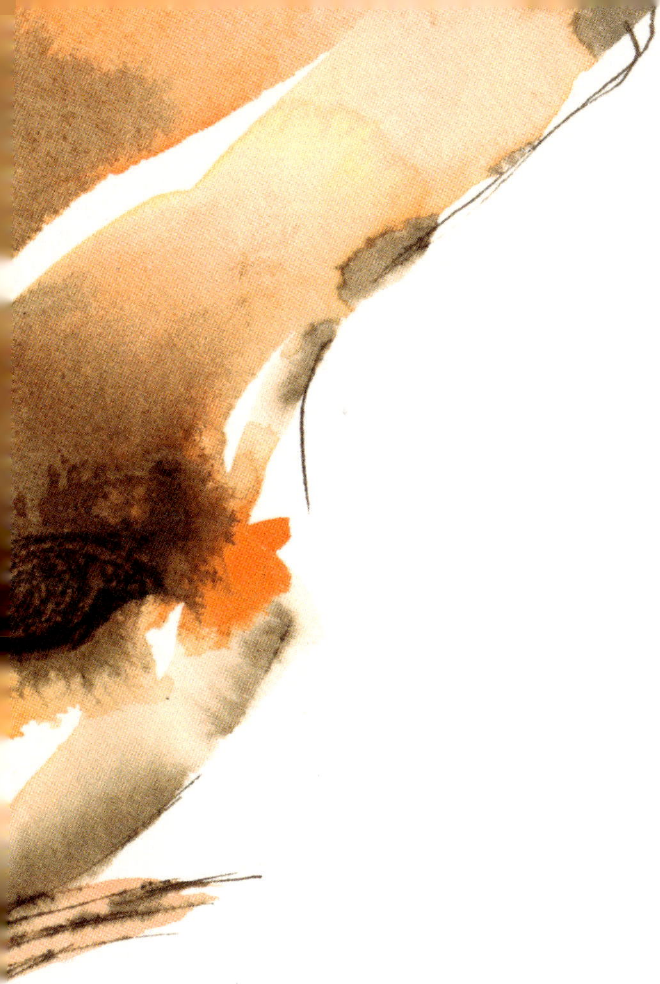

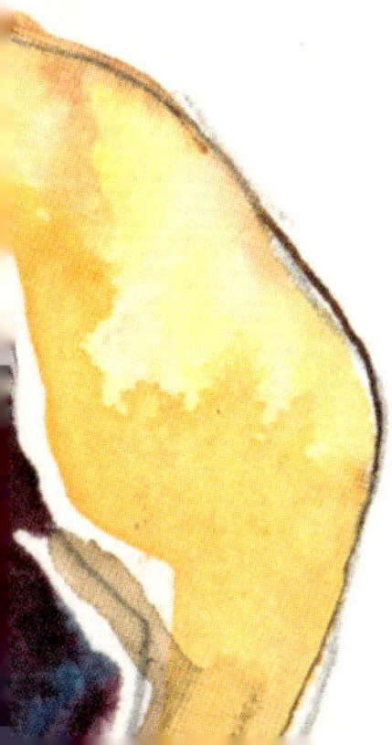

Die Papierarbeiten wurden auf dem Boot ganz anders als an Land. Die Aquarellistinnen würden sagen „jetzt fließt es aus mir heraus", aber so durchdringend bin ich nicht am Wasser gebaut, denn ich saß mit meinem Hintern auf der Badeplattform, hab das halbfertige Aquarell kurz dem See überlassen, es dann wieder auf den Tisch gepackt und auf dem feuchten Blatt weitergearbeitet. So habe ich experimentiert und erinnere mich an einen grünlichen Kinderkopf, den ich jetzt in einer der Schubladen suchen werde. Ich weiß noch, dass mir der etwas verflossene Mund des Kindes gefiel, ein Junge war es.

Immer versuche ich die Technik des Experimentierens auch auf die Leinwandarbeiten zu übertragen, indem ich mit Schellack arbeite, denn er ist unberechenbar und reagiert auf Zugluft. Da kann schon mal alles verschwinden, was zuvor gemalt wurde und das Bild ist im Eimer. Anders als bei den Papierarbeiten kann ich wie ein Berserker mit der Leinwand kämpfen. Die Papierarbeiten müssen sitzen, sollen leicht bleiben, wie eine flüchtig hingeschriebene Zeile, aus durchsichtigem Stoff. Und das Weiß des Papiers möchte ich erhalten und dort, wo nichts auf dem Papier ist, ist das Eigentliche, der Raum, den meine Figuren für sich beanspruchen: in selbst gewählter Einsamkeit, in Diskursverweigerung, im Zungenschlaf. Meine Figuren, das bin ich: verträumt, wenn man mich lässt, exzentrisch und ungeduldig, wenn man mir zu nah auf die Pelle rückt.

My works on paper were quite different on the boat from those I produced on land. Watercolourists would say "now it is flowing from me," but I'm not made to that extent for life on the water. I sat with my backside on the bathing platform, dipped the half-finished watercolour quickly into the sea, then put it back on the table and carried on working on the damp paper. I can remember a greenish head of a child which I shall now look for in one of the drawers. I know that I liked the way the child's mouth had run a bit; it was a boy.

I always try to transfer the technique of experimenting to my works on canvas, by working with shellac, because it is unpredictable and sensitive to draughts. Everything you have already painted can disappear and the picture is no good. Unlike the works on paper I can struggle with the canvas like a madwoman. The works on paper have to be right; they should remain light, like a hurriedly written line, made of transparent fabric. And I like to retain the whiteness of the paper, and the place wherethere is nothing on the paper is the important part, the space which my figures claim for themselves; in elective solitude; in a refusal to enter into discourse; with resting tongue. My figures are me myself: dreamy, when I am allowed to be, and eccentric and impatient when people crowd in on me too closely.

The collages are an exception, as I used them, for example to some extent in the "Finger Gottes" (God's Finger)

Eine Ausnahme sind die Collagen, wie ich sie u.a. teilweise auch bei der „Finger Gottes Serie" angewendet habe. Hier findet eine Verdichtung statt, da – wie bei den Leinwänden auch – in Schichten gearbeitet wird. Hier versammeln sich Figuren, hier gibt es kein Weiß, weil Gott schon ahnte, was er da schafft: erst den Adam, dann die Eva, zuvor das Paradies, was soll man da tun, außer Kinder kriegen, die sich dann den Schädel einschlagen.

Die Zeichnung und das Aquarell sind davon frei, haben nur eine Haut: meine Haut.

series. Here there is a concentration, since I also worked in layers as I do on canvas. Here figures are gathered together and there is no white, because God had an inkling of what he was creating there; first Adam, then Eve, and before that Paradise. What should you do there but have children who then beat each other's brains out?

The drawings and watercolours are free of that; they have only one skin, my skin.

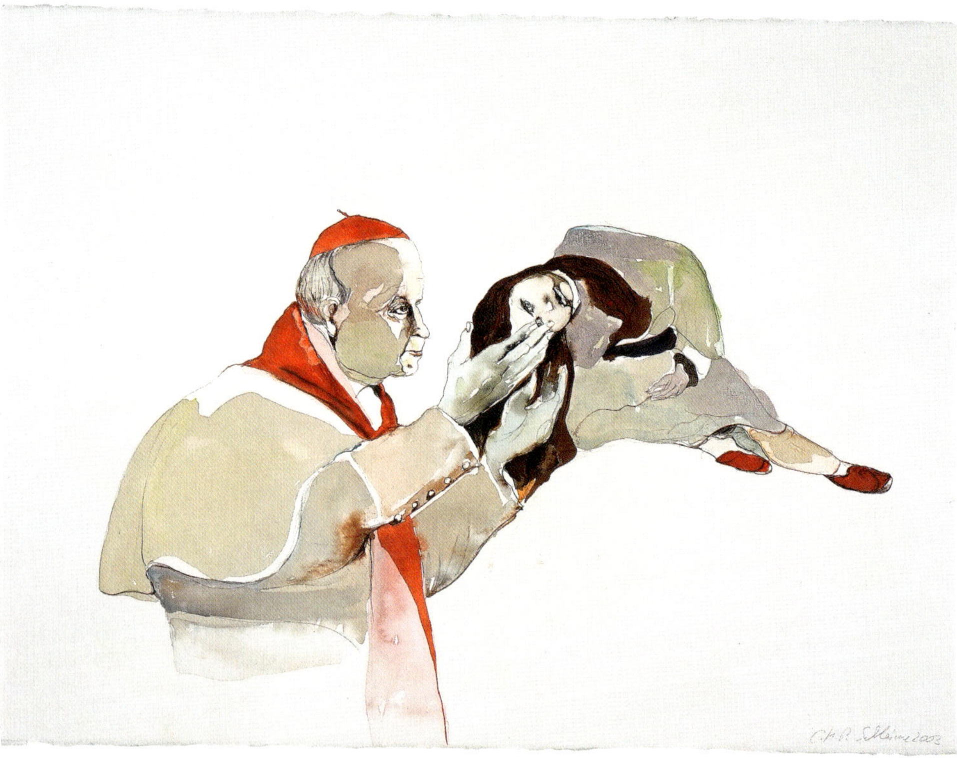

o.T. 2003
Aquarell & Tusche auf Papier Watercolour & Indian ink on paper
57 x 76 cm

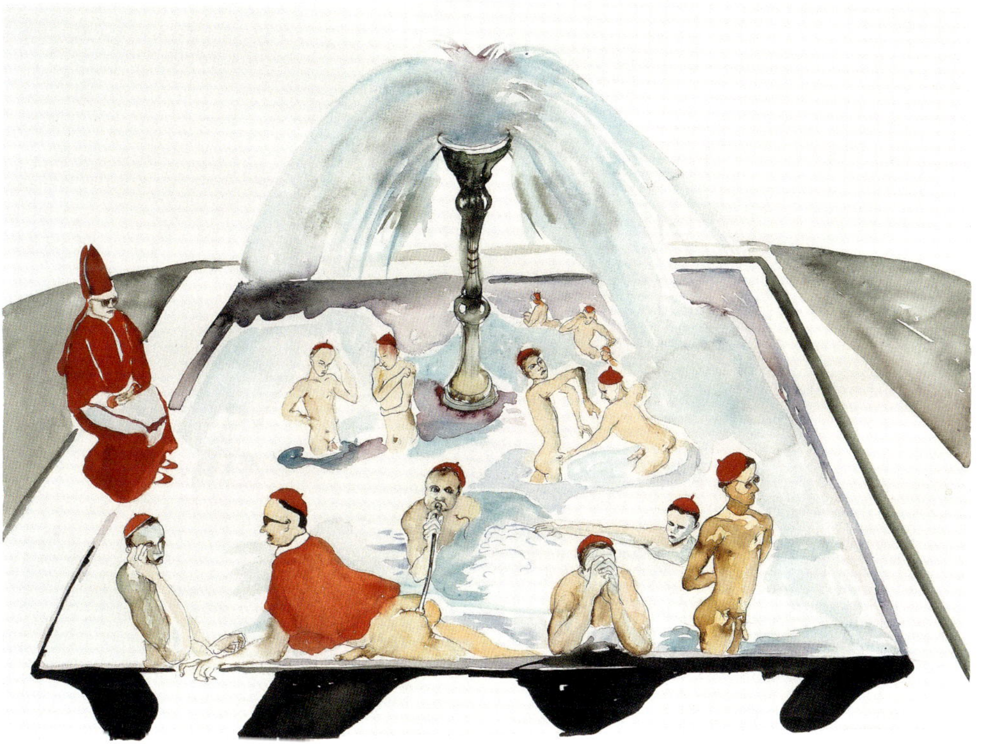

Gesundbrunnen 2003
Aquarell & Tusche auf Papier Watercolour & Indian ink on paper
57 x 76 cm

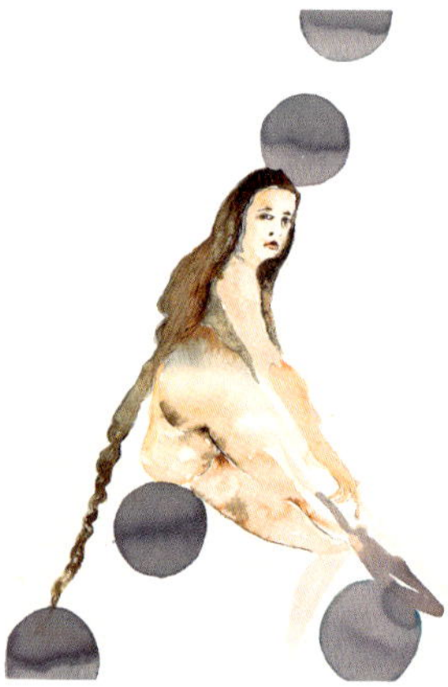

2010–2011

aus der Reihe „Halb unter Wasser“ 2010
Aquarell & Tusche auf Büttenpapier Watercolour & Indian ink on handmade paper
76 x 56 cm

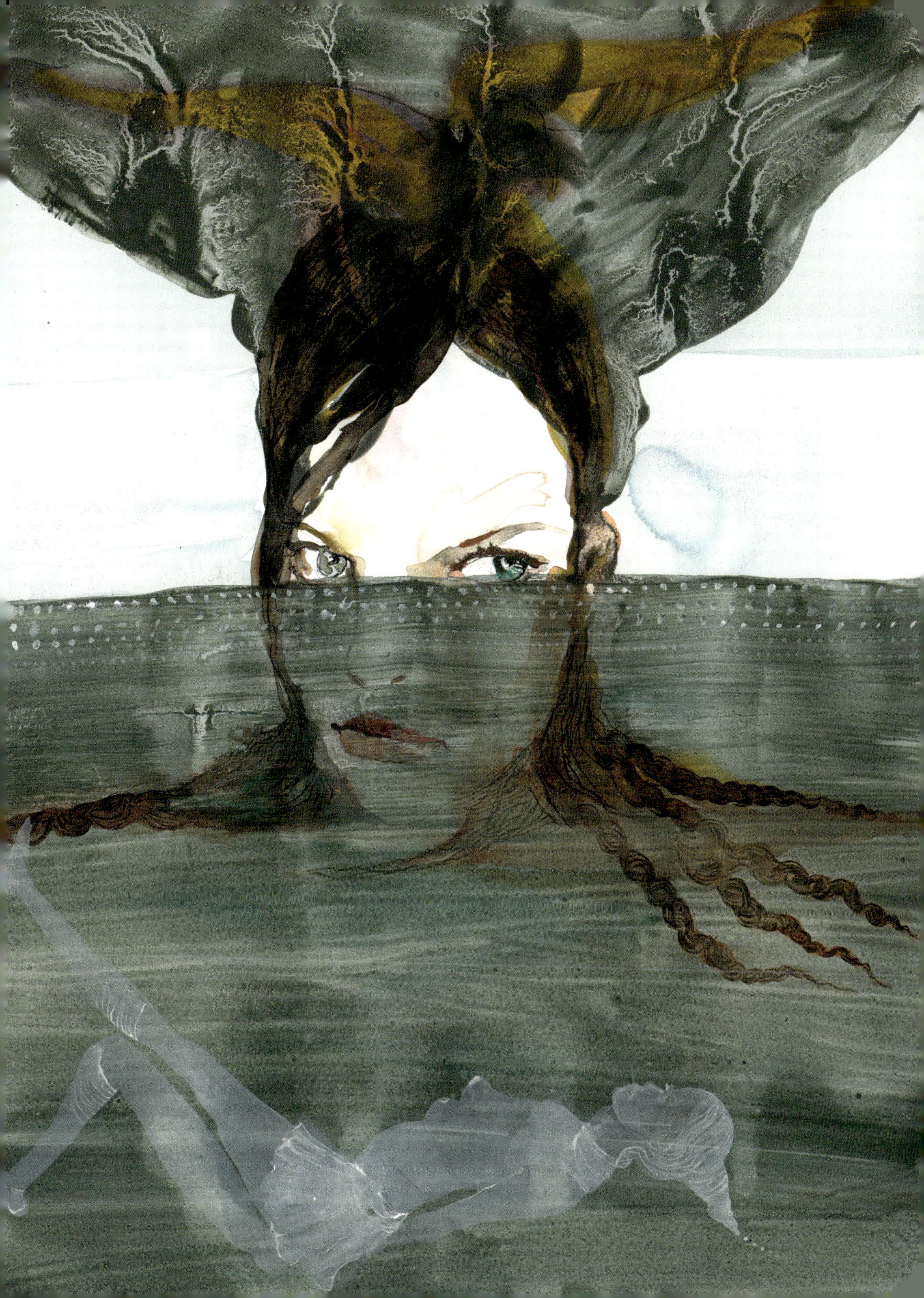

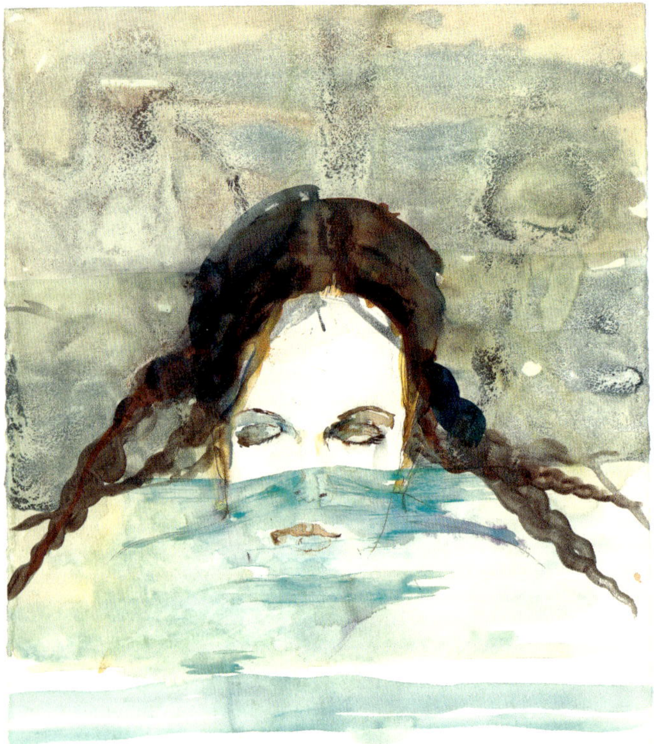

aus der Reihe „Halb unter Wasser" 2010
Aquarell & Tusche auf Büttenpapier
Watercolour & Indian ink on handmade paper
76 x 56 cm

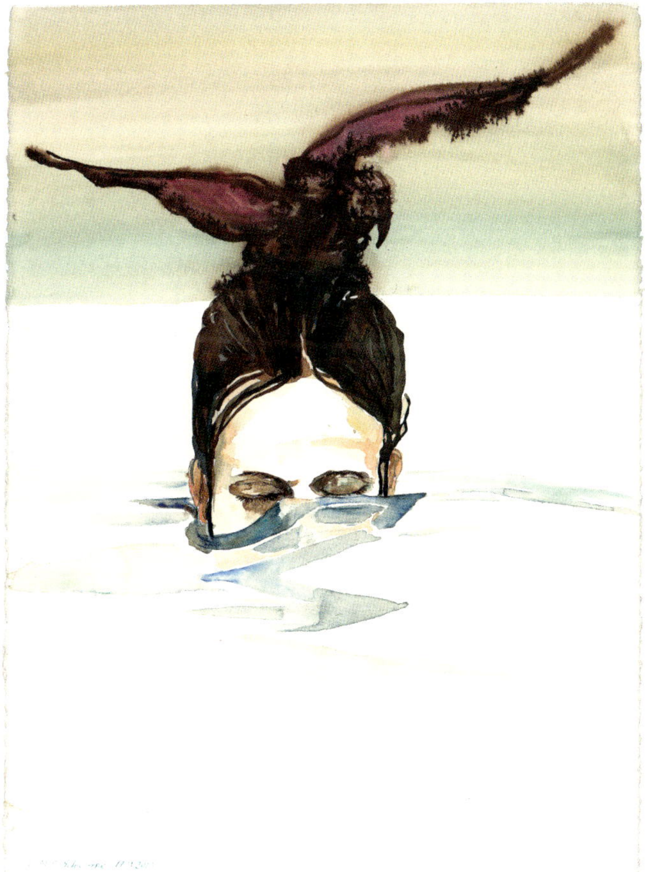

aus der Reihe „Halb unter Wasser“ 2010
Aquarell & Tusche auf Büttenpapier
Watercolour & Indian ink on handmade paper
76 x 56 cm

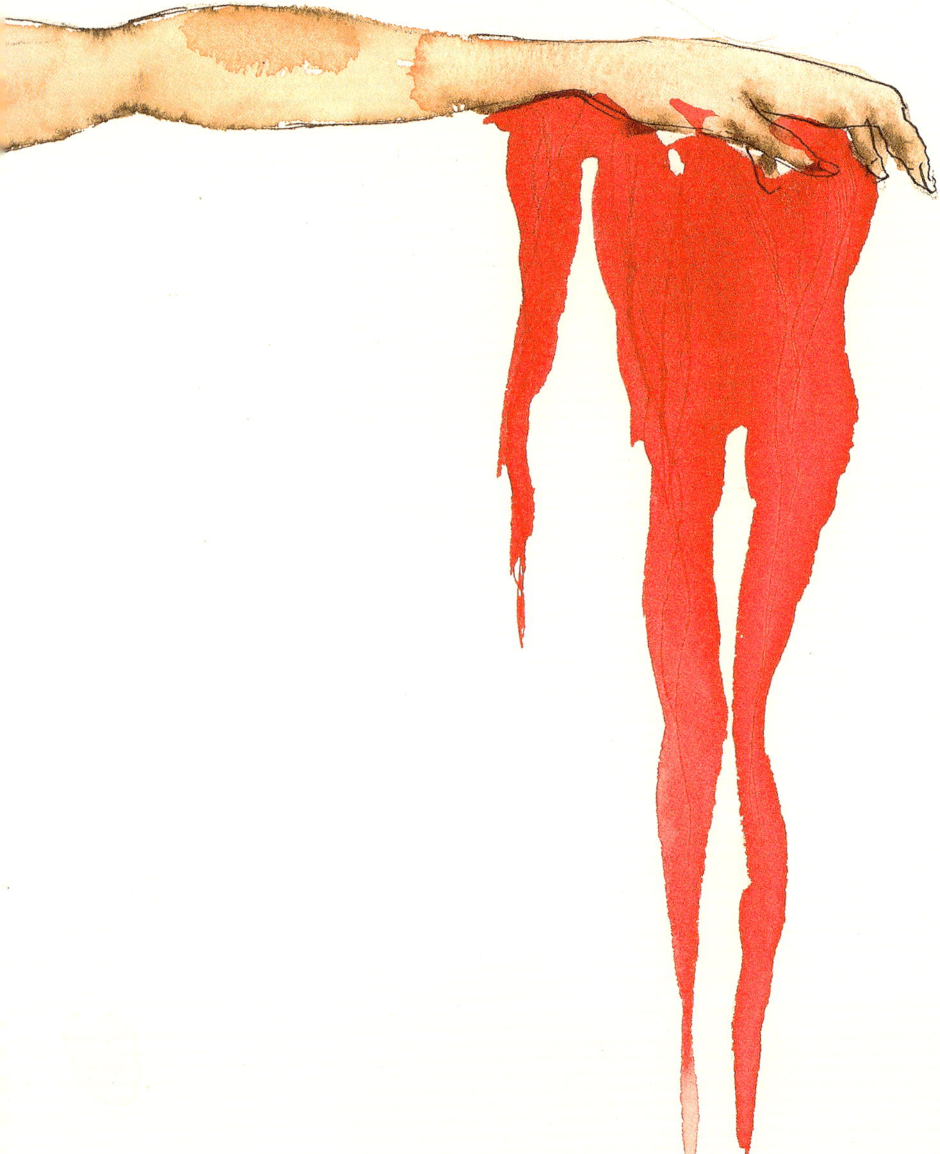

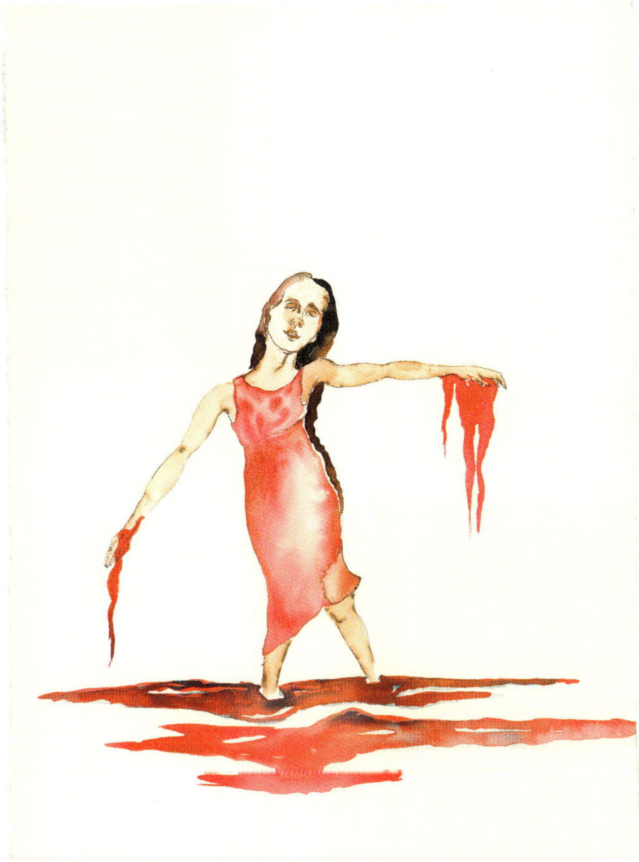

aus der Reihe „Halb unter Wasser" 2010
Aquarell & Tusche auf Büttenpapier
Watercolour & Indian ink on handmade paper
76 x 56 cm

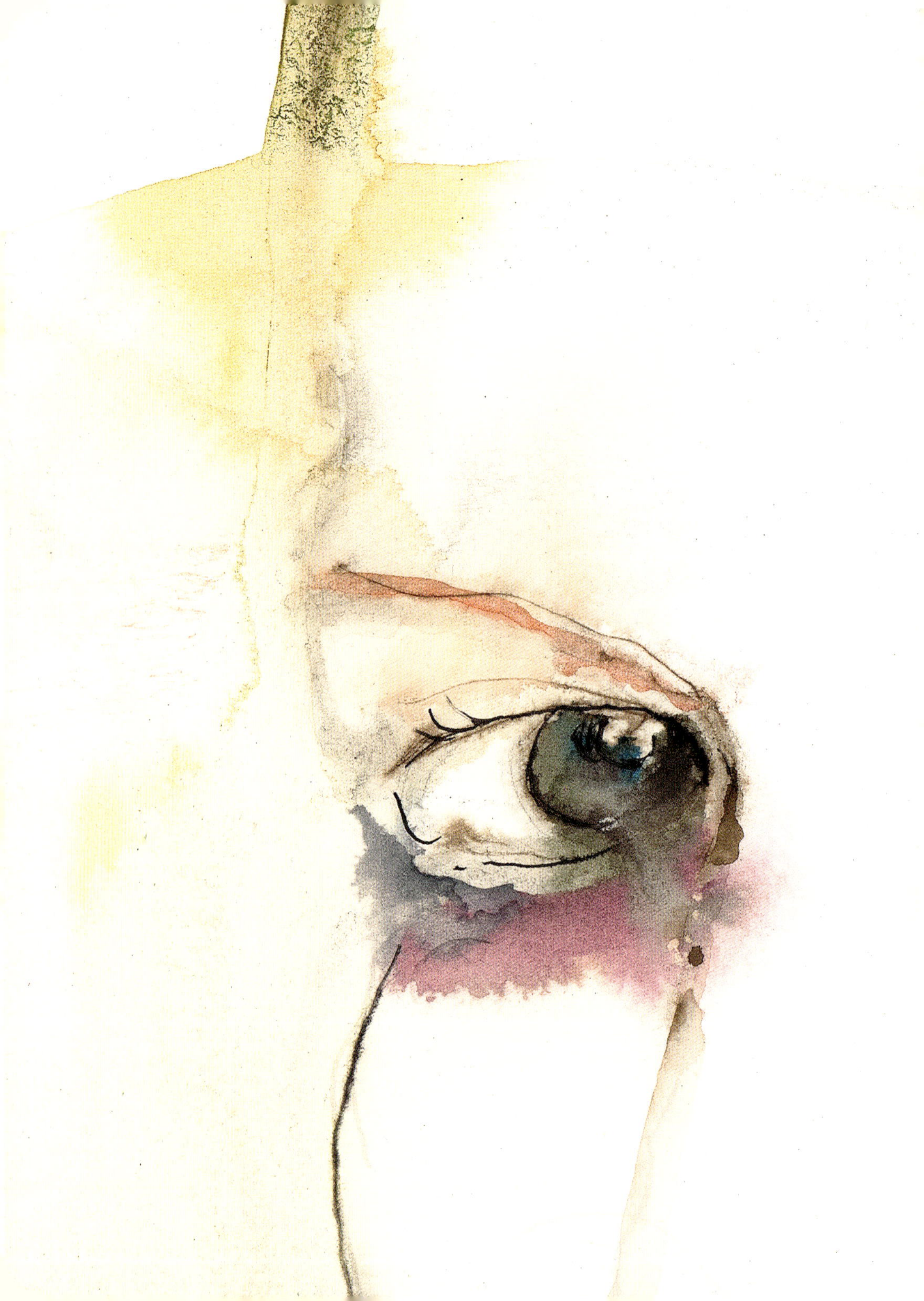

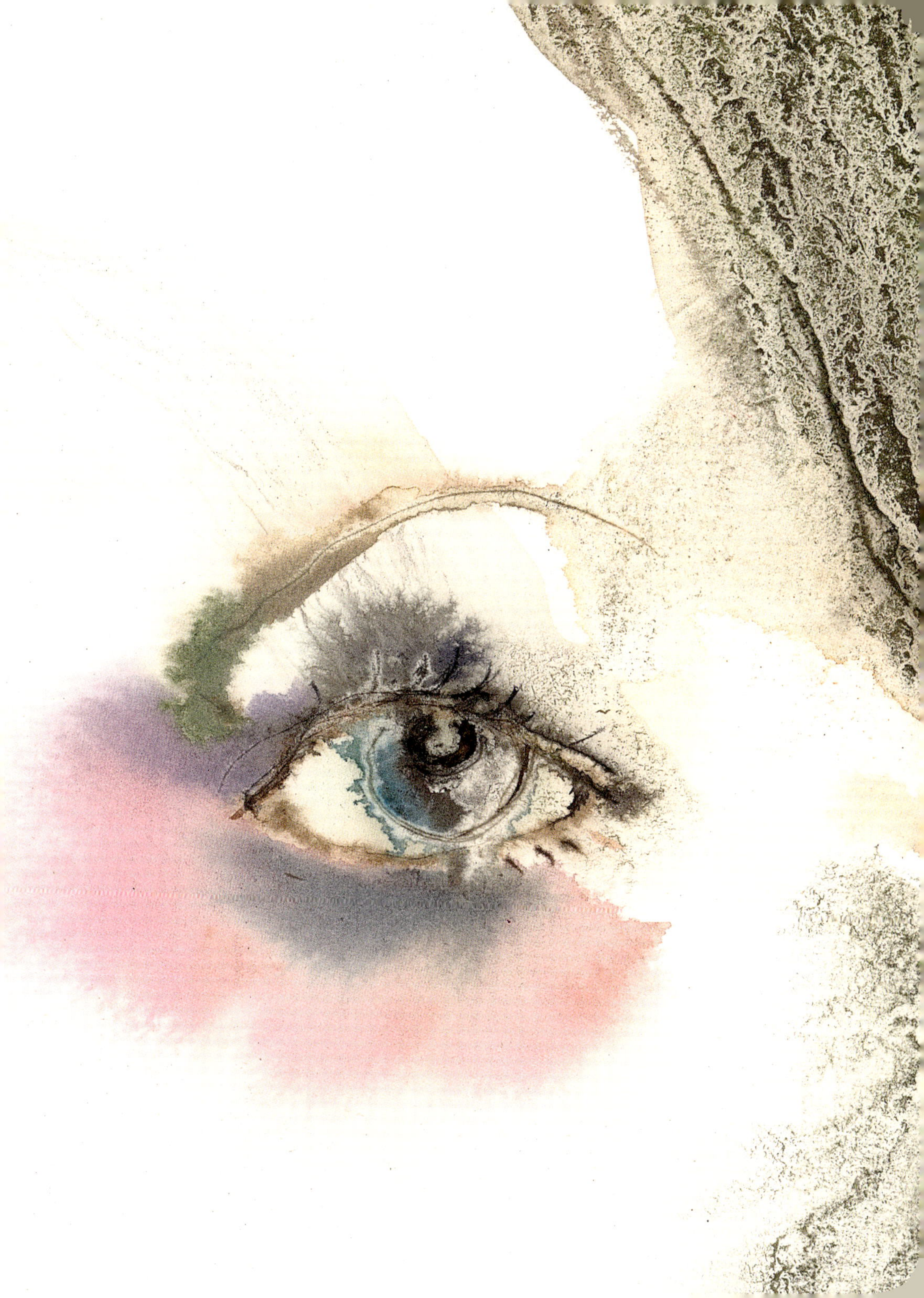

Ich begegnete einer Gräfin, als sie über eine lang gezogene Wendeltreppe auf mich zukam, dachte ich noch, es sei die Tochter des Gastgebers, als sie zehn Meter vor mir stand, hielt ich sie für seine Frau, als sie mir die Hand schüttelte, erkannte ich seine Mutter. Sie hätte die Demarkationslinie einhalten sollen. Distance ist für vielerlei gut.

Cornelia Schleime

I met a countess, when she walked towards me along a drawn-out flight of winding stairs, I still believed her to be the daughter of the host; when she stood ten metres away from me, I thought she was his wife; when she shook my hand, I recognised that she was his mother. She should have kept to the line of demarcation. Distance is good in a variety of ways.

Cornelia Schleime

Pestschwester 2011
Aquarell & Tusche auf Büttenpapier
Watercolour & Indian ink on handmade paper
57 x 38 cm

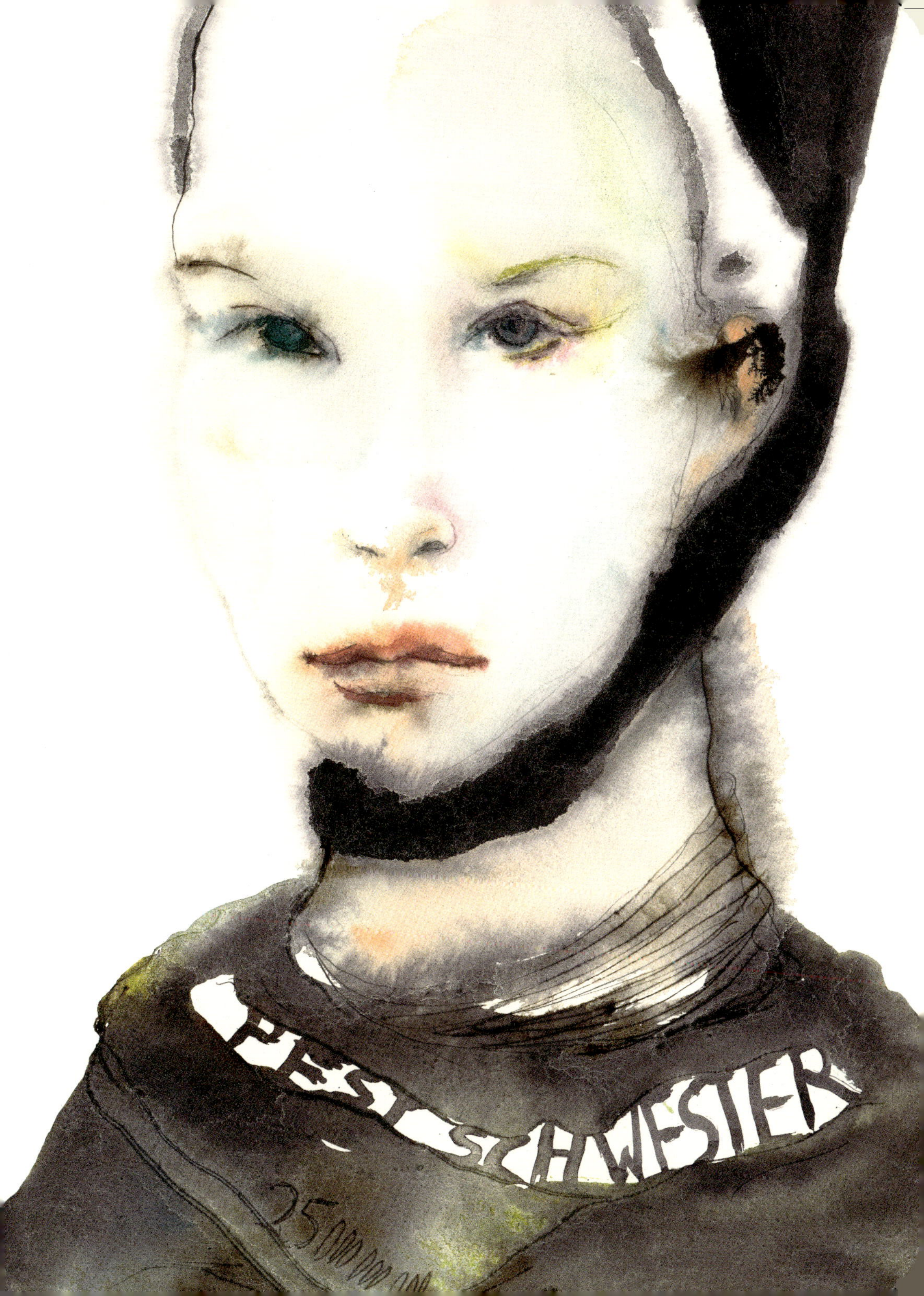
PEST SCHWESTER

rechte Seite right page **aus der Reihe „Köpfe“** 2011
Aquarell & Tusche auf Büttenpapier Watercolour & Indian ink on handmade paper 57 x 38 cm

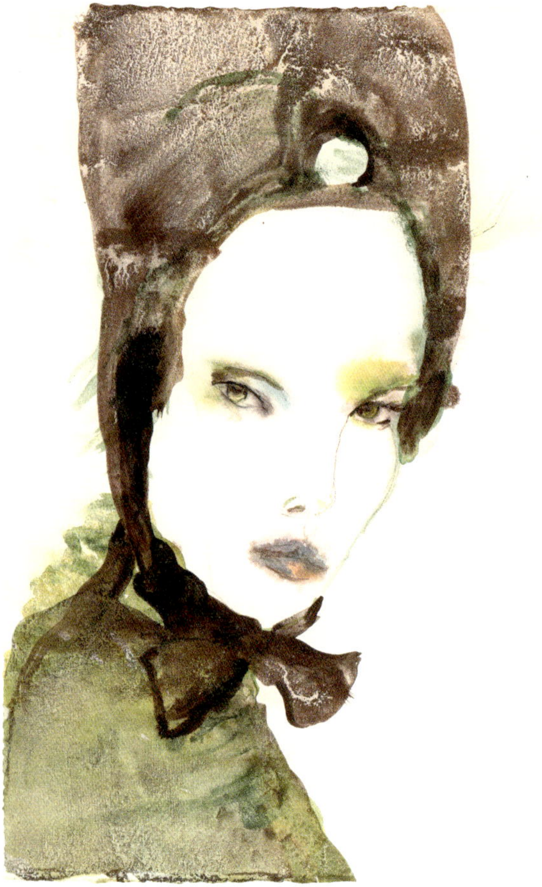

aus der Reihe „Köpfe“ 2011
Aquarell & Tusche auf Büttenpapier Watercolour & Indian ink on handmade paper
57 x 38 cm

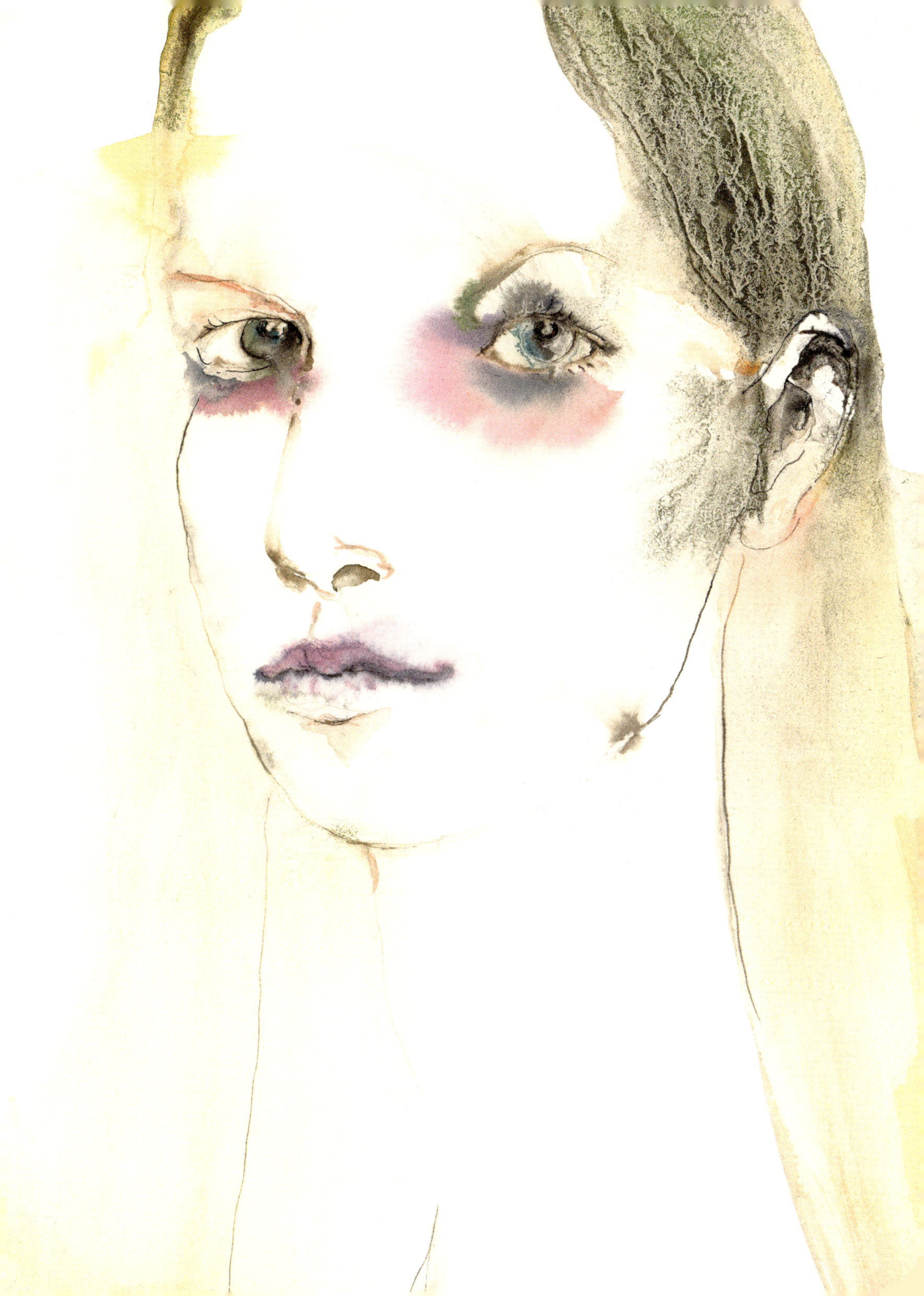

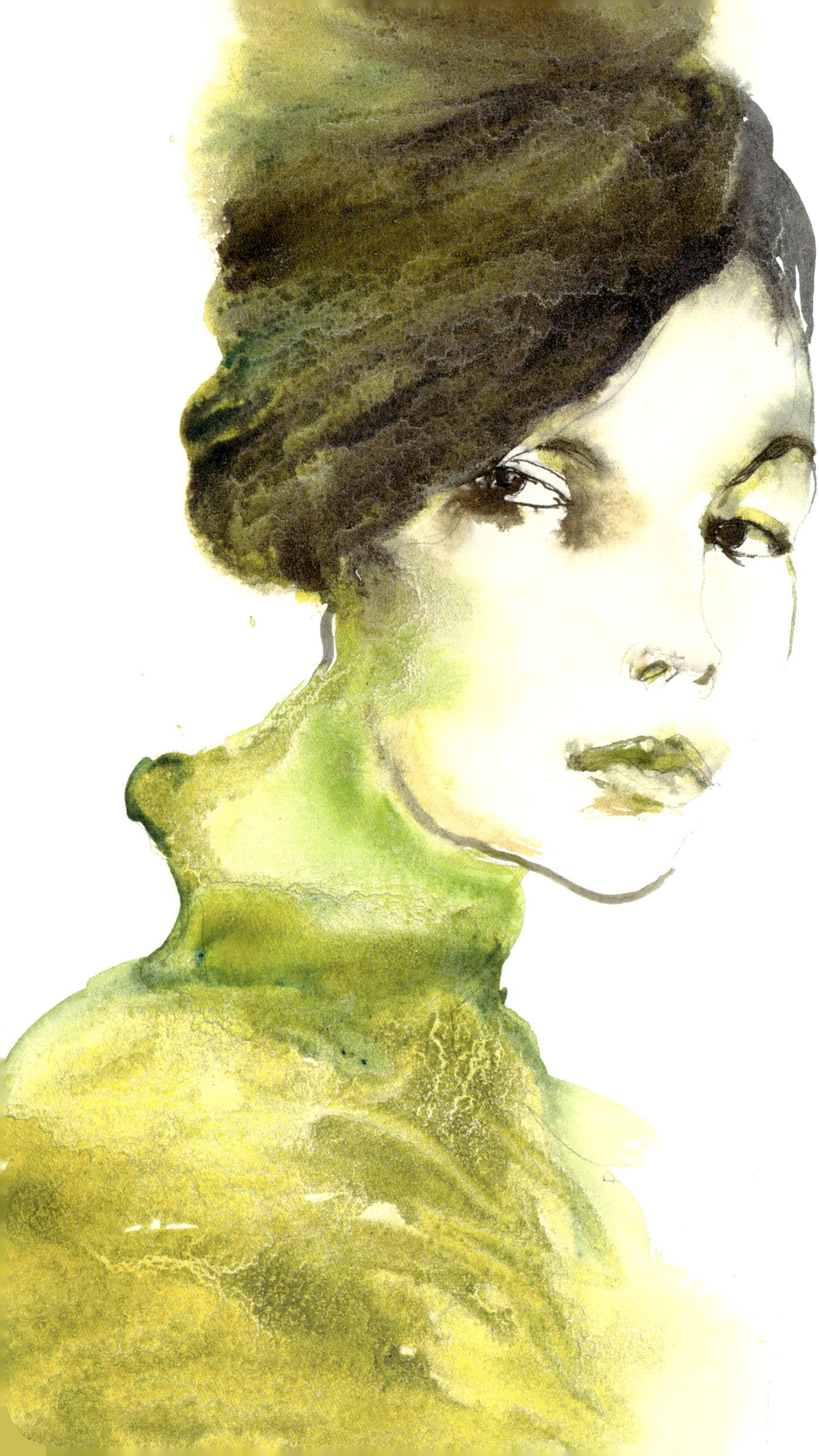

linke Seite left page **aus der Reihe „Köpfe"** 2011
Aquarell & Tusche auf Büttenpapier Watercolour & Indian ink on handmade paper 57 x 38 cm

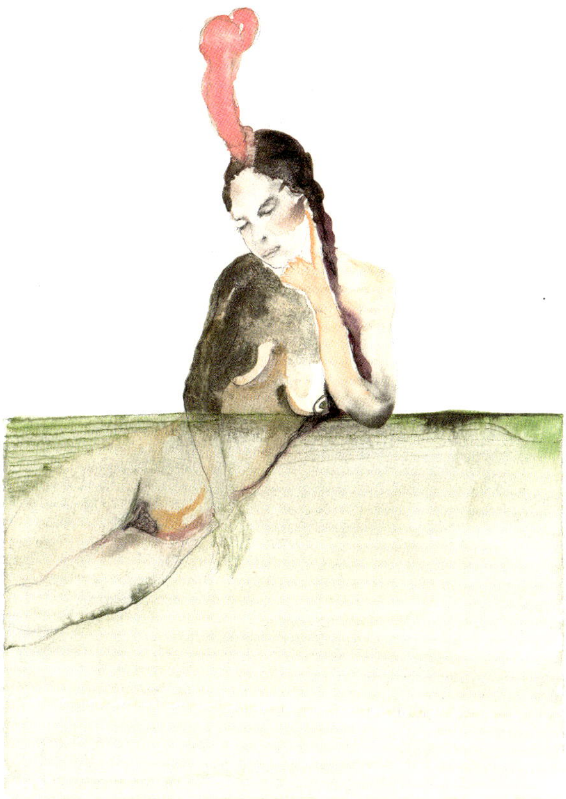

o.T. 2011
Aquarell & Tusche auf Büttenpapier
Watercolour & Indian ink on handmade paper
57 x 38 cm

rechte Seite right page aus der Reihe „Köpfe" 2011
Aquarell & Tusche auf Büttenpapier Watercolour & Indian ink on handmade paper 57 x 38 cm

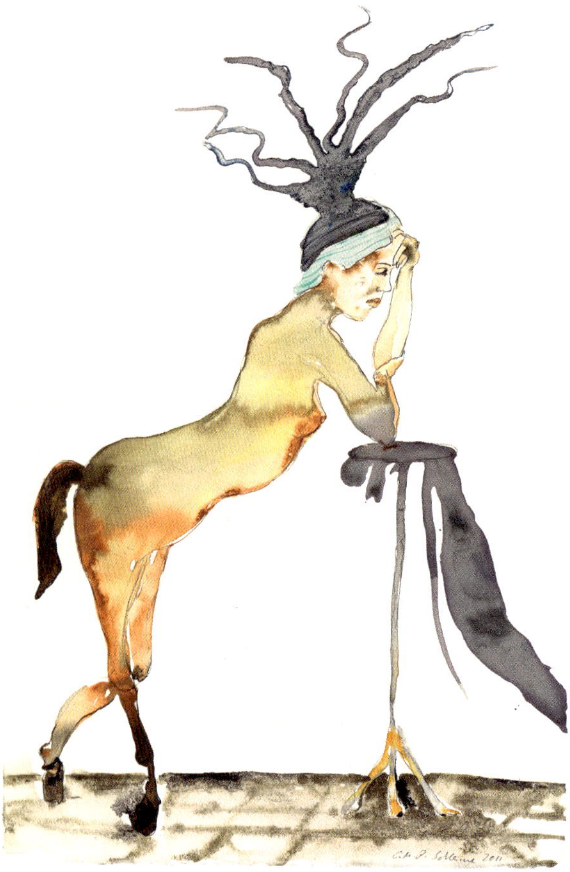

o.T. 2011
Aquarell & Tusche auf Büttenpapier Watercolour & Indian ink on handmade paper
57 x 38 cm

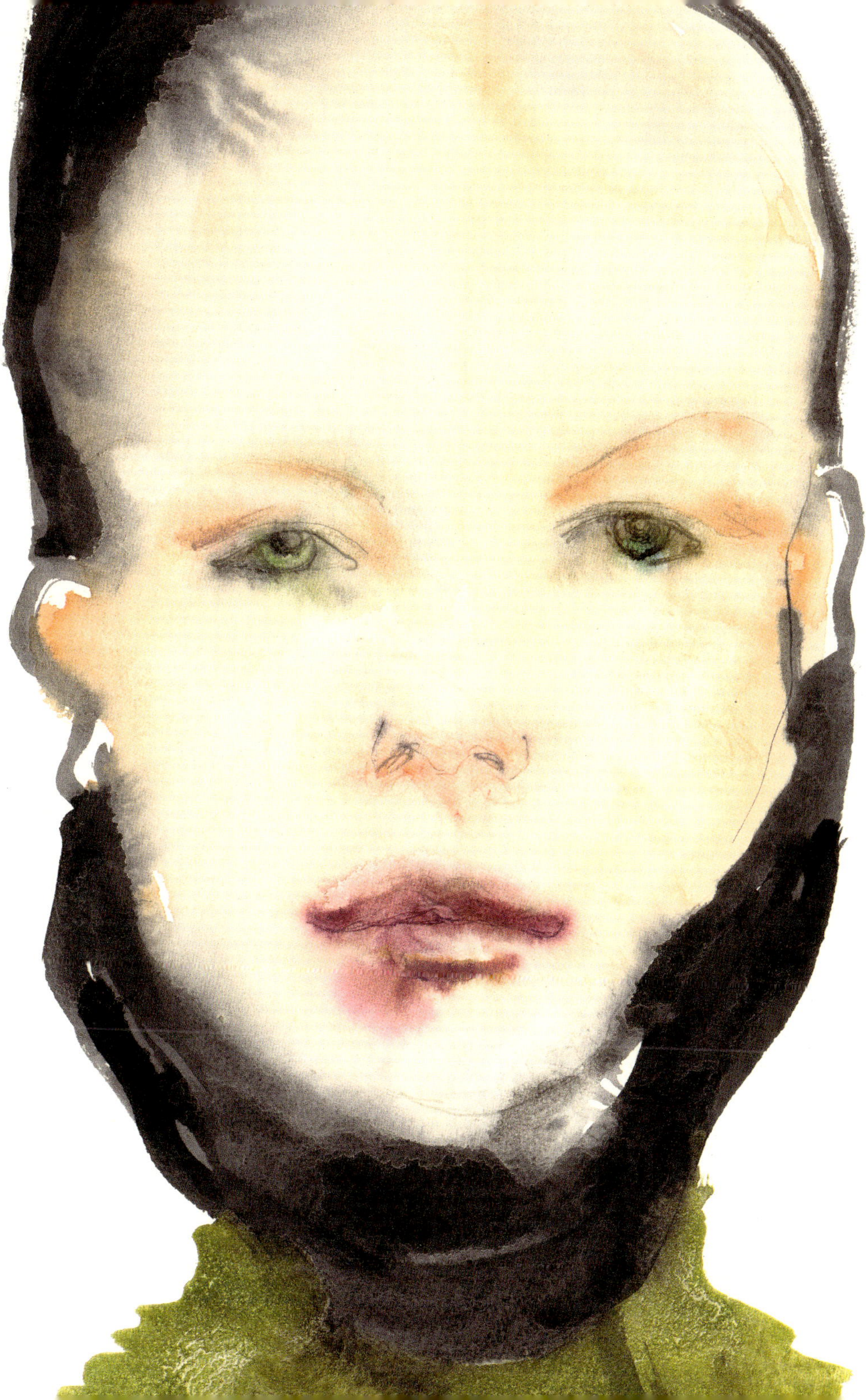

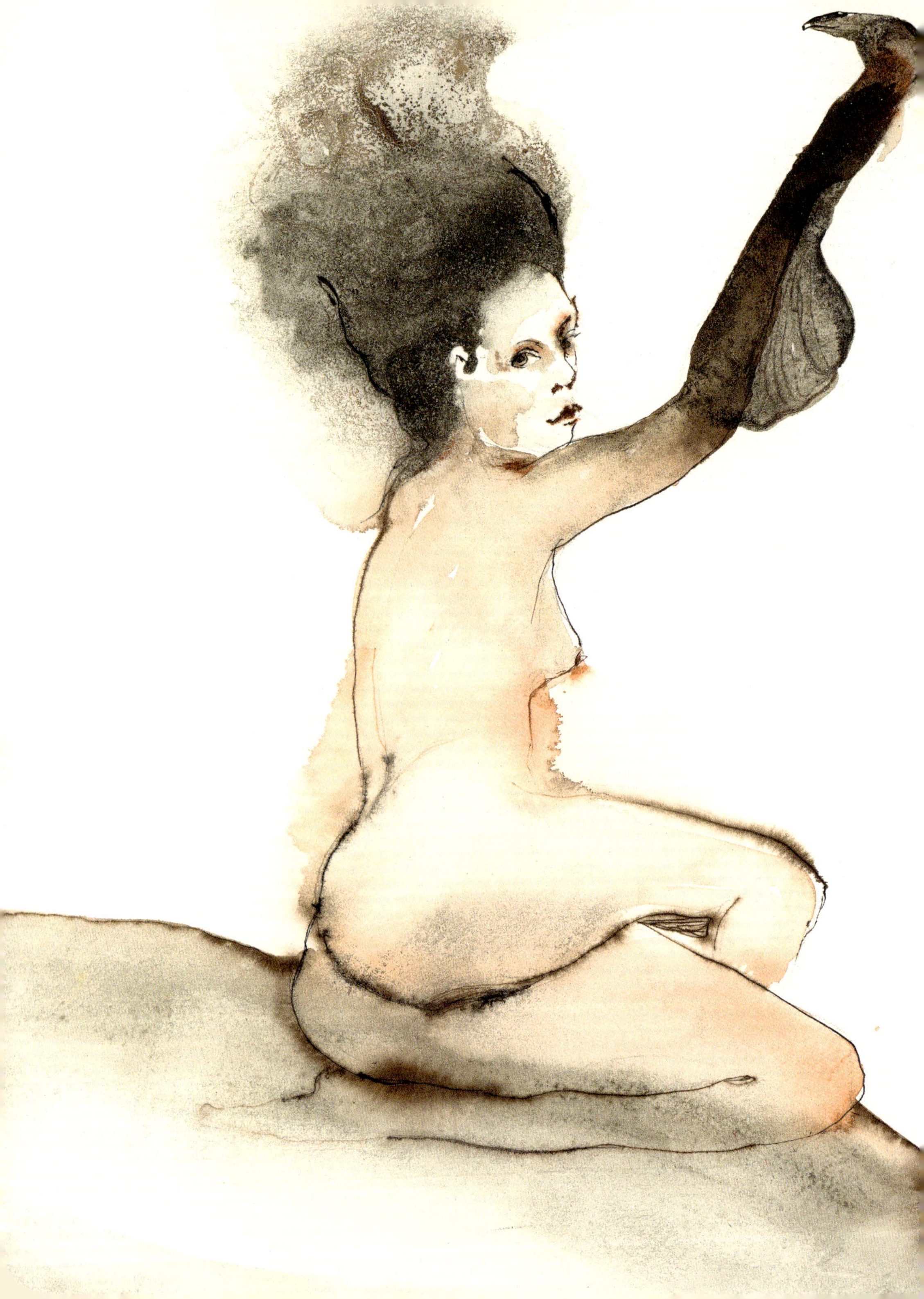

linke Seite left page „Die Puppenspielerin“ 2011
Aquarell & Tusche auf Büttenpapier Watercolour & Indian ink on handmade paper 57 x 38 cm

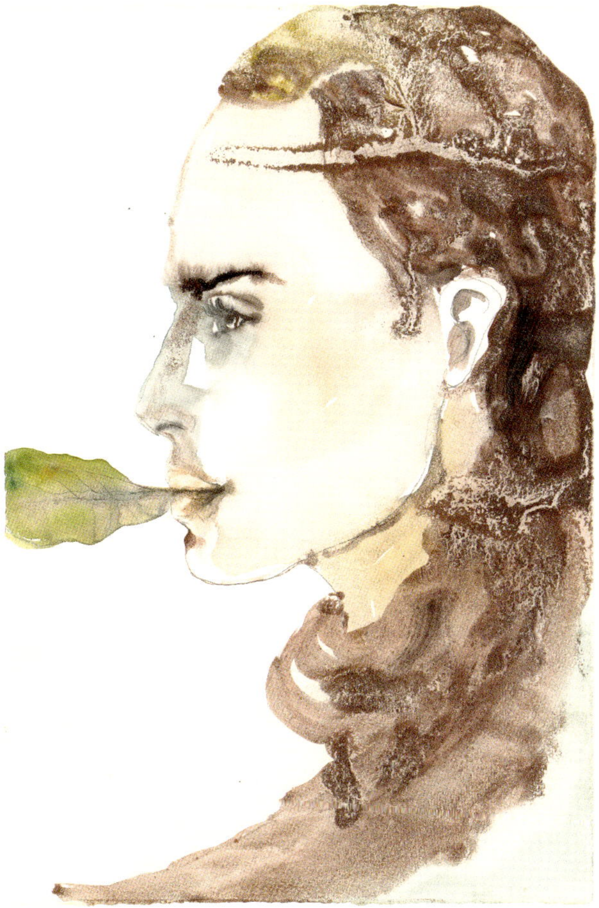

aus der Reihe „Köpfe“ 2011
Aquarell & Tusche auf Büttenpapier
Watercolour & Indian ink on handmade paper
57 x 38 cm

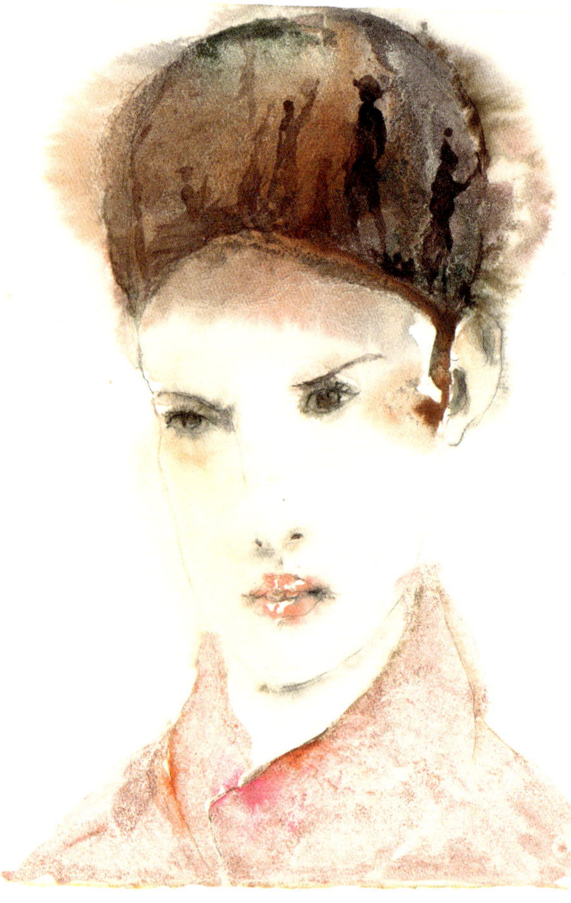

aus der Reihe „Köpfe" 2011
Aquarell & Tusche auf Büttenpapier
Watercolour & Indian ink on handmade paper
57 x 38 cm

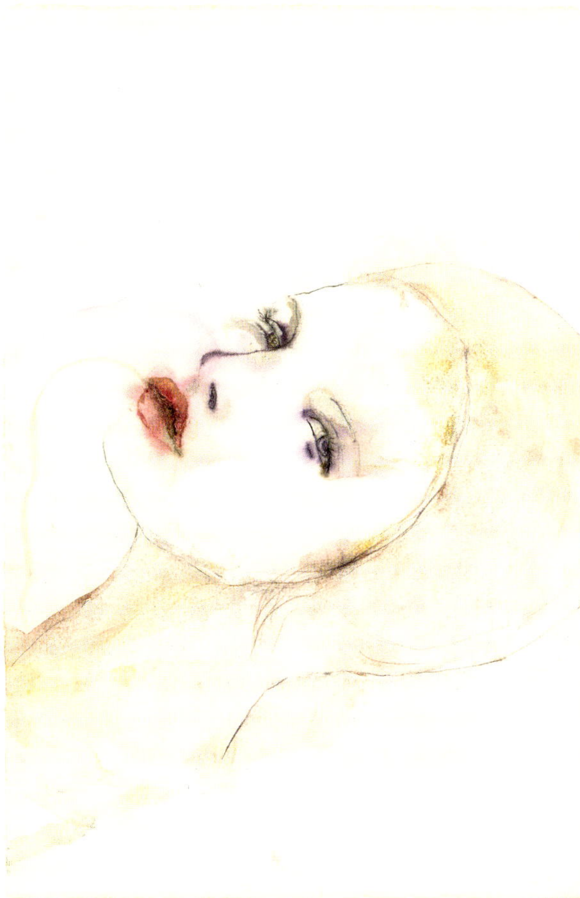

aus der Reihe „Köpfe" 2011
Aquarell & Tusche auf Büttenpapier
Watercolour & Indian ink on handmade paper
57 x 38 cm

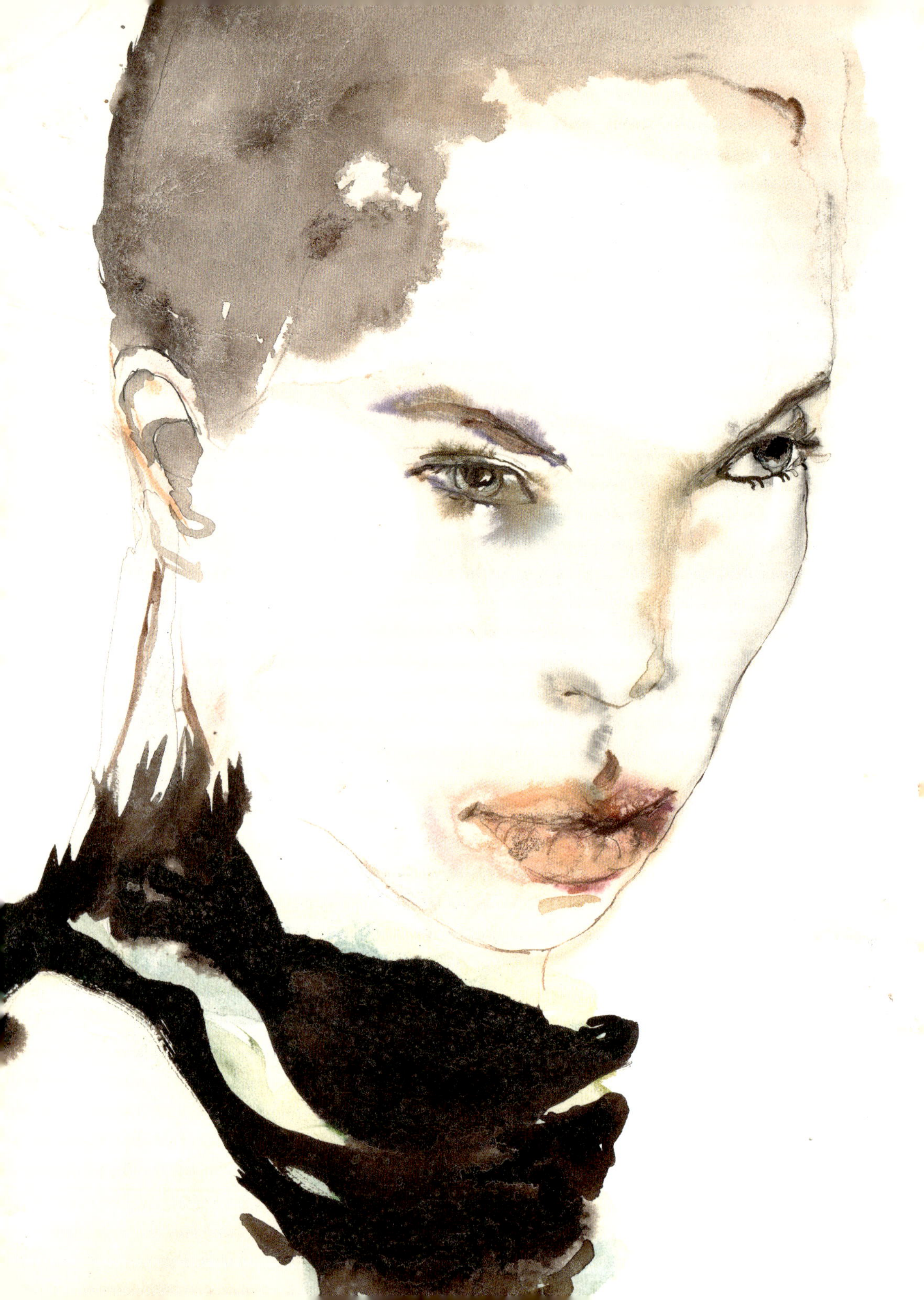

linke Seite left page **aus der Reihe „Köpfe“** 2011
Aquarell & Tusche auf Büttenpapier Watercolour & Indian ink on handmade paper 57 x 38 cm

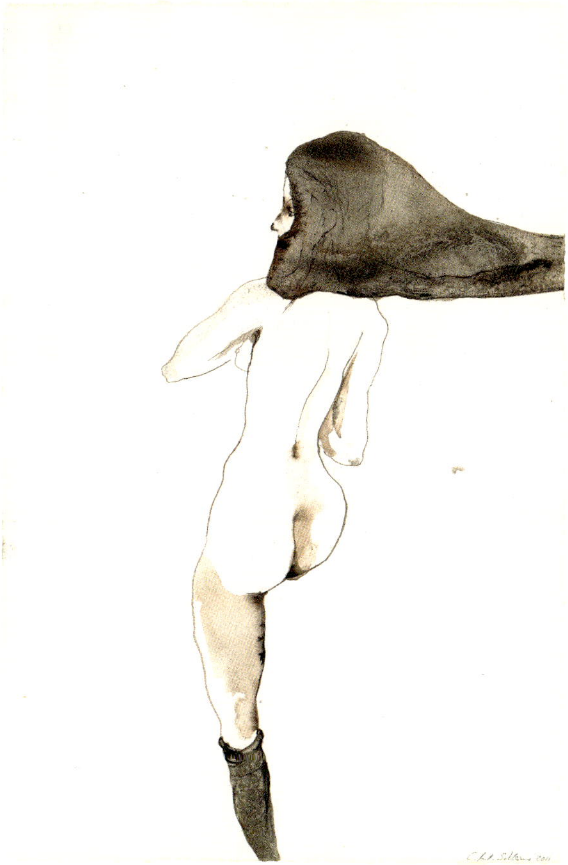

o.T. 2011
Aquarell & Tusche auf Büttenpapier
Watercolour & Indian ink on handmade Paper
57 x 38 cm

sein klapperndes Messer
wie es an meinen Träumen schleift

wie er sich ins Gedächtnis ruft
Jahrzehnte später

Als Schädelwind
Erklärt sein Tun

mal im Erinnern
meist im Vergessenen

Cornelia Schleime

his rattling knife
how it grinds at my dreams

how he conjures up thoughts of himself
decades later

As a wind of the skull
Explains his actions

occasionally in remembrance
usually in what is forgotten

Cornelia Schleime

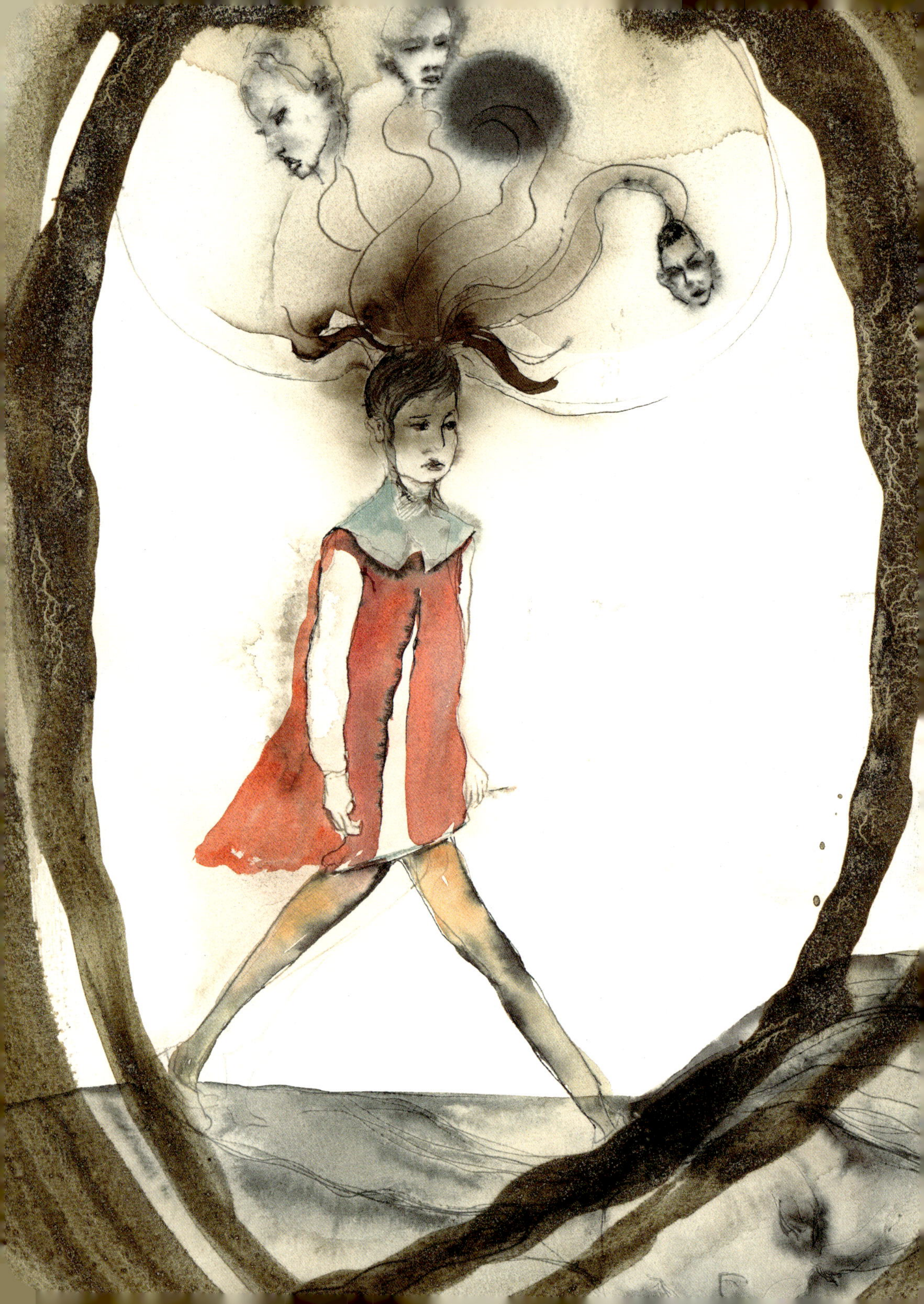

linke Seite left page **Die Gedanken wandern mit** 2011
Aquarell & Tusche auf Büttenpapier Watercolour & Indian ink on handmade paper 57 x 38 cm

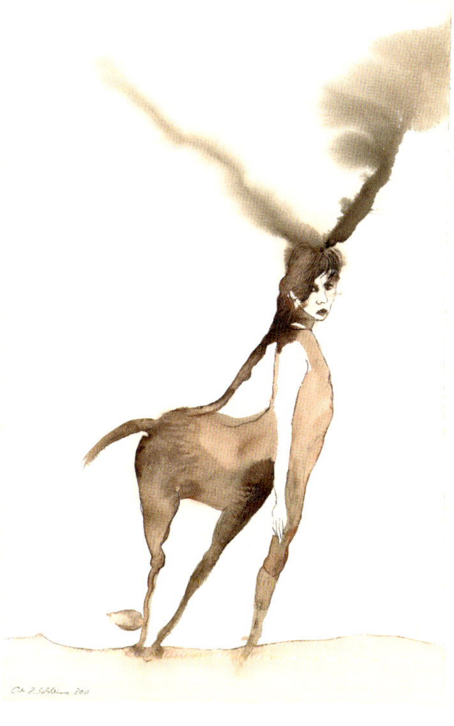

Die Windsbraut 2011
Aquarell & Tusche auf Büttenpapier
Watercolour & Indian ink on handmade paper
57 x 38 cm

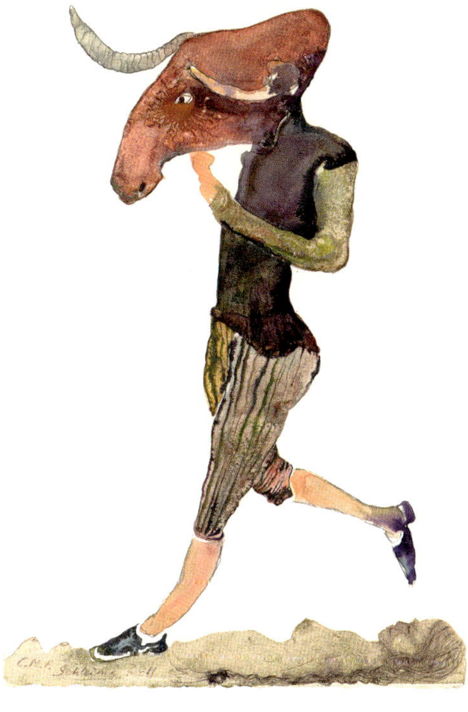

o.T. 2011
Aquarell & Tusche auf Büttenpapier
Watercolour & Indian ink on handmade paper
57 x 38 cm

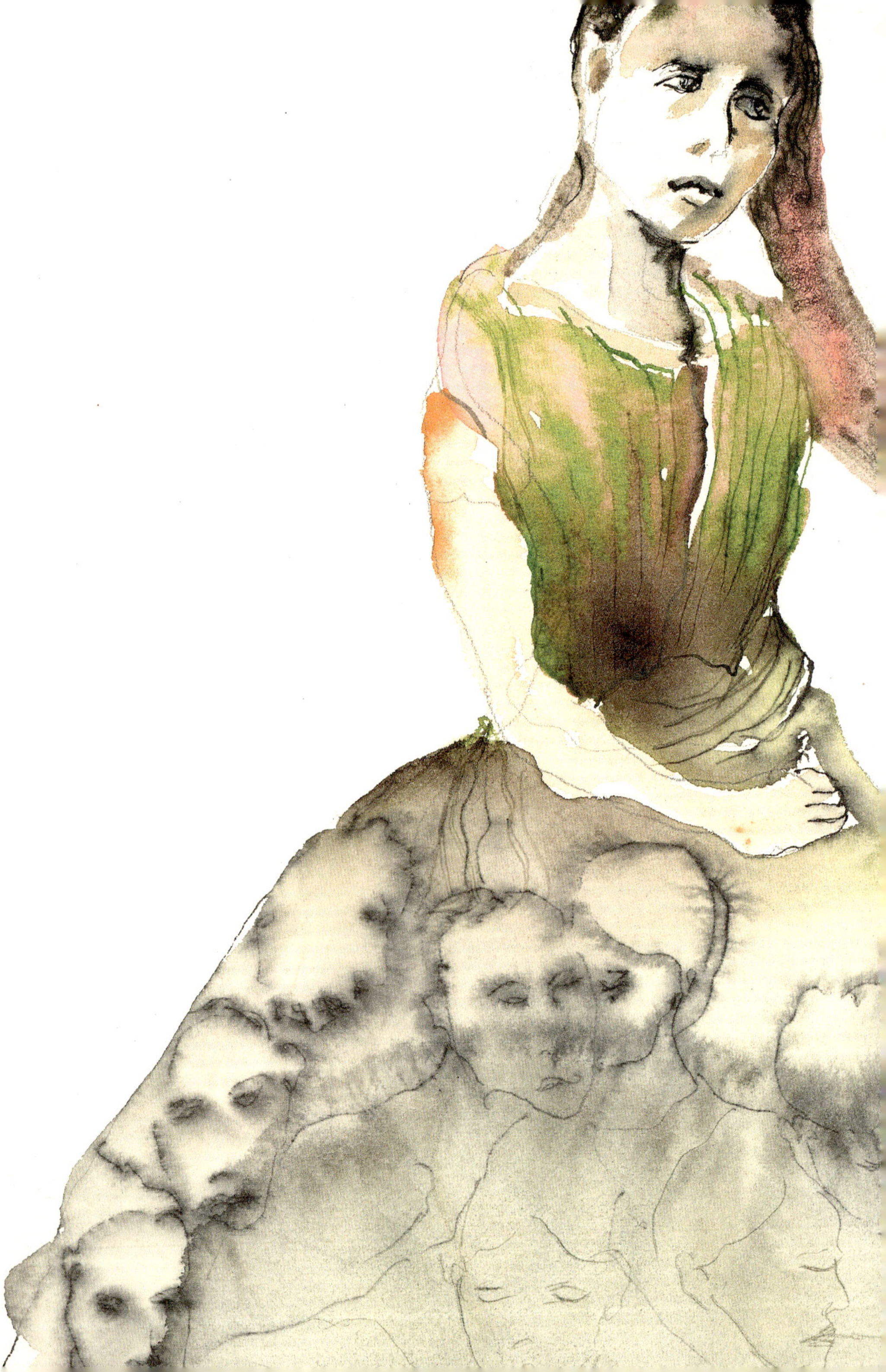

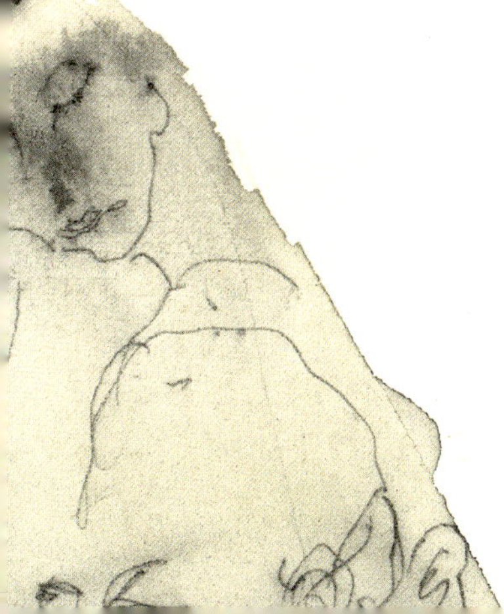

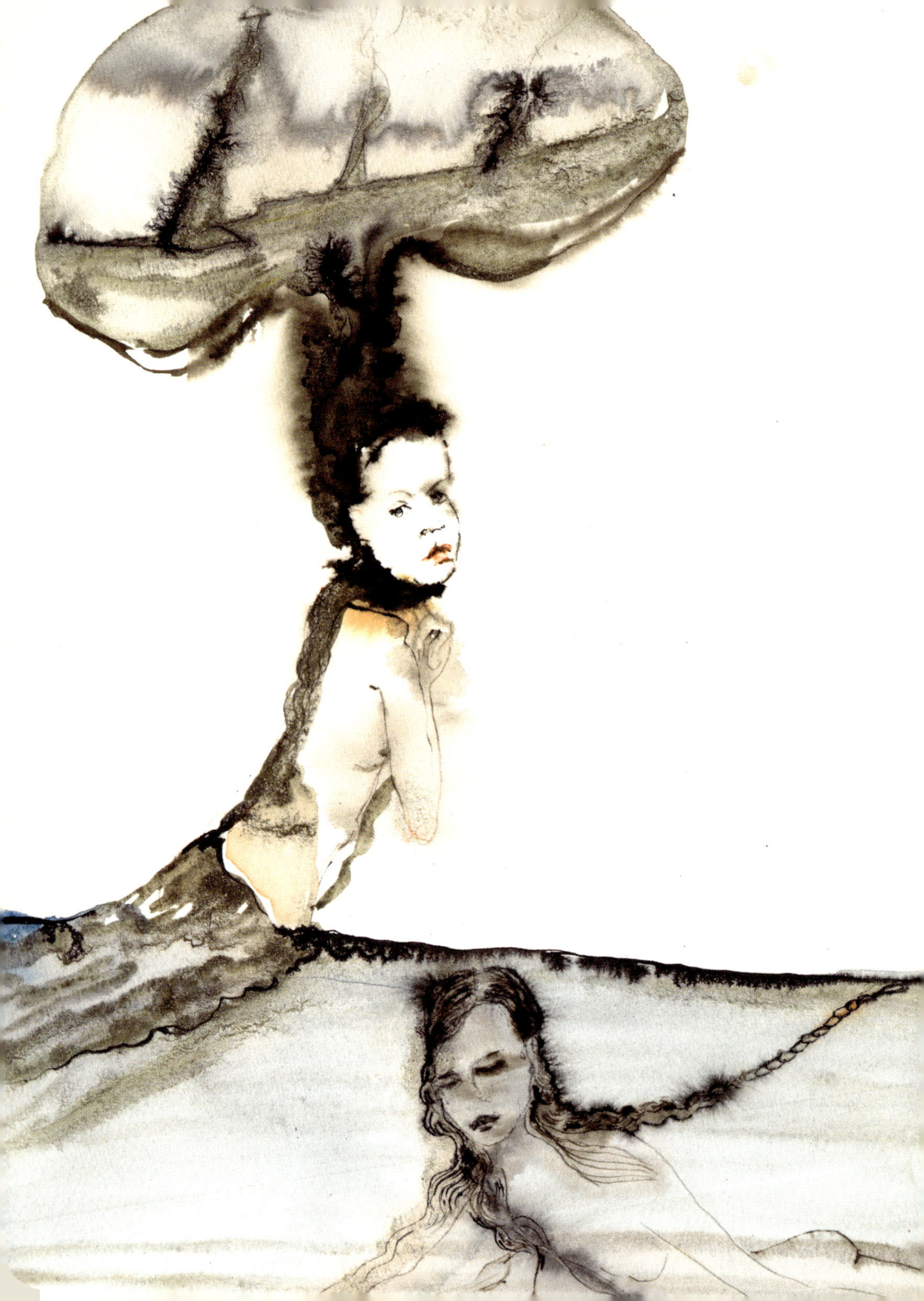

linke Seite left page **o.T.** 2011
Aquarell & Tusche auf Büttenpapier Watercolour & Indian ink on handmade paper 57 x 38 cm

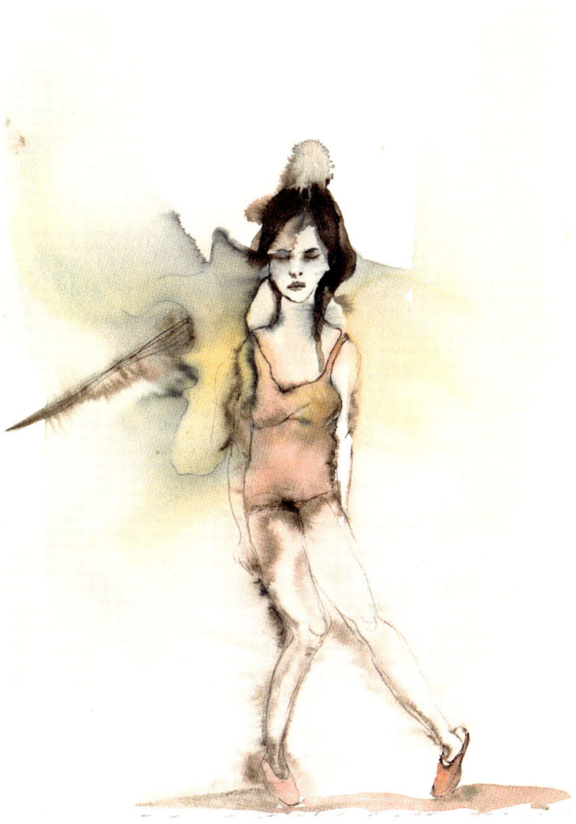

Fragil 2011
Aquarell & Tusche auf Büttenpapier
Watercolour & Indian ink on handmade paper
57 x 38 cm

rechte Seite right page **o.T.** 2011
Aquarell & Tusche auf Büttenpapier Watercolour & Indian ink on handmade paper 57 x 38 cm

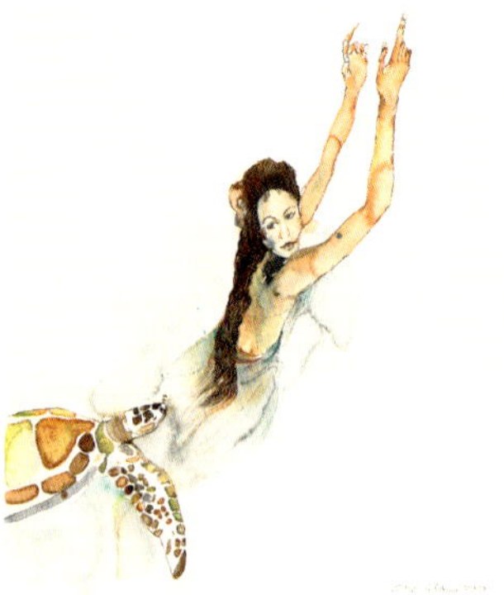
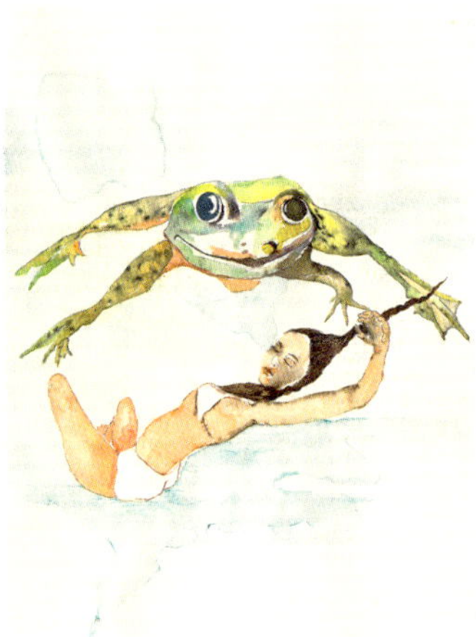
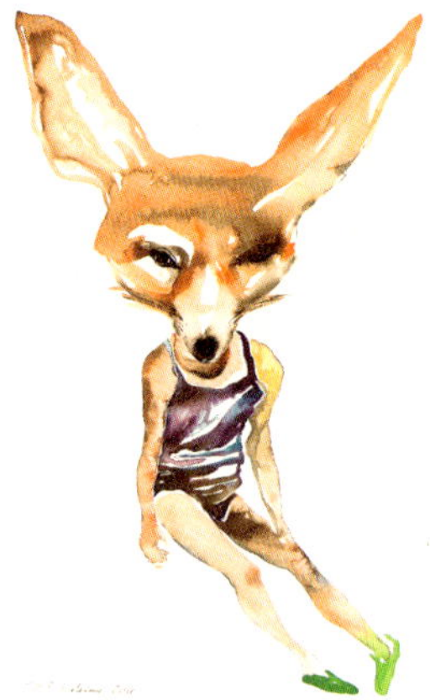
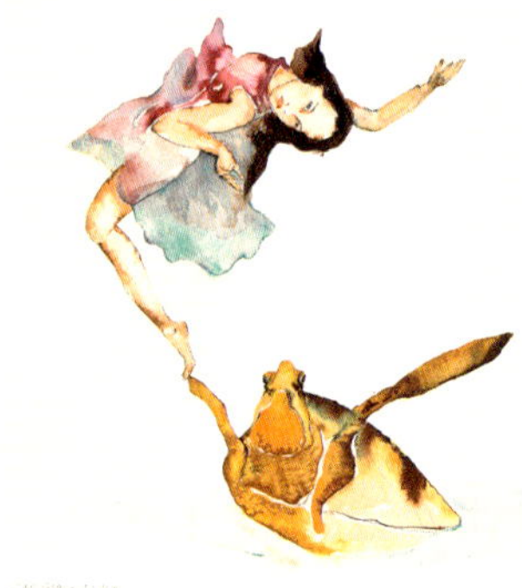
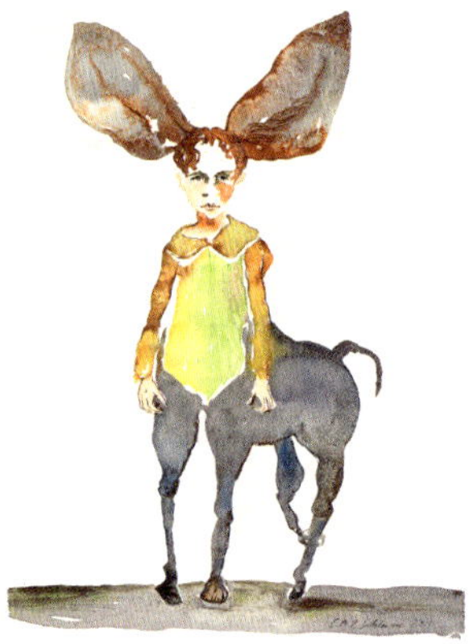
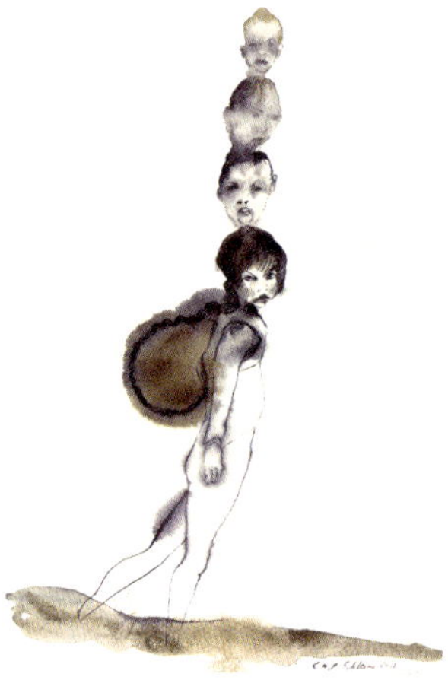

Abb. 1: **Verkündung** Abb. 2–5: **o.T.** Abb. 6: **Mitgift** 2011
Aquarell & Tusche auf Büttenpapier Watercolour & Indian ink on handmade paper
57 x 38 cm

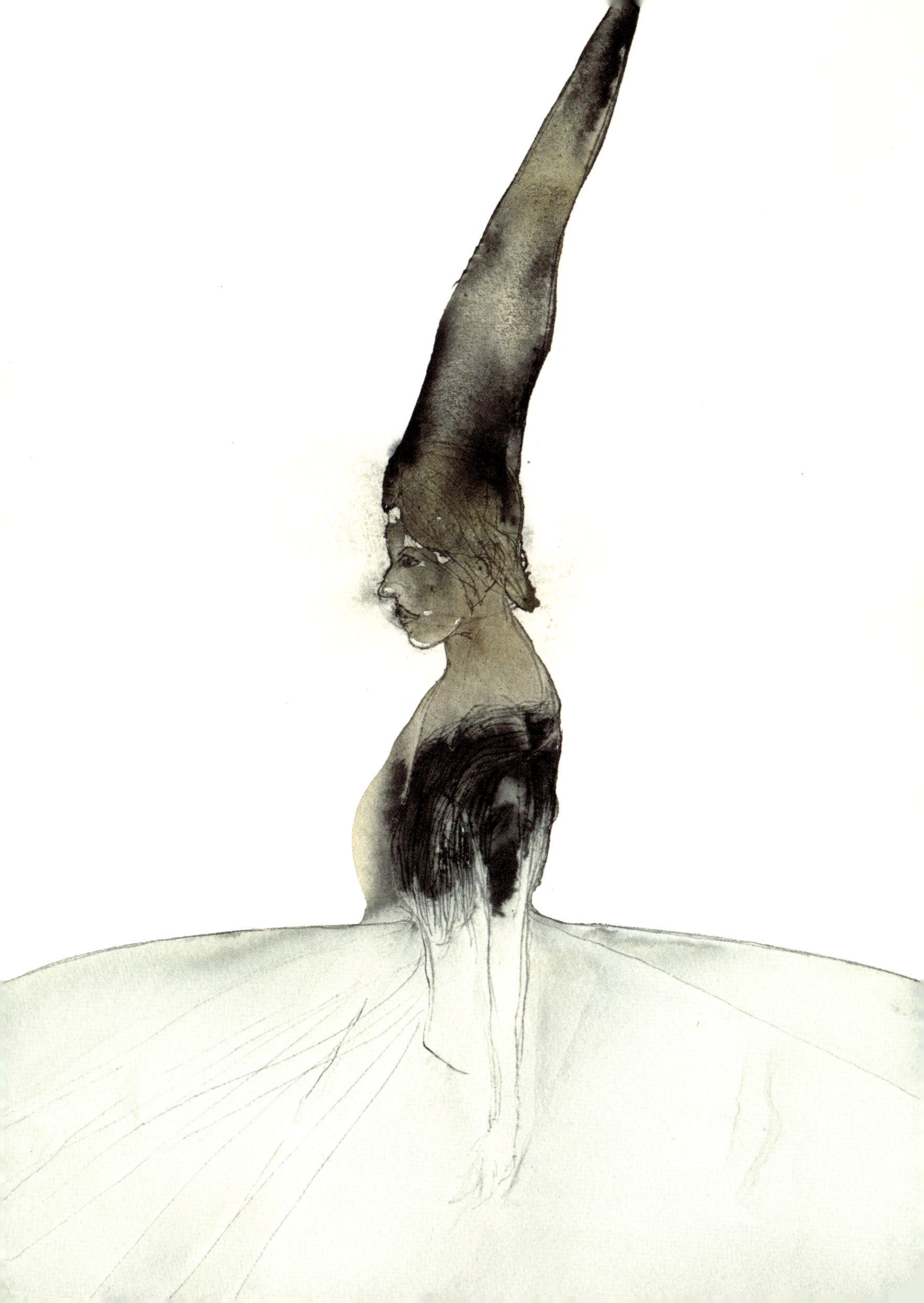

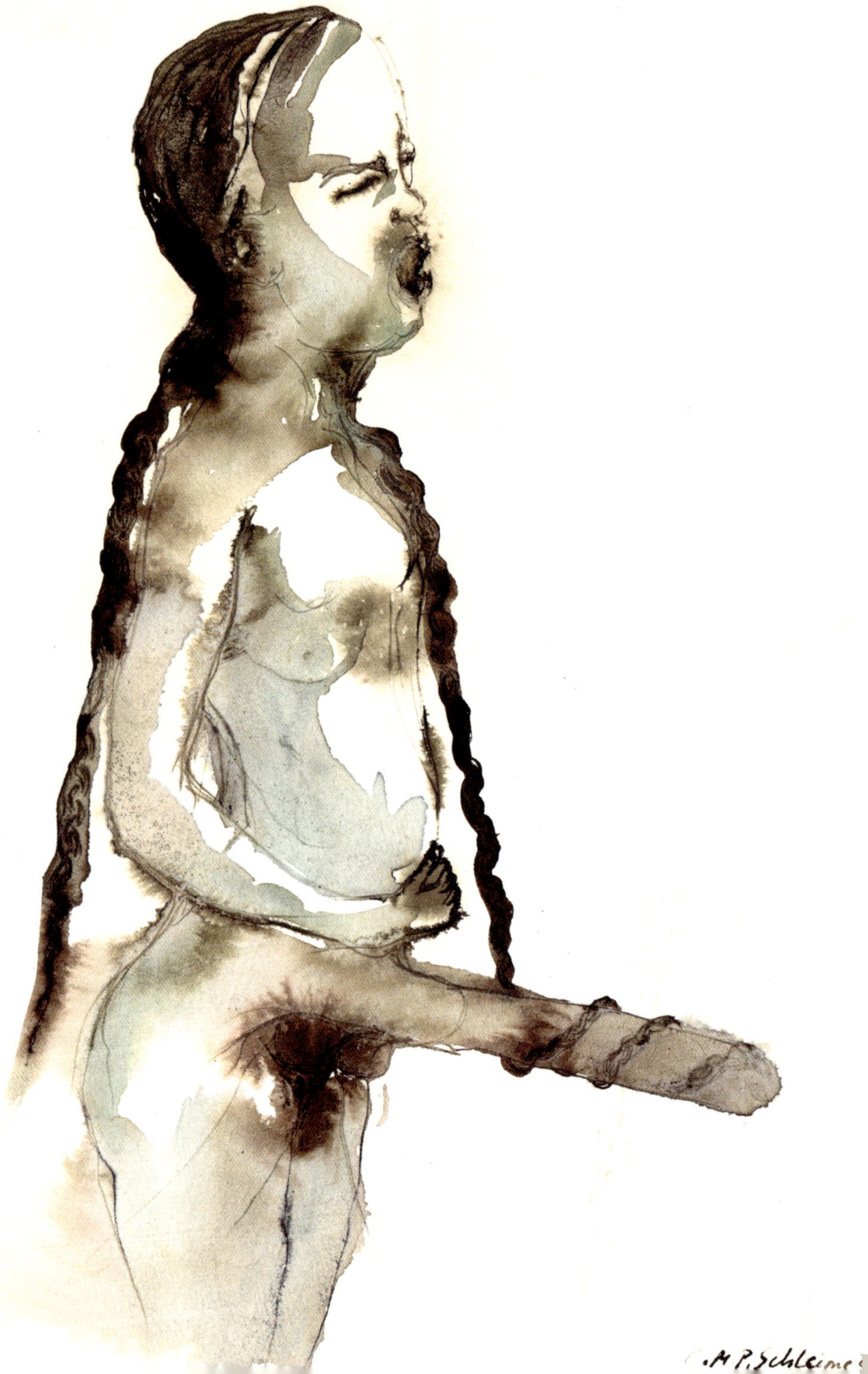

linke Seite left page **Waffenschmiede** 2011
Tusche auf Papier Ink on paper 57 x 38 cm

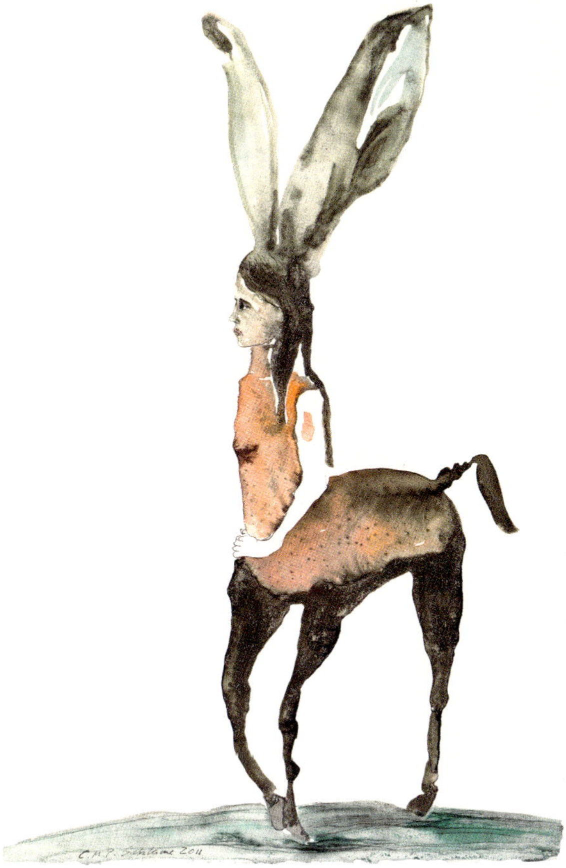

o.T. 2011
Aquarell & Tusche auf Büttenpapier
Watercolour & Indian ink on handmade paper
57 x 38 cm

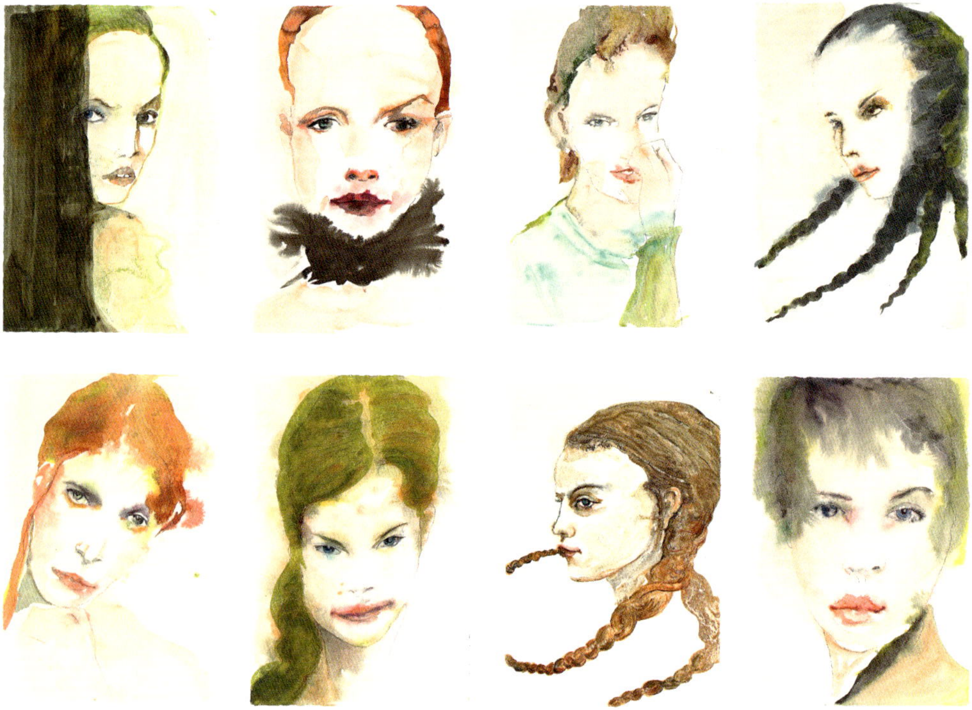

Zu diesem Buch erscheint eine auf 20 Exemplare limitierte Sonderedition ›Köpfe, 2011‹ Aquarell und Tusche auf Büttenpapier im Format 57 x 38 cm. Jedes Original ist von der Künstlerin auf der Rückseite nummeriert und signiert.

This publication is accompanied by the series "Köpfe, 2011", watercolour and Indian ink on handmade paper, 57 x 38 cm, in a special edition limited to 20 copies and with each original numbered and signed on the reverse by the artist.

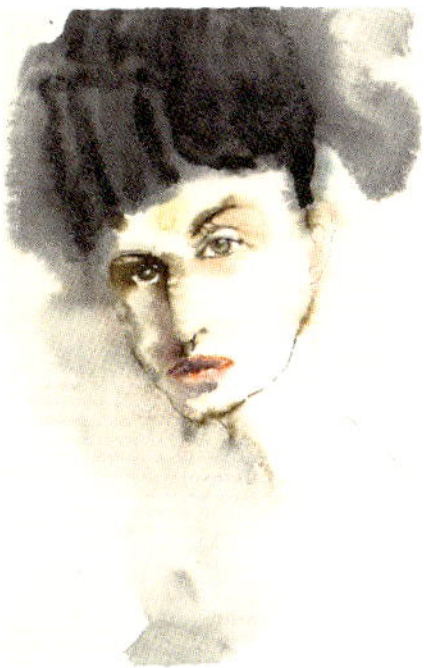
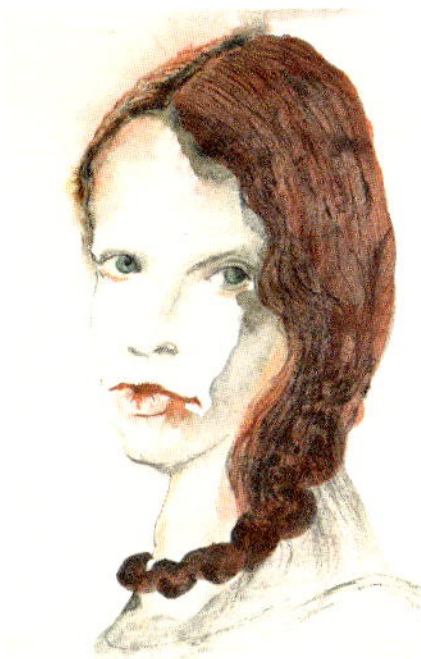
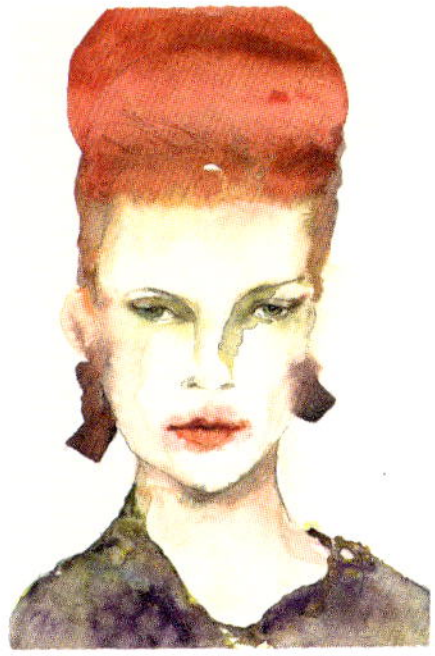
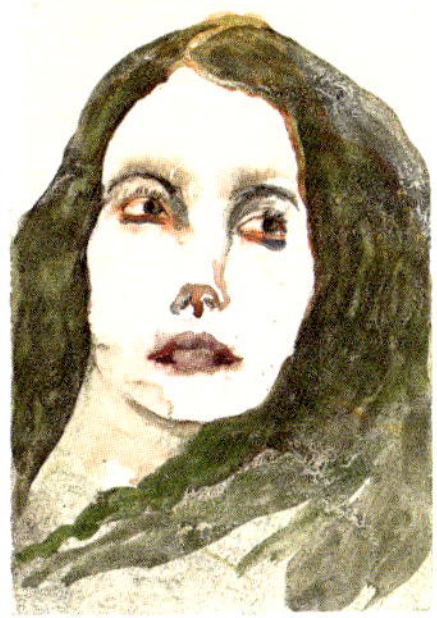
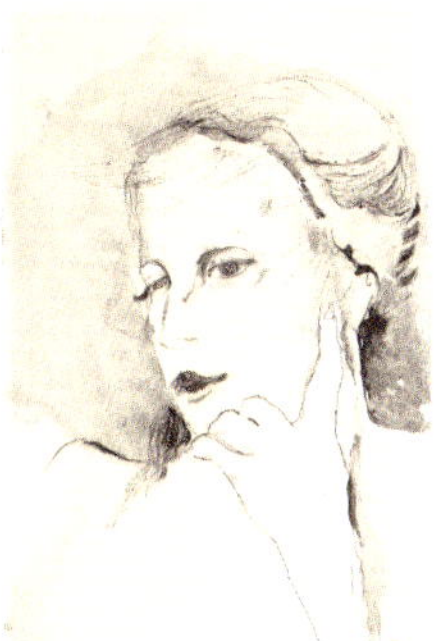
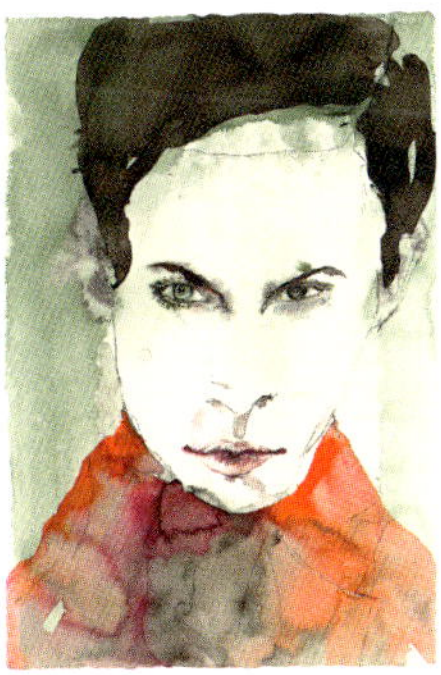
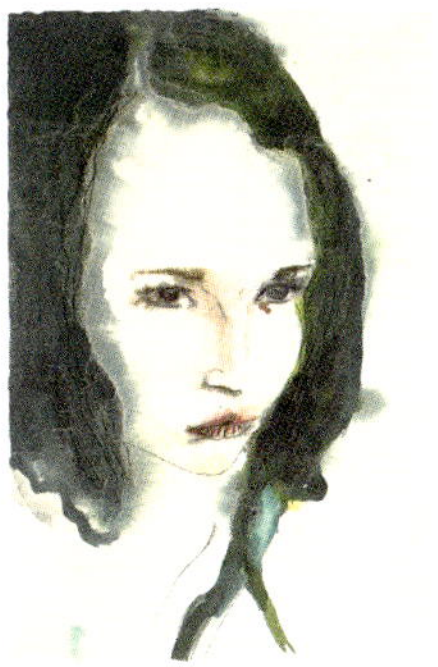
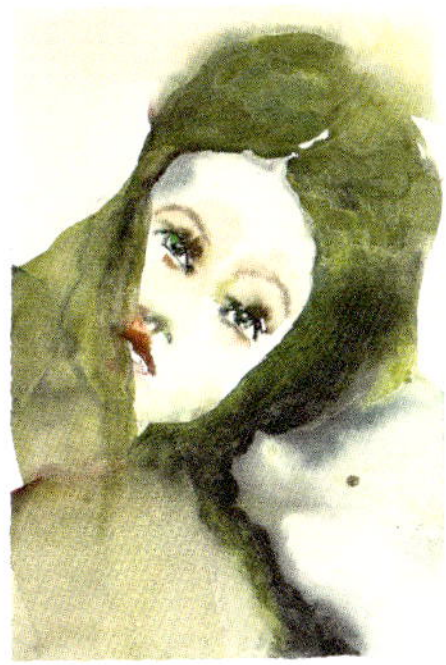
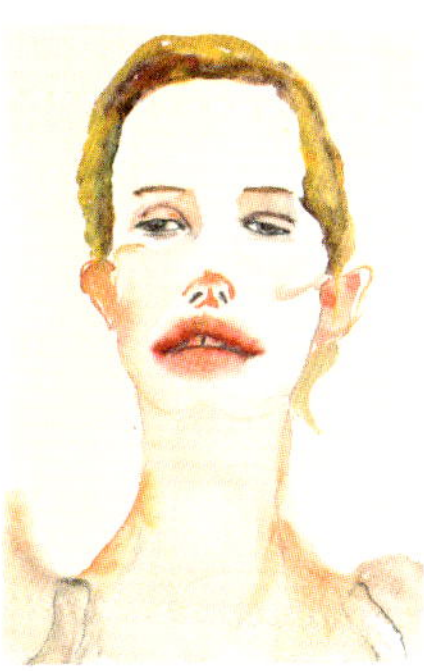
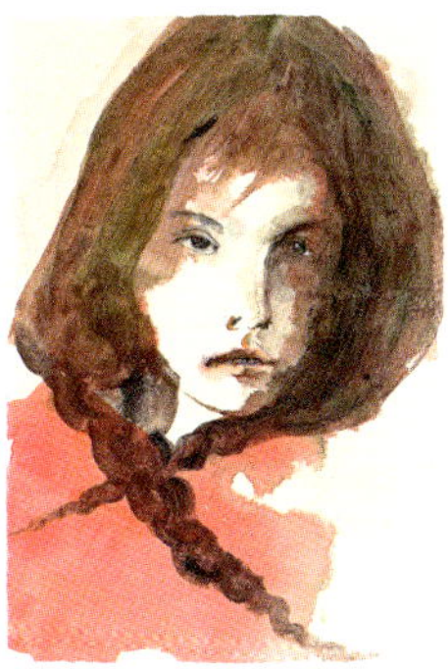
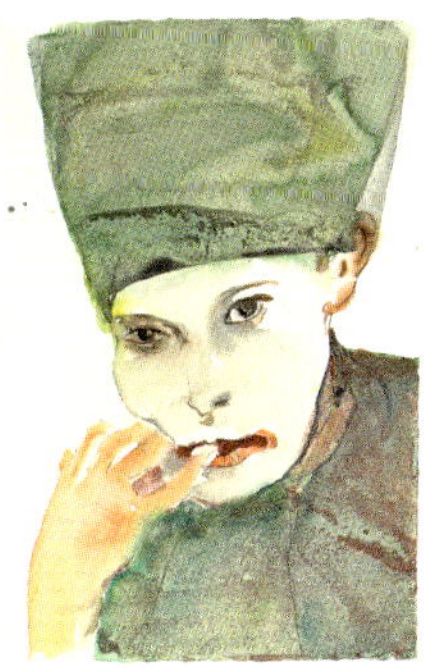
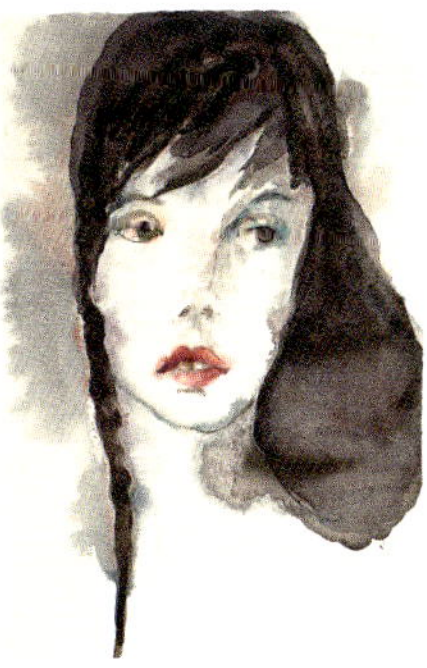

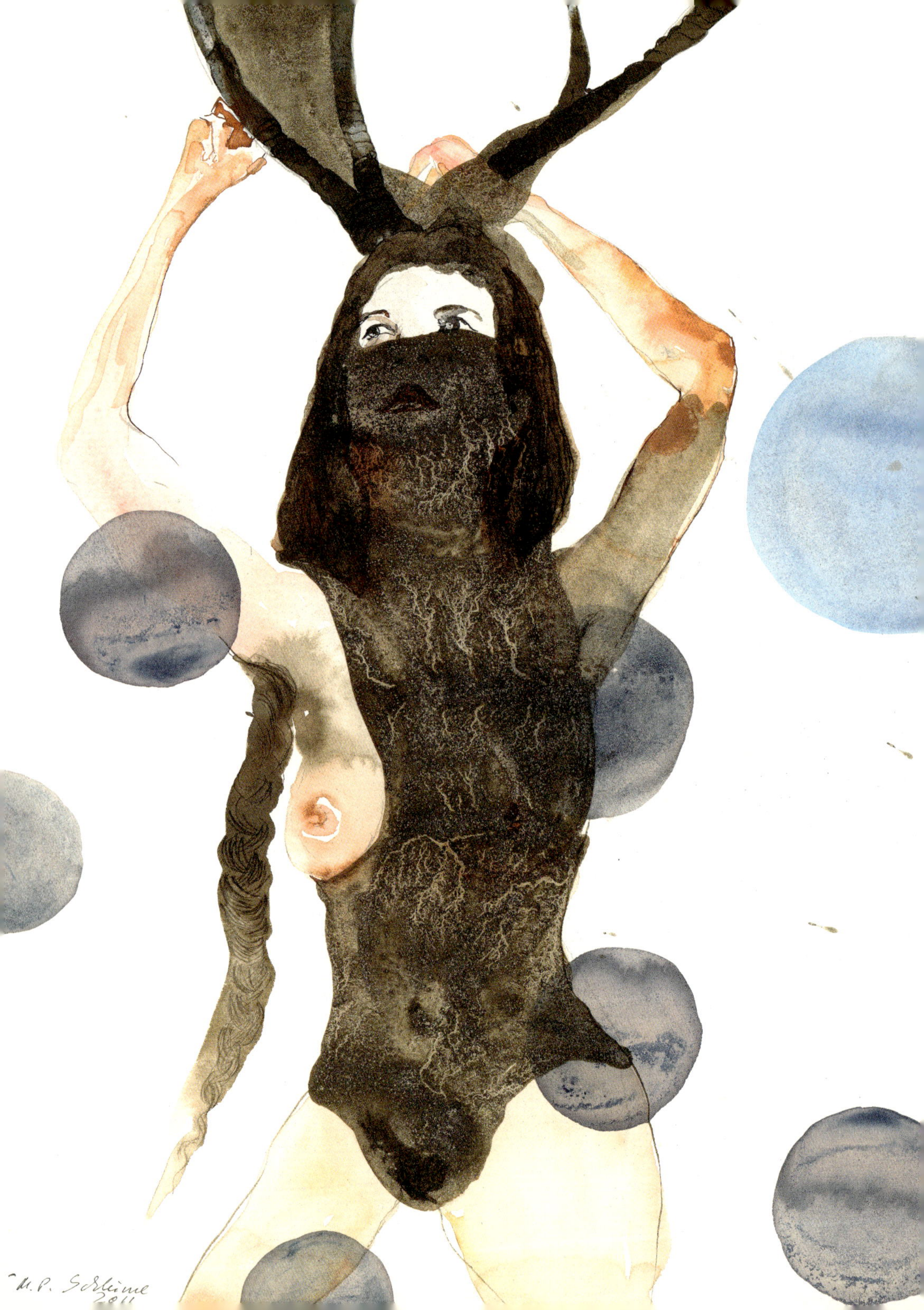
M.P. Schleime
2011

linke Seite left page **Ich zeig dir nicht alles** 2011
Aquarell & Tusche auf Büttenpapier Watercolour & Indian ink on handmade paper 57 x 38 cm

Impressum

Fotografie/Photography: Bernd Borchardt und Udo Hesse, Berlin und M.C. Hurek, München

Cover-Abbildung/Cover illustration:
‚Nicht nur die schwarzen, auch die roten Socken', 1996

Ein besonderer Dank an Christiane Bühling und für die Kooperation:
Galerie Michael Schultz, Berlin

Die Deutsche Nationalbibliothek verzeichnet diese Publikation in der
Deutschen Nationalbibliografie; detaillierte bibliografische Daten sind
im Internet über http://dnb.d-nb.de abrufbar.

Die Deutsche Nationalbibliothek lists this publication in the
German national bibliography, with detailed bibliographic data are
available http://dnb.d-nb.de available over the Internet.

Lektorat/Copy editing: Eckhard Hollmann
Übersetzung aus dem Deutschen/Translation from the German: Jane Michael
Gestaltungskonzept/Design concept: LIQUID | Agentur für Gestaltung, www.Liquid.ag
Layout: WE ARE INDEED, www.weareindeed.com, München
Herstellung/Production: Susanne Rösler, Berlin
Litho/Origination: Reproline mediateam, München
Druck und Bindung/Printing and binding: DZA Druckerei zu Altenburg GmbH

jovis Verlag GmbH
Kurfürstenstr. 15/16
10785 Berlin

www.jovis.de

jovis books are available worldwide. Please contact your nearest bookseller
or the address above for information concerning your local distribution.

ISBN: 978-3-86859-179-8

Ich danke allen Beteiligten für die Realisierung dieses Buches. Insbesondere: Jürgen Krieger, Eckhard Hollmann, der Galerie Michael Schultz, Christiane Bühling, Wolfgang Büscher und jenen, die mir still und schweigend Modell standen oder mein Leben begleiten.

My thanks go to all those involved in the realization of this book, especially Jürgen Krieger, Eckhard Hollmann, the Michael Schulz Gallery, Christiane Bühling, Wolfgang Büscher and all those who have sat still and silently as models or who accompany my life.

© M.C. Hurek

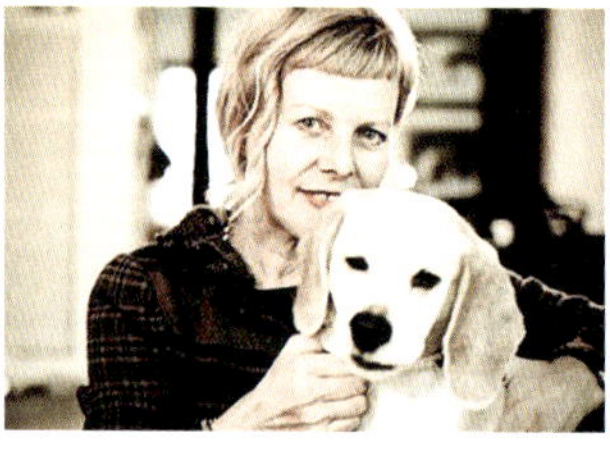

Cornelia Schleime lebt in Berlin und im Ruppiner Land.

Cornelia Schleime lives in Berlin and in the countryside near Ruppin.